Languages for Specific Purposes

Languages for Specific Purposes
Searching for Common Solutions

Edited by

Dita Gálová

Cambridge Scholars Publishing

Languages for Specific Purposes: Searching for Common Solutions, edited by Dita Gálová

This book first published 2007 by

Cambridge Scholars Publishing

15 Angerton Gardens, Newcastle, NE5 2JA, UK

British Library Cataloguing in Publication Data
A catalogue record for this book is available from the British Library

ISBN 1-84718-300-X; ISBN 13: 9781847183002

TABLE OF CONTENTS

Chapter II: ICT in Language Teaching

Chapter III: Languages for Specific Purposes – lexicology, terminology, translation studies

PREFACE

Globalization of the world economy requires professionals and specialists in various areas to communicate effectively in foreign languages. The success is conditional on their ability to manage language and cultural barriers, i.e. on the language skills and competences with respect to their professional areas.

The most of the book has concentrated on teaching English for specific purposes (ESP) rather than other languages. This clearly shows today's dominant position of English in the area of teaching foreign languages. The number of people using English for international communication is increasing, and English is often referred to as lingua franca or global language (Crystal, 1997). Based on Widdowson (1997) we may assume that English, being used this way, is always the language for specific purposes.

The study of languages for specific purposes represents a synthesis of linguistics and methodology of teaching foreign languages (L2) and includes the aspects of lexicology, terminology, translation and discourse analysis. In this book we therefore attempt to put together the theory and practice of languages for specific purposes, showing the procedures and relating course designs to learner's specific needs in learning foreign languages for academic, occupational or business purposes.

The authors tried to find solutions to the needs of learning LSP drawing on their experience with respect to the specificity of their learners' mother tongues (L1). We hope that it will be accessible to language teachers and LSP specialists, as well as graduate and postgraduate students majoring in foreign language teaching.

CHAPTER I:

TEACHING LANGUAGES FOR SPECIFIC PURPOSES

INTRODUCTION

DITA GÁLOVÁ

Teaching foreign languages to non-linguist students is a difficult but challenging task. There is hardly any branch where students would not need foreign languages (L2) for understanding of professional texts and where they would do without the skills to communicate effectively in the tasks connected with their study or work situations. The study of languages for specific purposes (LSP) is highly students-centred, focused on learners' professional linguistic needs, as well as teaching materials production. In general, it puts great emphasis on the practical outputs of language learning. LSP have to deal with a number of "sub-languages", i.e. language of business, science and technology, humanities etc., which makes it complicated to outline a methodology that would apply to all disciplines and professional activities the learners are involved in. As a result, the LSP methodology always integrates the language learning and subject learning approaches.

The origin of LSP is closely connected with recognizing the communicative role of languages and their functional styles. In the 1920s the Prague linguistic circle and the related works defined the functional language, which enabled description of different categories referring to the use in different disciplines and situations. This made it clear that in every language there are specific elements typical of different areas. In 1930s the German linguistics introduced the concept of *Fachsprachen*, and in the beginning of 1950s Savory published *The Language of Science. Its Growth, Character and Usage* (1953), which laid the foundations for the theory of languages for special purposes, later referred to as languages for specific purposes. Since the 1970s the linguists have agreed that LSP serve for the needs of individual fields of science, technology, economics, management, medicine, law, media, etc. In other words, the number of languages for specific purposes, in contrast to languages for general purposes (LGP), is relatively high.

With respect to English, there are different definitions of English for Specific Purposes (ESP), but probably the clearest one is Hutchison's and Waters's (1987, 1994) who see ESP as an approach rather than a product. This definition however suggests that ESP does not involve a particular kind of language or methodology. Here, the authors see the specificity in the specific end product the language teaching is aiming to achieve, i.e. to provide the learners with the language according to their learning context. Hence, ESP is defined by the needs and reasons for which the student is learning L2. The concept of languages for specific purposes shall always be related to the content; be based on the needs analysis and centred on language appropriate to particular disciplines and activities in syntax, lexis, discourse, semantics etc. (cf. Strevens, 1988, Robinson, 1991, Dudley-Evans and St John, 1998).

Dudley-Evans and St John (1998) date the origin of ESP study back in 1960s when it gained a well-established position as a component of applied linguistic research. Throughout its development, similarly to LSP, it has involved a close relationship between the theory and practice and has been influenced by the developments in education, business and computer technology.

Chapter I seeks to provide an overview of different approaches, issues, aspects, and practices in teaching LSP. The authors hope that readers will find the collection of papers a useful resource for understanding of current practices in teaching of languages for specific purposes.

DECISION-MAKING AND THE INTEGRATION OF THE FOUR SKILLS WITH LARGE, MIXED-ABILITY ESP GROUPS

ISABEL BALTEIRO

Introduction: the problems of teaching a large heterogeneous ESP University group

If the process of teaching a foreign language is quite complex in itself, it is even more complicated when we teach a language for specific purposes (English for Business, in this case), especially if the learners constitute a large and badly-defined (mixed-ability) group.

In this paper, we deal with ESP at University level, which apparently implies that we will face a well-defined intermediate group of mature students with a similar and acceptable background linguistic knowledge, acquired throughout the years spent at secondary school. However, unlike other countries, the reality of the teaching-learning process is not so idyllic in Spain as the ideal teaching environment with highly-motivated intermediate-level students is far from reality. We claim that only a very reduced number of Spanish students finish their secondary studies without a good command of English. Indeed, despite the fact that they have been learning English for at least eight years, their level is, in general, not higher than elementary. This would not be so dangerous if these two "types" of students did not meet in a University classroom. However, as we shall see below, University classes do not still group their students according to their levels. Obviously, this has important negative consequences for the teaching, for two main reasons: first, University teachers expect students with at least an intermediate level and prepare their materials accordingly, and, secondly, University teachers and their lessons are conditioned by students' deficiencies and variety of levels (and their consequences) and hence they are obliged to make drastic and difficult decisions to adapt their teaching to both the students' and the student's needs. To give an example, they have to decide whether to make a revision of or teach the basic general language skills and then attempt to continue with the expected syllabus and at the expected level or, rather, disregard such facts and teach what they were expected to. Of course, choosing one or the other option has serious implications for the learner's language development. Note, however, that, as Rinvolucri (1986: 29) argues "the problem of mixed abilities in the same room seems absolutely natural, and it is the idea of teaching a unitary lesson that seems odd".

In addition to the aforementioned difficulties regarding mixed-abilities and students' lack of the basic language knowledge, there are some others which also deserve our attention. That is the case of the large number of students that may be found in a classroom. ESP courses at Spanish Universities are usually offered as free-choice subjects, which means that any student may enrol as, surprisingly enough, there are no pre-requisites that may be used as filters to obtain quite homogeneous groups facilitating both the teaching and the learning processes. Therefore, unlike other ESP courses which are usually addressed to a very specific and reduced (apparently "homogeneous") group of individuals (as the group composition is established beforehand), ESP courses offered as free-choice subjects at University are a kind of jack-in-the-box or even, we could say, a dumping ground. The expression may sound exaggerated but it is not. Let us explain why. Offering ESP courses as free-choice subjects means diminishing the importance of ESP and makes it a "rubbish bin" for several reasons: firstly, free-choice subjects in the Spanish educational system are those in which students usually enrol for no specific reason beyond the number of credits they need to complete the academic year; secondly, students from any degree may enrol, even if not interested or if unrelated to their studies; thirdly, students of very different ages and different courses may be found in the classroom; fourthly, the best and the worst students may enrol; fifth, not only students but also professionals who have enrolled at University may meet in the ESP classroom. Therefore, it seems that there is room, literally, for everybody and for everything. Needless to say, as already mentioned, this enormous heterogeneity has serious negative consequences for the teaching-learning process, which is affected in all its components: from the selection of contents, materials, and the teachers' role to the situation of the better-motivated and more advanced students.

Apart from that, for economic and institutional reasons and despite the new European guidelines, the idea of creating both reduced and separate groups of learners, based mainly on their levels, is still far from feasible in Spain.

So far we have defined ESP courses at Spanish Universities and we have mentioned a series of actual problems that derive from the Spanish educational system, University study programmes, and, more particularly, from the offer of ESP as free-choice subjects which mainly means facing large and mixed-ability classes. We have also briefly mentioned the negative implications that these have for the teaching-learning process. Then, in an attempt to overcome such a problematic state, we should begin by reflecting on the fact that the complexity involving the teaching of ESP at University is mainly a consequence of classroom heterogeneity.

The heterogeneity found in the ESP Spanish University classrooms is a consequence of three main factors: the University as the institution that regulates the enrolment and the students' distribution in groups, the classroom as the place where the different learners meet, and the individuals themselves with their daily subjective needs and attitudes.

Firstly, as its name indicates "university" denotes heterogeneity, but here more than in other cases, as this is increased by both the offer of ESP as free-choice subjects and one peculiar characteristic of Spanish University classrooms, that is, large classes. Thus, we find learners from different degrees, from different nationalities and/or mother tongue (Socrates), from different linguistic and cultural backgrounds (students vs. students who are also professionals, for example), from different courses (from the first to the last year), with different ages (and degree of maturity), interests, purposes, etc. Secondly, university in Spain also implies large classes and therefore heterogeneity as regards number of learners or individuals, who bring with them an important diversity or variety of interests, purposes, motivations and attitude to language, their personalities, ages, linguistic and cultural backgrounds, both language and world knowledge, learning style, and even self-discipline. As Rinvolucri (1986: 29) states, "we do not teach a group but thirty separate people". Then, the larger the class, the more difficult and/or problematic it becomes. Thirdly, heterogeneity is also present at individual level since learners' involvement and motivation is different each day depending on diverse circumstances. In other words, we may say that each learner has an individual range of levels. Finally, we cannot forget that there are also other important discrepancies which may also be included within "heterogeneity", such as the differences between the learners' needs and their wants or wishes as regards the fulfilment of classroom activities. Students' needs and wants are sometimes hard to reconcile. Then there arises the question of whether we should make them happy by doing only what they wish or, rather, force them to do what they actually need. We think that there may be an intermediate point that allows teachers to adapt those activities the students are reluctant to do, so that they make them feel happier.

Needless to say, large and heterogeneous (mixed-ability) ESP groups, as just outlined, involve a series of difficulties and decision-making processes and, more importantly, are extremely difficult to teach. Hence it is really important to identify the group characteristics and the main problems that these may present (by means of a needs analysis) as well as look for practical ideas that can help and contribute to effective solutions, as explained below.

The solution to many of the problems (for both teachers and learners) posed by such large heterogeneous ESP free-choice University classes seems to be in (1) trying to vary topics and contents so that students are more likely to feel interested, (2) setting open-ended tasks so that learners may complete them according to their own levels, (3) providing activities with varying degrees of difficulty so that sometimes even more advanced students find them a challenge (which also will help to increase their motivation) or even giving them more difficult tasks, (4) using pair and group work so that one may help the other, (5) grouping them according to their levels so that no one may feel ashamed of his or her performance, (6) attending to particular individual difficulties (and advanced students), (7) providing additional material to those who may need it, etc. Obviously, the best solution would be to attend to individualised learning but this is nowadays still impossible at Spanish University as classes continue to be large, although some hope seems to lie ahead.

The preceding as well as other similar suggestions are found and explained in the following section, in which a practical example of teaching English for Business Purposes at a Spanish University is provided.

Pre-teaching considerations: an analysis of needs and attitudes towards the foreign language

Given the problematic nature of ESP subjects in Spanish Universities, it seems that a "solution" is urgently needed so as to be able to attend to the students' need as much as possible, specially if we consider that the most common and recommended teaching approach nowadays is learner-centred (see, Johns and Price-Machado, 200; Nunan, 1987; and, for a critique of it, Hutchinson and Waters, 1987). Our experience teaching a Business English course (a free-choice subject) at University level may provide the reader with some suggestions on how we may attend to mixed-abilities, diversity, heterogeneity and also to large number of students/learners.

It seems that the first best thing to do when facing a course with these or similar characteristics is to make a **needs analysis.** A needs analysis means obtaining "a picture" of our learners, as regards their needs and expectations, that is, objective needs such as their previous knowledge, what they know and the problems they have, their difficulties in learning, but also "subjective" needs such as passing the exam, working or studying abroad, etc., and ranking of preferences, that is, what they would like to learn and how they wish to study it, mainly concerning content and language skills. Knowing this will help and allow us to orient our decisions as regards classroom management, syllabus design, and, more particularly, the students' individual needs and, in general, their diversity or heterogeneity of levels. Accordingly, on the first day, students were given a questionnaire aimed at identifying the learners' needs, lacks, shortcomings, and competences, as well as their interests and purposes for the future. This made also evident and, consequently, made us conscious, from the very first moment, of the great heterogeneity of the group. The heterogeneity did not only concern the different levels or the mixed-ability in the class (some students had not had any contact with the English language for years, while others came directly from secondary school and apparently remembered some English), different purposes, etc. but, most importantly, students from very different and varied areas (from Economics, Business Administration and Management, Computer Engineering, English Studies, and a B.A. in English Translation), on the one hand, as well as students from very different cultural and linguistic backgrounds (besides the Spanish students, there were quite a few Socrates students, namely, twelve from France and three Russians). Special attention was devoted to the variety of interests and wishes that the learners put forward. Accordingly, some students wished to learn (general) English and had enrolled in this course only because they had no other opportunity to take English at University; others wanted to learn English related to the business world while others, the least, those from English Studies and Translation, intended to improve their knowledge in the field of Business English and were specially interested in learning vocabulary. Unlike these, the three Computer Engineering students cannot be disregarded as they are a good example of the demotivation in free-choice subjects classrooms, in particular, and, more generally, in present day classrooms. They were simply interested in "the credits needed to complete the required subjects for the academic year" and manifested that they had chosen Business English because it was suitable for their CVs and because the subject had been easy to pass in previous years (as grading was based only on class attendance). Note that they were not problematic in the sense of how to engage or motivate them, for several reasons: one did not attend lectures because he was working as a computer technician, a second one was completely demotivated and nothing could be done to help him, and the third attended and his level was above the average.

Apart from the questionnaire, they were asked to write a brief composition about their previous weekend. These revealed a good number of both lexical and grammatical problems. To give some basic examples and to make the reader conscious of the remarkable linguistic difficulties that we had to face and overcome, there appeared cases like the non-capitalization of the first person pronoun (**i*), the use of the third person singular of verbs without *–s*, or the misuse of prepositions like **in home*.

Given such a variety of interests, needs, and levels, and also considering motivation as well as style and speed in learning, some decisions were to be taken, mainly *what* to teach (and to whom), *how* to teach, and materials to be used. In addition to all this, there were other important decisions regarding the use of both the use of the L1 and the L2, the restriction to Business English teaching (without dealing with other relevant or basic issues related to general English), the teaching of the four skills, listening, speaking, reading, and writing, etc.

Decision-making and the teaching itself: Suggestions for an effective teaching in attempting the students to be competent in the four skills

Making decisions on what to teach and how to do it with such a large number of mixed-ability students is a real challenge for any teacher. However, the degree of difficulty to succeed is increasingly more complex when we deal with foreign language learners and even more with ESP. As Hemingway (1986: 18) notes, teachers face a range of problems such as (1) how to plan a lesson to meet the different needs of all the students; (2) how to give all students; equal attention, preventing the more advanced learners from feeling bored and the less able feeling lost or left out (on this, see also Nolasco and Arthur, 1988: 108); and (3) how to work through a given syllabus or textbook, but still allow for individual differences, among others. We think that the learners should be aware of the problematic situation and so they should be told about the importance of communication between learner and teacher and vice versa. Thus, the learners may also contribute and help the teacher in decision-making, although sometimes, of course, this will be done by using mere intuition.

Under the aforementioned circumstances, and with the aim of caring for learners' shortcomings in general English (note that only seven out of one hundred and eighty did not have important problems in relation to the basic language skills or competence), it seemed that alternating between Spanish and English was appropriate, despite the fact that there were Socrates students whose L1 was obviously not Spanish (but they were expected to have a good command of Spanish as they had been selected for the Socrates programme and lived in Spain). English was used most of the time, while Spanish was resorted to for relatively more complicated explanations or even for reinforcement. Nolasco and Arthur, however, consider the use of the L1 useful only if everything else fails. Moreover, they believe that the use of the mother tongue for instructions, for example,

> "removes the greatest single source of genuine communication in the language classroom and students can learn a lot by being asked to listen and do (oral instructions) or read and do (written instructions)".
>
> (Nolasco and Arthur,1988: 32)

Instead, they emphasize the importance of using the target language for classroom management.

The first two weeks of the course (six hours) were devoted to revision of basic aspects of grammar. Moreover, a book with basic grammar exercises and grammar summaries (Walker and Elsworth, 1986) was either provided or recommended so that they could reach the expected intermediate level or at least a lower intermediate one. This book was to be used at home and students should work with it at their own pace. Solutions to all those tasks were provided to the students once they had completed the exercises. Given all these measures, we focused on the teaching of "the" English for specific purposes with special reference to the general business world, banking, and companies or firms (as these topics attended to both the students' interests and purposes), as our main objective was to introduce the learners to the kind of language they will face and need to use and understand in their academic and professional future. In spite of this, at any time the students came across relevant grammatical issues (even if related to General English), these were commented upon.

Once the conflict General English – English for Specific Purposes was solved, there appeared the problem of how to prepare or obtain materials which attended to the group's heterogeneity, that is, to the diversity of levels and interests. The solution seemed to be in using open-ended tasks (either using existing materials, adapting them, or preparing new ones) so that they would allow different degrees of achievement (different levels and different types of answers) and to avoid using or preparing differential tasks that may, on the one hand, make the teacher feel frustrated if the students drop out on a given class and s/he realizes that he has lost time preparing specific activities for them, and, on the other, make some students feel either "different" or left out. As Hemingway observes,

> "a mixed level class can be demotivating for students if they are not encouraged to work to their own limits, and enabled to fully participate in the lesson. The student whose English is more advanced than the rest may feel cut off from the group if he/she is constantly given work to do alone, while the others catch up".
>
> (Hemingway, 1987: 18)

Apart from that, it must be remembered that most (if not all) textbooks are designed for an ideal homogeneous group. It is our role as teachers to overcome this restriction by adapting already existent materials and creating new ones. Thus, most of the activities were and had to be adapted from materials which had been specially designed for Business English, especially because students were not prepared to face authentic materials as such. In spite of this, authentic texts (without further adaptations) were provided twice along the course. The general tendency, however, was the use of adapted open-ended tasks or questions so that each student may achieve or perform at his or her own level. Moreover, more advanced students were given the opportunity, if they wished to, to use additional material so that they might advance at their own rhythm and according to their interests. In relation to this, it is quite noticeable that students were not interested in extra activities as their only purpose seemed to be to pass the subject and obtain (the) credits.

Another relevant question, probably the most important, as it was our main focus, was the study and introduction of the four skills in the teaching of such a heterogeneous course. At first sight, all of them seemed similarly relevant, specially if the learners' interests, purposes, and needs were taken into account, on the one hand, and, in particular, if we consider the importance that communication (both oral and written) skills have in the business world in general and in banking and firms (the two main targets that most students pointed out as their potential professional future), on the other.

However, as practice demonstrated, despite being conscious of their needs, these did not always coincide with what they wished or were willing to do. Thus, for example, despite the importance that listening tasks had to develop the communicative skills that they needed, they asked for them to be excluded from their classroom activities because, as they put it themselves, they "did not understand a word" and felt frightened by the situation. Accordingly, after the first listening activity (taken from Jones and Alexander, 1996: 11), most students showed their discontent and desperation; only more advanced learners, the least, expressed their satisfaction at having understood it and answered the questions correctly. As communication with students and the awareness of their needs and interests were used to orientate and manage the teaching (learner-centred approach), we decided to begin with simplified and adapted listening comprehensions, so that the teacher read texts aloud or said something and the students had to answer a number of questions. Later on, when the students felt more confident, cassette or CD recorded listening excerpts where provided: first, they listened to the cassette or CD; then, the teacher checked what they had understood; and, finally, the teacher repeated it (reading aloud or telling) to give the learners an opportunity to understand it better, successfully complete the tasks and, consequently, motivate them and make them feel better and more confident with listening. This was apparently a good measure, for several reasons: on the one hand, students felt more confident and less anxious; on the other hand, this allowed us to pay attention to the different levels in the class. For example, more advanced students were not allowed to talk until the rest had had a chance to answer the questions or participate in class. Moreover, the teacher used to mill around the class to check their degree of achievement in the written answers. In order to keep more advanced students engaged in the activities while the rest of the learners continued with their attempts to complete the tasks, they were asked to fill in as much information as possible. At correction time, as already suggested, primary attention was paid to basic information and then they were asked to complete the missing data, telling aloud to the whole class, so that more advanced students also had their opportunity to participate. Therefore, all students, independently of their levels and degree of achievement, had a chance to contribute with their answers at one time or another.

As regards speaking activities, different types were used throughout the course. Most of the students were first reluctant to talk, especially when they realized that more advanced students, including the Socrates ones, had a good level of oral skills and could speak fluently. Speaking tasks were always used as a complement to another task, for example, a listening or a reading comprehension, which was used as the motivator or engagement element. To increase their motivation and make them more conscious of the importance of speaking, they were usually told about the importance of communication (and, as a corollary, of oral skills), especially in the business world. Moreover, we attempted to engage them by asking referential questions, that is, questions related to economy or the business world and to which the teacher (who was only an English teacher and not a Business specialist) did not know the answer. Thus, the lecture became a more natural environment to learn Business English. Apart from that, speaking activities were presented as an exercise to "rest" and relax (with their colleagues) for a while. Thus, students worked either in pairs or groups, and they were grouped together depending on their levels. Lower-level students were never grouped with the more advanced ones, in order to avoid the sense of unease. Quite exceptionally, however, if there was to be a leader in a group, for example, an advanced learner may work with the lower level students. Nevertheless, intermediate and elementary students were usually combined. Note, however, that many researchers concerned with mixed-ability problems usually consider that combining lower-level students with advanced ones is the most appropriate way of grouping learners (see Maddalena, 2002: 5). Furthermore, our experience tells us that groups formed by elementary students only should be avoided. The reasons for such a conclusion derive from the fact that, in speaking tasks, apart from their tendency to use their L1, instead of English, they tended to make efforts to write down in English what they had said in the L1, Spanish in our case (as all the foreigners had an intermediate level), so that, when asked, they simply tried to read what they had written. Modifying such behaviours was specially complicated or rather, almost impossible.

Unlike with listening and speaking, learners, above all lower level students, seemed more confident with reading and writing. However, we cannot disregard the fact that, like with the aforementioned skills, lower-level students were quite reluctant to participate in the reading tasks, especially at the beginning. But their participation improved as the course advanced, to the point that at the very end they participated in them of their own accord. Obviously, a factor that contributed to this was telling them that they were not being evaluated or assessed, but the point was simply to make them pay attention, fix, learn, improve, and acquire both oral and written skills. Reading comprehension tasks were also used for the teaching of grammar, vocabulary, and even pronunciation as students were asked to read the texts aloud and the teacher used to correct their pronunciation. Quite noticeable is the fact that the students commented their satisfaction for the amount of vocabulary that they were learning and they also felt happy about the correction and feedback as regards pronunciation. As regards group heterogeneity, especially in relation to the different levels and backgrounds in the class, this was almost imperceptible when students were given texts with very specialised vocabulary. Their level of comprehension did not differ greatly since more advanced students had a good command of general English only. This fact was quite motivating for all of them because the more advanced made great efforts to continue with their "status" of being the best in the class, whereas lower-level learners were happy to know that the others did not recognise the vocabulary.

As regards written tasks, they did not present problems of adaptation to the group heterogeneity, as compositions naturally allow for different levels of achievement and none is necessarily incomplete or incorrect. For the correction different techniques were used. On the one hand, the teacher may correct the text so that the student is given individual feedback (thanks to corrections on paper) and also group feedback as the most important and recurrent errors were collected and an explanation was given in a one-hour session. On the other hand, guided corrections were also made so that the student himself should re-write the text, following the teacher's indications, and give it back to the teacher, who would correct it again and attend the student in a tutorial. For obvious reasons, those with higher levels were not asked to re-write their writings for their level did not require it.

Along the preceding paragraphs we have tried to offer some suggestions and share our experience dealing with a large heterogeneous ESP University group. Note that special attention was paid to level differences which eventually appeared as the most relevant in such course. As seen, we mainly tried to prevent better students from feeling bored and the weaker ones from being left behind. Moreover, we also touched upon other questions, such as the contradiction between students' needs (of which they were perfectly conscious) and their wants. Thus, as seen, despite the importance of oral skills for their potential future jobs and their awareness of such a fact, they were reluctant to do speaking and listening tasks and they even tried to eliminate them from the syllabus. Apart from that, as regards other matters related to heterogeneity, it must be said that the differences imposed by the free-choice nature of the subject, were specially noticeable as regards the main degree studied (students from English Studies and Translation were always eager to do the oral tasks and completed them successfully), their age or course at University (more mature students showed more interest and their cultural background knowledge was relatively important) and the demotivation in the case of those who were just looking for credits to complete the curriculum (as explained above, in the case of the Computer Engineering students). Finally, two French male students who wanted to disrupt lessons cannot be disregarded. The question is whether this was due to their own personalities or rather to their demotivation. The problem was solved by keeping an eye on them all the time and by forcing them to do the tasks.

Conclusions

With the preceding decisions, we apparently had quite efficiently solved or overcome most of the difficulties; however, we needed to ask the learners how they felt about it. In the last class of the term, students were asked to fill in a questionnaire. Emphasis was given to questions related to what they had learnt and enjoyed, on the one hand, and to what they would improve, modify or change, on the other. Opinions were, like the group itself, quite diverse and heterogeneous and apparently (cor)responded also to the individual levels. Even though all of them considered that the teaching method was good, that they had learnt quite a lot, and that they were happy but afraid of the final grade (which was their most important objective), some were satisfied with the use of both Spanish and English, whereas others would have preferred only English. Similarly, while some manifested that they would have preferred only cassette or CD listening tasks for the challenge that this implied, others expressed their satisfaction and stated that the teacher's contribution in reading or telling aloud had helped them to improve their listening skills. Therefore, as expected, it is very difficult to find suitable activities for the whole class and make all of them happy. However, the teacher should always consider the students' feedback to make new decisions on his/her teaching but sometimes they may also use intuition as the main boost for decision-making.

As just remarked, teaching ESP at University, especially when the courses are offered as free-choice subjects, is not an easy task. Heterogeneity and, with it, mixed-abilities and large classes make the teaching-learning process a challenge for the teacher. This entails a number of decisions regarding such fundamental aspects as *what* to teach (syllabus, materials, topics, etc.), *how* to teach (lesson planning, preparation, involvement, management, pair and group work interaction, feedback, etc.) and *to whom* (for example, should all students be taught the same and use the same materials if their interests and levels are so different?). However, despite the difficulties, nothing is impossible. Accordingly, if the teacher has good disposition and with some effort and reflection, taking into account the students' needs and wants (which should be identified from the very first day) and trying to strike a balance between both the problems imposed by free-choice ESP subjects at

University will surely, though not exempt of difficulties, be not impossible to cope with. An example of how this could be done is provided in this paper; however, we cannot disregard the fact that every ESP subject, every class, and even every student (depending on the day), will be different, and therefore we will have always to keep an eye on the situation at every moment and be aware of the difficulties and demanding peculiarities of the (free-choice ESP) language classroom. In general, we should take into account the communicative principles that apply to any general purpose class. Among others, the importance of creating opportunities for discovery learning and genuine exchange of information, using the language in problem-solving processes; (2) collaboration between learners; (3) open-endedness (to avoid the sense of frustration that many students in large mixed-level classes have when they are denied the opportunity of using the language available to them at their own different levels of competence), and (4) enquiry (questions without closed predictable answers), which Pulverness (2002: 2) regards as "key factors in the large mixed-level EAP class".

Finally, we cannot end this paper without saying that the ideal teaching situation would be that in which the learner receives individualised attention (on this, see McDonough and Shaw, 1993: 243 ff), however, as seen, this seems impossible in so large groups as Spanish Universities have. Instead, we can consider that "a heterogeneous class can also be addressed as a whole class of individuals who have a symmetry of learner needs" (Millrood, 2002: 135) and so attempt to achieve as much success in the teaching as possible.

References

Hemingway, P. (1986) "Teaching a mixed-level class" in *Practical English Teaching*. September 1986, pp. 18-20.

Hutchinson, T. & Waters, A. (1987) *English for Specific Purposes*. Cambridge: CUP.

Johns, A. & Price-Machado, D. (2001) "English for Specific Purposes: Tailoring courses to student needs – and to the outside world" in M. Celce-Murcia. Ed. 2001. *Teaching English as a Second or Foreign Language*. Boston: Heinle and Heinle, pp. 43-54.

Jones, L. & Alexander, R. (1996) *New International Business English. Communication skills in English for business purposes*. Cambridge: CUP.

Maddalena, S. (2002) "Using High Level Students As Teaching Assistants in a Mixed Ability Classroom" in *TESL-ES 6/1*. (http://tesl-ej.org/ej21/cf1.html; 20/03/2007)

McDonough, J. & Shaw, C. (1993) *Materials and Methods in ELT*. Cambridge, Mass.: Blackwell.

Nolasco, R. & Arthur, L. (1988) *Large Classes*. London: Macmillan Publishers.

Nunan, D. (1987) *The learner centred curriculum.* Cambridge: CUP.

Pulverness, A. (2002) "Squaring the circle: Teaching EAP to Large Mixed Groups" in http://www.melta.org.my/ET/2002/wp01.htm (25/03/2007)

Rinvolucri, M. (1986) "Strategies for a mixed ability group" in *Practical English Teaching 7/1,* pp. 29-30.

Walker, E. & Elsworth, S. (1986) *Grammar Practice for Intermediate Students*. London: Longman.

AUTONOMY IN ESP: SOLUTION OR RECIPE?

NOÉMIA BÁRBARA

Introduction

To those involved in Higher Education it is clear that tertiary institutions are undergoing a reform which was triggered by a two-page document – the Bologna Declaration of 1999 – corroding its very structures while laying the foundations for the European academia in the 21st century (Reinalda & Kulesza, 2005: 3). Thus started the overwhelming steam-roller of bureaucratic recommendations of what is now known as the Bologna Process.

Battling against the loss of ground in higher education to Asia and the USA[1], Europe strives to achieve greater compatibility and comparability in the courses it offers so as to increase its competitiveness. Having defined the strategy: to create the most dynamic and competitive economic space of the world in a knowledge-based society, and the deadline – the European Area for Higher Education should be completed in 2010 – the "eurocrats" are urging higher education institutions to become actors in this process of change and to compete "more resolutely than in the past for students, influence, prestige and money in the worldwide competition of universities" (Reinalda & Kulesza, 2005: 124).

Portugal should be no exception. However, as the emphasis in our country was laid not so much on the strategy and the goals but on detail, namely on the duration of learning cycles 3 + 2, or 4 + 1, we lagged behind the adoption of measures. This will probably lead to unemployment of teaching staff rather than the deep reform and innovation envisaged by European planners. The adopted strategy was

---

[1] Blight, Davis and Olsen discuss the diversity of higher education on a global scale focusing, among others, on Universitas 21, an association of major research-intensive international universities where 16 member universities from the U.K., U.S.A., Asia, Australia and New Zealand (each participating with 4 universities) provide services of assistance to local universities to advance their plans of internationalization since 1997.

perceived by some as changing the least, joining in the last minute, and considering change just because we are told to by Europe (Neves, 2005:5).

If what is at stake is a reform of higher education, in Portugal, in my understanding, the implementation of the Bologna Process seems to be a superficial "facelift" of the degrees offered, focusing only on course duration, on form, and not on content, nor new methodologies which are at the core of a new knowledge paradigm to modernise higher education European institutions (Bárbara, 2005). And yet great many changes are demanded of the new bachelor and master students. According to the Portuguese Higher Education Act of 2006 that regulates the new courses in a "Bologna format", following the Dublin descriptors, bachelors should, among other competencies, have the competence to learn in a lifelong process with a high degree of autonomy. Not only are there new demands in terms of student profile, but the desired student attitudes should be different and aimed at self-directed learning and autonomy.

Globalization and the new role of languages

A buzzword such as globalization pervades today's academic discourse, among others, focusing on worldwide political, social, and cultural interactions (Sousa Santos, 2001), regardless of geographical boundaries, which immediately raises questions about language (Block & Cameron, 2002). In fact, globalization is changing the conditions under which language learning is taking place. As English has been adopted as a *lingua franca*, not so much as a remnant of a British imperialism but as a synonym of the United States economic imperialism, the rise of transnational corporations contribute to the spread of English and therefore to its demand as these corporations disperse into more "flexible centres of production". Again, with the increase of world organizations and new global networks, English continues to be in great demand globally (Gray, 2002). A new area where English is dominant as a commodity to serve other commodities is the internet, in itself a worldwide web of ongoing growth.

Nowadays, languages are more and more treated as language commodities and this new role has been transforming language departments into service units "providing skills additional to the core capacities required by other areas of professional activity" (Phipps & Gonzalez 2004: 8). General English courses are more and more becoming English for Specific Purposes courses in order to guarantee their survival. While the language loses its human environment, its social experience, it becomes more and more instrumental, devoid of educational values, and embedded with training features to win out in the marketplace. According to Moreira:

> "Higher Education has been forced to question its value for money, but also its usefulness, it has been required to re-package itself in attractive wrappings promising financial and social rewards to consumers, but also to reflect on and redefine learning outcomes, desired exit profiles, skills and attitudes".
>
> (Moreira, 2005: 55)

Due to its strong connection to the marketplace and its practical features, ESP may be a strong field in the difficult world of job hunting for teachers of L2. Almost all Polytechnic Schools in Portugal have at least one semester of English for Specific Purposes, usually connected to Business, Communication or Engineering courses. The latter have managed to include English across the curricula for more than a decade now. Such is the case with Escola Superior Agrária de Coimbra, which offers classes of English for Engineering since 1985 as well as French and Spanish for the course of Ecotourism since 1999 (Bárbara, 2005), and Biotechnology since 2005.

And yet even Languages for Special Purposes seem to be under threat due to the Bologna framework in which reformulation of courses set to competition for contact hours the *hard skills,* connected to the engineering core of he courses, and the *soft skills.* The latter seen as complementary but superfluous at a time where the decrease from 5 to 3 years will tend to obliterate this niche of language learning and teaching. The irony lies in the fact that while Bologna sets out to promote employability and the use of languages in mobility programmes:

> "If higher education programmes are to be relevant to the European labour market, graduates have to be able to communicate in a number of languages and to expand their repertoire in changing needs. It is the responsibility of higher education institutions to provide opportunities and incentives for students to acquire these abilities"
>
> (CEL/ELC, 2002)

employability is being mistaken by early specialisation and professional training. If a student is to be "processed", to use Barnett's term[2], in less time, it can be understood to be prepared for the profession in less time as

---

[2] Barnett uses the idea of universities as enterprises where the logic of competition amongst them compels to the treatment of students as products to be processed quickly so as to improve the university's comparative position in benchmarking.

well, therefore shedding all the complementary subjects which do not have immediate bearings with job performance.

To some, the promotion of employability may mean a more general curriculum for the student to be supplemented with later specialisation. To others, it may mean the defence of one's own employability: defending one's job and one's departmental power by including in the new syllabuses the disciplines one has always taught, overlooking new goals and the new exit profiles of the courses. For ESP teachers there are not many solutions but to observe the contest among departments and to watch the reduction to a bare minimum of contact hours for language learning while engaging in the debate.

On the one hand we are witnessing a crisis in the humanities and in traditional language learning, and on the other hand the increase in global demand for speakers of English in remote areas of the globe. In the dawn of a of new capitalist era with the dominance of new regions, such as China and India, Europe is trying to define its place in the world by reinforcing its economic dimension, visible with the creation of the Euro; and its educational dimension in the knowledge society, visible through the creation of the Bologna area, overcoming the European Union boundaries of its 25 members. Language teachers of European countries have certainly a role to perform and a word to say in this new European dimension in helping its citizens in their mobility.

Why learner autonomy? A rationale

It is commonly accepted that autonomy is a precondition for *effective* learning, therefore when learners succeed in developing autonomy they become better language learners and enhance their capacity for critical thinking and responsibility (Holec, 1981), (Dickinson,1992), (Dam,1995), (Benson, 2001). Autonomy, once seen as an idealistic goal distracting students and learners from the real business of teaching and learning languages, in recent years, however, school reforms in European countries have resulted in new national curricula more attuned to the idea of learner autonomy and more likely to promote innovation in the language classroom (Trebbi, 2003), (Moreira, 2001). The aforementioned Dublin descriptors which determined the Portuguese Higher Education Act of 2006, are an example of how autonomy steadily has made its way into a new teaching/learning paradigm.

Two years after signing the Bologna Declaration, the European ministers in charge of higher education met in Prague and furthered some of the goals already accepted, but emphasized other aspects. To quote from the Prague Communiqué of 2001:

> "Lifelong learning is an essential element of the European Higher Education Area. In the future Europe, built upon a knowledge-based society and economy, lifelong strategies are necessary to face the challenges of competitiveness and the use of new technologies and to improve social cohesion, equal opportunities and the quality of life".

First of all, autonomy is a *desideratum* in a society where lifelong learning is valued and since teachers cannot provide students with all the knowledge and skills they need or would like to learn, they can perhaps serve the students better by equipping them with strategies to learn how to teach themselves. In view of the speed of technological developments and the subsequent needs of today's society, learning cannot be understood exclusively in a primary, secondary or tertiary context (Van Esch, 2003), and autonomy as a goal may draw formal education to life (Vieira, 1998).

Secondly, it is also important to equip the learners with tools and strategies that will empower them in a world where the teacher is only one of the many providers, or sources, of language exposure and communicative practice (Van Esch, 2003). For instance, the internet is a tool of paramount importance offering multimedia sources and language opportunities and easily accessible to higher education students.

A third reason for this rationale has to do with the nature of learning itself. Because learning is a personal process it can only be efficient if the learner wants and wills to learn. Students recognition of responsibility for their learning is considered as a first step towards autonomy, and what is more, they should exercise this accountability by being fully involved in all aspects of their learning process – planning, implementation, evaluation - to fully understand the why, the what, and the how of their learning (Little, 2003). Ultimately, the teacher cannot take the final responsibility for a student's learning.

So why should we want our students to be accountable for their learning? As many have pointed out, preparing learners for a changing future will allow them to better function in an ever-changing society that values independent initiative and adaptability to change and would also maximize their life choices (Cotteral, 1998), or lifelong strategies (Prague Communiqué, 2001).

Autonomy in ESP: Possibility or constraint?

Once the goal of language pedagogy was to find the "right method" – a methodological magic formula that would work for all learners at all times (Nunan, 2003). Although not a method but an approach or a philosophical orientation, autonomy does not claim to be the right approach, but a possible solution to many problems in language learning. For those used to teaching large heterogeneous classes of English for Special Purposes where the students' previous preparation is highly mixed, autonomy can be an answer for it may provide a plan for one-to-one teaching and learning. The right method may not exist but autonomy is an approach which can be methodologically holistic, or comprehensive, and student-centred.

It is nowadays acknowledged the failure of the transmission system of education where students are the mug to be filled by the jug – the teacher – but do not participate much in the decision of the teaching/learning process. The model of higher education perceived as a succession of lectures given by professors to large and small audiences as the method of transferring knowledge as information is questioned in terms of its effectiveness. Nowadays, in the new learning paradigm skills replace knowledge as the primary objective of education (Hills, 2003). It may be that we are in a throwaway society, cognitively speaking, as Barnett puts it, discarding knowledge *per se* and adopting knowledge as operation.

> "What modern society is calling on higher education is to develop on all students the capacities to be able to *operate* effectively in society (…) and so we find demands for 'flexibility', 'communication skills', 'teamwork'."
>
> (Barnett, 1994: 15)

We may debate the negative impact of replacing the *know-what* for the *know- how*, but we cannot dismiss that this is a reality and we have to adapt our students for this new reality. Educating students to be passive consumers of knowledge receiving it from teachers as the sole providers of authority is doomed to failure. Students should be transformed into

> "critical consumers of knowledge, envisaging teachers as facilitators of learning, as mediators in the relationship student-learning, as partners in the pedagogical relationship where knowledge is dynamic, transitory and differs from subject to subject."
>
> (Vieira, 1998: 38)

According to Dudley–Evans & St John, ESP is designed to meet specific needs of the learners and makes use of the underlying methodology and activities of the disciplines it serves. It is also centred on the language (grammar, lexis, register) skills, discourse and genres appropriate to these activities. It may have a different methodology from that of General English, is designed for adult learners either in a tertiary level institution or in a professional work situation who are intermediate or advanced students. Moreover, "the key stages in ESP are needs analysis, course (and syllabus) design, materials selection (and production), teaching and learning, and evaluation" (Dudley–Evans & St John, 1998: 121) which overlap and are interdependent. Needs analysis establishes the *what* and the *how* of the course while evaluation checks and establishes its effectiveness. Although students may not be fully aware of their language learning needs, they may give a good contribute in designing the course and in the production of materials to be used in contact hours based on their *own* needs analysis. As they are usually transferring knowledge from core disciplines into English, they can help in planning the units and their contents, consequently turning autonomy in ESP into a feasible goal.

Indeed, the learner should be able to take charge of his/her own learning for no teacher can know what is best for each learner or predefine the learning process and its outcomes (Trebbi:2003, 169). So students have to learn what their needs are in order to become successful learners by learning how to learn and developing awareness of their own learning; it is up to the teacher to provide good conditions for language learning and the material for knowledge construction. Therefore learning depends on collaborative investigation by teachers and learners from their different perspectives. The concept of learner autonomy and successful learning are seen as two sides of the same coin. There should also be a balance between "openness" in the syllabus design and on the other hand, "direction", so the teacher may respond to the diverse learning needs in the classroom and at the same time make it the locus for innovative pedagogical change.

If the concept of autonomy seems to be brewing of possibility it also contains many constraints. Due to the crisis in higher education in Portugal, the reduction of students in higher education institutions set off great competition between universities and polytechnics in dire straits because of Ministry financial policies based on student entries. If less students means less government funds, then a common worry can be to save resources in teaching staff, and thus the philosophy of autonomy in teaching may be perceived as students working independently on their own, or technologically dependent, which implies less need for teachers. In this context autonomy can be a recipe. If you lack financial resources it is convenient to support such an approach to learning.

One other constraint to learner autonomy has to do with the cultural background of the students in Portugal. Secondary school in Portugal is characterized by a total dependence of learners on the teacher as a transmitter of knowledge. As far as EFL learning is concerned:

> "... students tend to suffer from the symptoms of a pedagogy for dependence: a general lack of motivation, an extreme dependence upon the teacher, a passive role in classroom discourse, an inability to learn how to learn the language, and a normative view of the teaching/learning process".
> (Vieira, 1999: 150)

If autonomy is to be understood as a solution to *effective learning* one can consider the constraints and work out solutions, namely that there are several degrees for autonomy and that it can be gradually introduced in syllabuses in order to achieve change, even if only in the long run, or to contribute to the training towards a different mentality. It can be an open process where the teacher who has delineated the syllabus framework decides when to direct the syllabus towards a different path after assessing the dynamics of the group he/she is working with. The tutorial hours ascribed to the new courses may help the teacher make this an easier task and help transform the student into an accountable learner by monitoring his/her progress more often, personalizing the teacher /student relationship, giving feedback and guidance more often while trying to set students to a freer environment.

Developing a course strategy for the promotion of autonomy

Given the constraints of having only 1 or 2 hours of contact with students per week in the first year of a course, the methodology of language teaching/learning is bound to change to achieve successful results or it will only be a means of keeping one's job. If contact hours are not enough to transmit knowledge in a traditional course then the course outline has to be redefined.

Although our institution has not adopted a Bologna model for its courses yet, in the academic year 2007/08 all Portuguese higher education institutions are compelled to have their courses re-formed and so will we. Thus, in our institution, English for Specific Purposes will be taught to seven courses: four engineering courses, one ecotourism course, one organic farming course and one biotechnology course, whose contents are currently being planned and whose objectives are under discussion. For the Languages and Communication Sector the discussion is centred on how to find mechanisms for autonomy promotion with highly unmotivated students whose vocational area is very far from language learning, who are almost totally dependent on the teacher and who usually study on the eve of exams. We do not have recipes; we do not know if we have solutions for these problems, we only have strategies to try to foster autonomy. In our draft of course objectives we have considered the following components:

1 Foster learner/teacher dialogue
2 Learn how to learn a language
3 Learn how to build classroom materials
4 Use the European Language Portfolio
5 Use the virtual resource centre
6 Work in collaboration with teachers of specific subjects
7 Continuous assessment

Foster learner/teacher dialogue

From the beginning students have to understand what is asked of them and they should have encounters with the teacher in tutorial hours to discuss their study plan, their material research, their self-assessment, extra work, etc. Every student should have at least 3 compulsory interviews at the beginning, mid-point and end of the school year. In each interview the aims are different. In the first, the establishment of a relationship between student and teacher is central as well as clarifying the objectives of the course. In the second the goal is to assess and discuss the learner's progress and to offer advice. In the final interview there should be an overall assessment on how the work was carried out, on positive and negative aspects, etc. Of course, students should have less formal encounters with the teacher during the whole year formally, in tutorials, or informally, after classes.

Learn how to learn a language

After a placement test the students should be confronted with their weaknesses and strengths and start to devise a plan to learn how to learn the language. Each student will have advice on which strategies to choose to foster their learning. As tools will be needed they will have to learn how to use the dictionary and the grammar book as effective tools. Guidance will be also offered on how to elaborate their personal portfolios and their materials for language learning.

Learn how to build classroom materials

Although the first units are taught in a more traditional teaching/learning paradigm, to give time for the student to adjust to the objectives of the course, each student is responsible to prepare a unit for the classroom a "coursebook" to be built according to their needs and objectives. The course tasks to be designed in these units replicate those which students confront in the use of the foreign language in their profession. Students should prepare oral presentations on specific subjects to be assessed by the teacher, by their peers, and by themselves.

Use the European Language Portfolio

Students should be familiar with the descriptors of the European Language Portfolio and use it to assess their progress, to develop their biography as learners and to seriously engage in self-assessment.

Use of the virtual resource centre

As the institution does not have independent study facilities, a virtual resource centre will be used as a portal for *e-learning* and for a reinforcement of teaching hours. Learners will find on-line different *loci* to go to for particular information, *e.g.* in the resource centre they will have a library where they will find on-line dictionaries and grammars, encyclopaedias, course materials, etc. Students will be encouraged to create their e-portfolios so that the whole institution could have access to the work they have developed. These e-portfolios should also be on the electronic library files of the virtual resource centre. Learners will also contact the teacher by e-mail, so that *blended learning* could be feasible, and clarify their doubts before the next contact hours.

Work in collaboration with teachers of specific subjects

Near the end of the year the teachers of English should have the participation of teachers of core disciplines, specially with the first year discipline that introduces the relevant topics relevant to the students′ profession, presenting short lectures akin to the contents they are studying and interacting with the class in the target language. Team-teaching includes also the creation of a dossier with articles and materials in English to be handed out to students in the second and third years, so as to confront them with the materials they will have to read and work from in later semesters. On the other hand, this dossier will also broaden the students' choice when elaborating their class materials or their oral presentations.

Continuous assessment

If the students are used to studying on the eve of exams their effective learning is null. If the teaching/learning model has to change it cannot do so if what is valued is the end-product and not the process. The building of a portfolio of assignments and of a "coursebook" is something gradual and the assessment system should follow it. An exam is the same for all students; a portfolio has a tinge of uniqueness, of being personal. A part of the portfolio to be included is a personal dictionary, or glossary elaboration, an already tried out strategy that emphasizes the unique characteristics of portfolios, for as the personal dictionaries are elaborated according to the needs of the learner and on the materials chosen and developed, so should the portfolios. Because focus should be laid on learning how to learn and on how to self-assess the personal process, the final mark should have a percentage considering the mark the student has attributed to himself/herself for the work carried out.

Concluding remarks

The Bologna Process represents a challenge not only to students, but in particular to teachers since we have learned how to teach and now we have to unlearn it in order to relearn it. Teachers have to learn to share power, to share decisions, and to constantly adapt to ongoing change in the classroom and in the world. They have to be sharp on judging what is to be under his/her supervision and direction and what is to be the student's decision. No innovation takes place without risk taking. A pedagogy for autonomy based on a threefold strategy namely, contact hours, blended-learning and tutorials for building self-tailored syllabuses for heterogeneous classes of engineering courses may not bear fruit immediately, may not be a recipe for success, but it may offer some solutions in a trialling process such as learning.

References

Bárbara, N. (2005) "Who's afraid of the Bologna Process? – Perspectives on ESP in Engineering courses" in Moreira, G. & Howcroft, S. (coord.) *Línguas e Mercado Languages and Marketplace Marktplatz* *der Sprachen Langues et Marché Idiomas y Mercado.*Aveiro: Universidade de Aveiro, pp. 275-283.

Barnett, R. (2003) *Beyond All Reason: Living with Ideology in the University.* Buckingham: Open University Press.

—. (1994) *The Limits of Competence: Knowledge, Higher Education and Society*. Buckingham: Open University Press.

Benson, P. (2003) "Learner Autonomy in the Classroom" in Nunan, D. *Practical English Language Teaching.* New York: McGraw-Hill Contemporary.

—. (2001) *Teaching and Researching Autonomy in Language Learning.* Harlow: Pearson Education.

Benson, P., Voller, P. (1997) *Autonomy and Independence in Language Learning*. Harlow: Longman.

Blight, D. *et al*. (2000) "The Globalization of Higher Education" in Scott, P. (ed.) *Higher Education Re-formed.* New millennium Series, London and New York: Falmer Press, pp. 95-113

Block, D. & Cameron, D. (eds.) (2002) *Globalization and Language Teaching.* London and New York: Routledge.

Bologna Declaration: Joint Declaration of the European Ministers of Education Convened in Bologna on the 19th of June 1999

Conseil Européen pour les Langues/European Language Council (CEL/ELC) (2002) "The Bologna Process and the Issue of Languages". Brussels

Conselho da Europa (2001) *Quadro Europeu Comum de Referência para as Línguas. Aprendizagem, Ensino, Avaliação*. Porto: Edições Asa.

Cotterall, S. & Crabbe, D. (eds.) (1999) *Learner Autonomy in Language Learning: Defining the Field and Effecting Change.* Bayreuth Contributions to Glottodidactics, vol 8 . Frankfurt am Maim: Peter Lang.

Cotterall, S. (1998) "Developing a Course Strategy for Learner Autonomy" in Wallace, M. *Action Research for Language Teachers.* Cambridge: Cambridge University Press.

Dam, L. (1995) Learner Autonomy 3: From theory to Classroom Practice. Dublin: Authentik.

Dickinson, L. (1992) *Learner Autonomy 2: Learner Training for Language Learning.* Dublin: Authentik.

Duddley-Evans, T. & St John, M. J. (1998) *Developments in English for Specific Purposes: A Multidisciplinary Approach.* Cambridge: Cambridge University Press.

Ellis, G. & Sinclair, B. (1989) *Learning to Learn English; A Course in Learner Training.* Cambridge: Cambridge University Press

Gray, J. (2002) "The Global Coursebook in English Language Teaching" in Block, D. & Cameron, D., (eds.) *Globalization and Language Teaching*. London and New York: Routledge.

Hills, G. (2003) "The New Learning Paradigm and the Importance of Technology" in J. GOMES, (coord.) – *Reflectir Bolonha: Reformar o Ensino Superior*. Porto: Universidade do Porto. CD-ROM, PDF.

Holec, H. (1981) *Autonomy and Foreign Language Learning*. Oxford: Pergamon Press.

Little, D. *et al.* (2003) *Learner Autonomy in the Foreign Language Classroom: Teacher, Learner, Curriculum and Assessment*. Dublin: Authentik.

Moreira, G. (2005) "Meeting the Needs of the Market vs. Building a Better World… The Campus Europae Initiative." in Moreira, G. & Howcroft, S. (coord.) *Línguas e Mercado Languages and Marketplace Marktplatz der Sprachen Langues et Marché Idiomas y Mercado.*Aveiro: Universidade de Aveiro, pp. 51- 60.

—. (coord.) (2001) *Programa de Inglês – 10º, 11º e 12º Anos (Nível de Continuação). Componente de Formação Científico-Tecnológica.* Lisboa: Ministério da Educação, Departamento do Ensino Secundário.

Neves, F. S. (2005) *Quem Tem Medo da "Declaração de Bolonha"? A "Declaração de Bolonha e o Ensino Superior em Portugal.* Lisboa: Edições Universitárias Lusófonas.

Nuan, D. (ed.) (2003) *Practical English Language Teaching.* New York: McGraw-Hill Contemporary.

Phipps, A. & Gonzalez, M. (2004) *Modern Languages. Learning & Teaching in an Intercultural Field.* London: Sage Publications

Reinalda, B. & Kulesza, E. (2005) *The Bologna Process – Harmonizing Europe's Higher Education.* Opladen & Bloomfield Hills: Barbara Budrich Publishers.

Santos, B. S. (org.) (2001) *Globalização: Fatalidade ou Utopia?* Porto: Edições Afrontamento.

"The European Higher Education Area". Joint Declaration of the European Ministers of Education Convened in Bologna on 19th June 1999. http://www.bologna-berlin2003.de/pdf/bologna_declaration.pdf

"Towards the European Higher Education Area". Communiqué of the Meeting of European Ministers in charge of higher Education in Prague on19th May 2001.
http://www.bologna-berlin2003.de/pdf/Prague_ communiqueTheta.pdf

Trebbi, T. (2003) "Curriculum Development and Learner Autonomy in the Foreign Language Classroom: Constraints and Possibilities" in Lillte,

D. et al. *Learner Autonomy in the Foreign Language Classroom: Teacher, Learner, Curriculum and Assessment.* Dublin: Authentik.

Van Esch, K. & St John, O. eds. (2003) *A Framework for Freedom. Learner Autonomy in Foreign Language Teacher Education.* Vol. 8 , Frankfurt am Maim: Peter Lang.

Vieira, F. (1998) *Autonomia na Aprendizagem de Língua Estrangeira. Uma Intervenção Pedagógica em Contexto Escolar*. PhD Thesis at the University of Minho in Methodology and English Teaching. Braga: Instituto de Educação e Psicologia.

—. (1999) "Pedagogy for Autonomy: Teacher Development and Pedagogical Experimentation" In Cotterall, S. & Crabbe, D. (ed.s) *Learner Autonomy in Language Learning : Defining the Field and Effecting Change.* Bayreuth Contributions to Glottodidactics, vol. 8. Frankfurt am Maim: Peter Lang, pp. 149 – 158.

THE IMPACT OF THE CEFR ON TESTING LANGUAGE COMPETENCE IN HIGHER EDUCATION

JANA BÉREŠOVÁ

English for specific purposes (ESP) is based on designing courses to meet learners' needs, using the underlying methodology and activities of the disciplines it serves, being centred on the language, skills, discourse and genres appropriate to these activities. Designing a course is a matter of asking questions in order to provide a reasoned basis for the subsequent processes of syllabus design, materials writing, classroom teaching and evaluation. Most of ESP teachers use the recommended questions What, Why, When, How, Where and Who the answers to which cover language description, learning theories and needs analysis (Hutchinson & Waters, 1991). There are a number of ways in which information about needs can be gathered. The most frequently used are: questionnaires, interview, observation, data collection, informal consultations with stakeholders such as firms/companies, associations, governments, and so on.

The definition of language learning objectives is assisted by a transparent and coherent Common European Framework produced by John Trim, Daniel Coste, Brian North and Joe Sheils. After piloting with two internal editing distributed by the Council of Europe in 1996 and 1997, the Common European Framework of Reference for Languages: Learning, teaching, assessment (CEFR) was published with Cambridge University Press for English and with Didier for French and is currently available in 23 languages. In the past few years it has been increasingly widely adopted by schools in mainstream and adult education, by publishers and by examination providers.

The Common European Framework of Reference (CEFR) was written with the aim to establish a metalanguage common across educational sectors, national and linguistic boundaries that could be used to talk about objectives and language levels to make easier for practitioners to tell each other and their clientele, what they wish to help learners achieve and how they attempt to do so and to encourage practitioners in the language field to reflect on their current practice, particularly in relation to learners' practical language needs, the setting of suitable objectives and the tracking of learner progress (North, 2005).

The present reform of the school-leaving examination in Slovakia is based on the materials of the Council of Europe. The new system of assessment provides a free choice for the students studying English at secondary schools. The students can choose between the basic level (compatible with Level B1 of the CEF) and the advanced level (compatible with Level B2 of the CEF). The former one is recommended for those who start to learn English at secondary schools and the latter one for those who continue learning the same language at secondary level and for those who want to use the language for academic purposes or in their future professions.

The next level is Level C1 which is defined as a proficient user who can understand a wide range of demanding, longer texts, and recognise implicit meaning. The learner should express him/herself fluently and spontaneously without much obvious searching for expressions and is expected to be able to use the language flexibly and effectively for social, academic and professional purposes. In writing skills he/she is expected to produce clear, well-structured, detailed text on complex subjects, showing controlled use of organisational patterns, connectors and cohesive devices. This global description provides teachers and curriculum planners with orientation points.

The Faculty of Health and Social Care of Trnava University prepares students to become professionals in two fields of study: Public Health and Social Work. Most of them completed their secondary-school studies passing the B1-level school-leaving examination in English, only some of them passed Level B2 and feel enough confident to reach Level C1 during their university studies. At our faculty, the students are obliged to study general English for 4 semesters which means that the main emphasis is put on general English and acquisition of language communicative competence: linguistic competences (defined as knowledge of, ability to use, the formal resources from which well-informed, meaningful messages may be assembled and formulated), sociolinguistic competences (knowledge and skills required to deal with the social dimension of language use) and pragmatic competences (the user/learner's knowledge of the principles: discourse competence, functional competence and design competence). Communicative language activities are organised in three main categories: reception, interaction and production (CEFR, 2001).

After four semesters of general English in two levels: B2 and C1, students can choose English as electives and the specific programme, based on the occupation for which English is required, is implemented. If the specific occupation for which English is required is public health, for which the central duty is identified as health services and hospital managements, the occupational classification will be managers in health services. We presume that many of our students will work for international health companies providing health materials or for any health institutions such as state public health departments or local ones referring to sanitation inspections, environmental health, tuberculosis screening, epidemiology, dairy product supervision, state laboratory services, etc. Our ESP programme contains the topics like team work, how to be a good manager, how to make meeting work and how to negotiate. What is more, most of them will try to get money from various organisations and foundations, therefore project work is an inevitable part of the syllabus. The students are trained how to search for grants, how to prepare a project, how to draw up a budget, how to plan activities, how to balance profits and looses and so on. Some of them are likely to become official representatives of international companies, and will need presentation techniques, therefore presentation preparation and presentation delivery are included. In addition to this, students should be aware of how to get and retrieve information, which is achieved through Information and Communication Technologies (ICT).

The skills which have to be acquired are understanding (listening and reading), speaking (spoken interaction and spoken production) and writing. In real professional life, our graduates are expected to read long and complex factual texts, specialised articles and longer instructions. In writing they are expected to express themselves in a clear, well-structured text, expressing points of view at some length, to be able to select a style appropriate to the reader/the audience. Writing CVs, formal letters, summaries, reports and essays is included in the syllabus so the students can achieve strategies necessary for real life.

Our students' communicative language competence in ESP is activated in the performance of the various language activities, involving reception, production, interaction and mediation (processing), both in written and oral forms. Mediation involves translation, interpretation, a paraphrase, reformulation of the text and summary or record. At the faculty, the ideas of Alan Maley (1989:3) that translation develops three qualities essential to all language learning: accuracy, clarity and flexibility are followed and different activities to develop language awareness are used. It is emphasised that there might be alternative ways of expressing meanings and our students are aware of the fact that if they understand the different language systems (Slovak and English) they will never have the problems of interference of the mother tongue in the English texts and interference of English translating texts into their mother tongue.

Language competence which includes phonology, morphology, syntax, lexis, stylistics should be enhanced as well. Our intensive programme deals with functions in ESP communication:

- the passive (as it is more frequent in formal English which is influenced by the impossibility to use agentless sentences without subject and needs of achieving the right distribution of communicative dynamism)
- to-infinitive and in order to-infinitive (to express purpose)
- expressions like it causes..., it is caused by… (to express cause)
- expressions like it is responsible for... it is due to... it is the result of... it results from... (to express result)
- modals such as may, might (to express possibility)
- be+likely+infinitive, it is likely that... (to express likelihood)
- modals such as must, have to, should, ought to (to express obligation)
- must, have to (to express necessity)
- expressions such as like, unlike, more than, less than, a great deal, in contrast with, compared to (to express comparing).

In the mid to late 1990s, the issues of linking assessments, tests and examinations to the CEFR was still hardly discussed at an academic level. The achievement was the Manual "Relating Language Examinations to the Common European Framework of Reference for Languages: Learning, Teaching, Assessment" (Council of Europe, 2003) which is currently being piloted. The Manual proposes a linking process undertaken through three sets of procedures: specification of the context and purpose of the examination plus of the coverage of its tests and sub-tests in relation to the CEFR, standardisation of the interpretation of the CEFR levels by those involved with the examination, and empirical validation including external validation that the results reported by the test-in-operation relate to the CEFR in the manner intended (North, 2005). Some materials such as the videos/CD-Roms giving samples of levels for the setting of certification tests have been launched by The Council of Europe's Language Policy Division. It was proposed for the development of language programmes that are consistent with one another, from one language to another and also with the common tools which already exist.

English is an essential tool for any health manager working with international matters. It is the lingua franca of the management profession, of business and international affairs. Employers of international health companies need to know that the public health staff they appoint have a sufficient level of English to be able to communicate with clients and professionals in other countries, and to handle information written in English.

It is necessary to take into account that there is a need for tests of ESP and to follow the steps such as how to create them, what issues should be involved in test development, how we can test specificity and how it affects results. Specific purpose language testing used to be criticised in the past mostly on the grounds: specific purpose language proficiency is just general purpose language proficiency with technical vocabulary thrown in, specific language tests are unreliable and invalid since subject knowledge interferes with the measurement of language knowledge. Douglas (2002) focused on two aspects of language for specific purposes (LSP) tests: authenticity of the task and the interaction between language knowledge and specific purpose content knowledge. Authenticity means that the test taker will carry out the test task in the same way as the task would be carried out in the actual target situation. Bachman (1991) proposes two aspects of authenticity: situational and interactional. The former aspect comprises authentic characteristics derived from an analysis of tasks in the target language use situation. The latter one involves the interaction of the test taker's specific purpose language ability with the test task. In LSP testing background knowledge is a necessary, integral part of the concept of specific purpose language ability.

> "The interaction between language knowledge and content, or background knowledge is perhaps the clearest defining feature of LSP testing, for in more general purpose language testing, the factor of background knowledge is usually seen as a confounding variable, contributing to measurement error and to be minimized as much as possible. In LSP testing, on the other hand...background knowledge is a necessary integral part of the concept of specific purpose language ability."
>
> (Douglas, 2002)

In general, there is a need and companies would recognise the tests if they are relevant, objective, reliable and validated. Developing a test, we should start by interviewing experienced professionals, company supervisors, heads of international divisions, and managers who typically deal with international colleagues who know what people involved in a specific subject area should be able to conduct their business in a foreign language.

The first step in test development is to produce test specifications, including a statement of the purpose of the test, description of what it is that is intended to be measured, a description of the contexts and tasks, details how the test will be scored, and an indication of how scores on the test should be interpreted.

The issues involved in test development are reliability, construct validity, authenticity, interactiveness, and practically. Reliability is defined as consistency of measurement, and construct validity pertains to the meaningfulness and appropriateness of the interpretations that we make on the basis of test scores. The minimum acceptable level of authenticity might be stated in two ways: in terms of task characteristics and in terms of expected perceptions on the part of test takers and test users (Bachman, Palmer 1996). Interactiveness is defined as the extent and type of involvement of the test taker's individual characteristics in accomplishing a test task. Practicality pertains primarily to the ways in which the test will be implemented.

The ESP test should be geared to the field of study, the task/questions should be more subject–related, should contain the task which students will be exposed to in real professional life, so the texts, topics, tasks and resources should be authentic. Balance between specific subject areas and more general subject matter seems to be good and justified. We should be aware of the fact that if the balance is not right, it becomes a test of knowledge, accessibility is limited, test construction and marking/ examining are impractical, generalisability is limited, and impact on teaching and learning is negative.

In testing speaking tasks need to be examined by a language professional as well as subject specialist speaking English. Language skills cannot be distinguished from professional skills. Thus, the more process questions, the more accurate the test is as an indicator of ability to use professional skills.

In test development it is necessary to collaborate with content experts, test users, testing experts, examiners, candidates and teachers because ESP tests must impact positively on learning. The ESP test writer must involve practitioners from the specific purpose field in question to work with the test development team on the selection and use of appropriate texts. Test development is best carried out as a collaborative effort involving a wide range of people for whom the test is important (Davidson, Lynch, 1993). This range includes experts in technical, professional, and academic fields that are the target language use domains of interest. Our faculty involves professors and associate professors and professionals from two areas: public health and social work. The tests contain authentic texts, topics and tasks, appropriate to health and social care English domains (public health or health management and social work). Input for reading comprehension is authentic public health/health management-related texts or social work related texts testing reading for gist and global meaning, reading for structure and detail, understanding general points and specific details, discourse features, etc. The testing techniques appropriate for testing these skills are matching, multiple-choice, cloze, rational deletion and open cloze. Testing listening comprehension is assessed through gap-filling, multiple matching and multiple-choice on the monologues linked by theme or topic or dialogues from 2 or more different speakers with the focus on listening for specific information, to identify topic, speaker's opinion, listening for gist, specific information, attitudes, etc.

Productive skills are assessed through tests of writing and speaking. Communicative tasks like describing or comparing figures from graphic input, describing and summarising, explaining, apologising, complaining, recommending are usually tested through writing reports, formal letters and essays. Speaking involves speaking production as well as speaking interaction. A presentation on a public health/health management or social work theme provides useful information about a candidate if he/she is able to organise a larger unit of discourse, giving information, expressing and justifying opinions. Interaction is assessed on a discussion on a public health/health management or social work topic through two-way conversation between students or between the interlocutor and a student. The interlocutor should be a subject lecturer to provide professional input. The number of tasks depends on the given time for the test of speaking. The test is designed to minimise the possibility of attempts to use rehearsed speech.

Draft tests are usually given to colleagues, students and subject specialists to get feedback from them on such matters as the appropriateness of test content, approximate level of difficulty of tasks and the likelihood of obtaining the expected responses. In formal piloting we try to give a test to trial candidates. The examiners are trained how to score the performances of students to be objective as much as possible. We are aware of the fact that "the higher stakes dependent on test performance, the more important it is to find the resources necessary for thorough piloting" (Douglas, 2002: 254).

Advantages of placing ESP tests on the CEFR are numerous. It allows candidates and teachers to ascertain level of language ability necessary for success, allows test users to compare performance across exams and provides test users with a description of what candidates can do. ESP tests can be placed on the CEFR by relating language exams to the CEFR Manual. The test must be valid, reliable and have detailed test specifications. Positive results from developmental trials, socio-cognitive framework (Weir, 2005), expertise of item writers, test designers, examiners, item response theory, can do statements help ESP tests be placed on the CEFR.

If teachers want to prepare students for exams it is necessary to accept the model of team teaching. There are two main types which are recommended: the first one which involves two teachers (the ESP teacher and the specialist lecturer) being present in the classroom together or the second model subject – language integration, which may involve only one teacher teaching at a time (Robinson, 1991). At our faculty the second model is preferable. A specialist is obliged to present the topic and is in charge that the speciality will be correct. The task of the language teacher is to act as constant check to see that any questions of problems of structure, vocabulary or pronunciation were given immediate attention.

Participation in professional life requires from our graduates to function in specific purpose contexts where precision, clarity, range and flexibility of language use are called for. ESP teachers should be prepared to measure accurately and make valid interpretations of test performances if they want to know how well their students can use language in specific contexts of use.

ESP teachers should be flexible, willing to try new approaches and methods. Being an ESP teacher requires a lot of effort, searching for information in the field of study of their students, trying new methods, participating in additional training, making learners aware of their needs and they have to play a lot of additional roles. However, orienting themselves to a new environment is enriching.

References

Bachman, L. F., Palmer, A. S. (1996) *Language Testing in Practice*. Oxford: Oxford University Press.

Bérešová, J. (2005) *Angličtina pre špecifické účely v zdravotníckom manažmente*. Trnava: Trnavská univerzita.

Common European Framework of Reference for Languages. Learning, Teaching, Assesment (2001) Cambridge: Cambridge University Press.

Davidson, F. & Lynch, B. (1993) Criterion-referenced language test development: a prolegomenon. In Huhta, A., Sajavaara, K., and Takala, S. (eds.) *Language testing: new openings*. Jyvaskyla, Finland: Institute for Educational Research, University of Jyvaskyla, pp. 73-89.

Douglas, D. (2000) *Assessing Languages for Specific Purposes*. Cambridge: Cambridge University Press.

Duff, A. (1989) *Translation.* Oxford: Oxford University Press.

Hutchinson, J. & Waters, A. (1991) *English for Specific Purposes*. Cambridge: Cambridge University Press.

Manual. Relating Language Examinations to the Common European Framework of Reference for Languages: Learning, Teaching, Assessment (2003) Preliminary Pilot Version. Strasbourg: language Policy Division.

Munby, J. (1997) *Communicative Syllabus Design*. Cambridge: Cambridge University Press.

North, B. (2005) *The CEFR Levels and Descriptor Scales*. 2nd ALTE International Conference, Berlin 19-21 May 2005.

Robinson, P. (1991) *ESP Today: A Practitioner's Guide*. Prentice Hall International.

Weir, C. (2005) *Language Testing and Validation: an Evidence-Based Approach*. Hampshire: Palgrave-Macmillan.

STRATEGIES AND LANGUAGE COMPETENCE IN THE ELP – SCOPE, PURPOSE AND ADAPTABILITY FOR LSP PORTFOLIOS

NATAŠA GAJŠT

Introduction

The introduction of the European Language Portfolio has made an important positive and qualitative advance as regards the awareness of key participants in the process of learning languages, i.e. the students and the teachers alike. This useful instrument has provided the teachers with a concise and practical insight into the complexities of language teaching and learning while the benefit for the students lies mainly in their more active role in language learning, self-assessment and in the greater awareness of language use. Apart from that, it provides a certain level of learner autonomy as the students may use the portfolio without the supervision of the teacher. As regards the LSP portfolios, they provide a valuable insight into their users' knowledge also for employers who may be able to see either the progress or the level of their employees' linguistic knowledge in a specific area, e.g. business, engineering, law, etc.

Setting aside the entire portfolio with all its constituent parts and its usefulness for the users, this contribution looks in more detail at the descriptors for strategies and language competence. Moreover, it examines their scope and their purpose as well as their adaptability for LSP portfolios.

Strategies and language competence in ELP – "What to say and how to say it?"

Communication, as the exchange of information, news, ideas with other people, either in writing or orally, cannot be accomplished without language. Ludwig Wittgenstein's famous words that the limits of one's language mean the limits of one's world well correlate to the issue of language competence and, consequently, to strategies used in communication. The strategies of language use and language competence are closely interconnected since one can hardly apply any strategy using language to obtain certain results without adequate language competence. Moreover, language competence per se is useless without the ability of speaker to apply it in practice, i.e. to carry out the tasks set.

At the beginner stage of language learning, for example, i.e. when the learner has only limited language competence, he or she is usually able to apply only limited and the most basic strategies to communicate his or her message. Here, it should be noted that there are no descriptors for strategies available in the CEF for A1 level. As the linguistic competence widens or increases, so does the scope of various strategies one can apply.

However, even with limited linguistic knowledge, but with well-developed strategies for production of language, the reception as well as for interaction, a person may achieve the goal of communication, i.e. convey the message or carry out a certain task. On the other hand, if a person lacks the ability to apply strategies for communication, then even a vast linguistic knowledge cannot be put to practice effectively. In general, nevertheless, it can be argued that the greater the linguistic competence a person has, the greater his or her repertoire of language strategies is. One has, therefore, to bear in mind the great interconnectedness of language competence and strategies since it is equally important what you say as how you say it.

(a) Strategies in ELP

What exactly is a strategy? According to the Oxford Advanced Learner's dictionary strategy is "a plan that is intended to achieve a particular purpose", or "the process of planning something or carrying out a plan in a skilful way". CEF provides even more complex definition:

> "A *strategy* is any organised, purposeful and regulated line of action chosen by an individual to carry out the task which he or she sets for himself or herself or with which he or she is confronted."
>
> (CEF: 10)

Therefore, in order to carry out the individual tasks, one must apply a particular strategy. The user of a particular language may choose among a great variety of strategies.

The CEF includes a number of different types of strategies. For the *language production*, the language user may choose the strategy of *planning*, *compensating* or *monitoring and repair*. On the *reception* side of communication, the strategy of *identifying cues and inferring* both in spoken and written communication channel is applied. The third category of strategies comprises *taking the floor*, *co-operating* and *asking for clarification*, all of which are *strategies for interaction*.

The total number of different descriptors in the CEF for strategies is 46. It has to be pointed out that in some cases the descriptors that are valid for more than one level of language knowledge.

The distribution of these descriptors is presented in Table 1.

	Level:	***A1***	***A2***	***B1***	***B2***	***C1***	***C2***
Production strategies	***SP1***	–*	1	2	1	1	1
	SP2	–*	2	4	1	1	1
	SP3	–*	–*	3	2	1	1
Reception strategies	***SR***	–*	1	2	1	1	1
Interaction strategies	***SI1***	–*	3	3	4	1	1
	SI2	–*	1	3	2	1	1
	SI3	–*	2	1	1	1	1

* – = no descriptors available

Table 1 Strategies in CEF

(b) Language competence in ELP

Communicative language competence comprises linguistic, sociolinguistic and pragmatic competences. The first type of competences, i.e. *linguistic competences* include lexical, phonological, syntactical knowledge and skills and other dimensions of language as a system (CEF, 13) without considering the sociolinguistic value and the pragmatic functions within language use. Here, we include lexical, grammatical, semantic, phonological, orthographic and orthoepic competence and the CEF provides the following descriptors for "linguistic language competence": "*General linguistic range*", "*Vocabulary range*", "*Vocabulary control*", "*Grammatical accuracy*", "*Phonological control*", "*Orthographic control*".

Sociolinguistic competences, as the second type of competences, refer to the knowledge and skills needed to deal with the social dimension of language use. This component strictly affects all language communication between representatives of different cultures (CEF, 13). They incorporate the linguistic makers of social relations, politeness conventions, expressions of folk-wisdom, register differences and dialect and accent. The "sociolinguistic language competence" is defined by the "*Sociolinguistic appropriateness*" descriptors.

Thirdly, *pragmatic competences* mainly deal with the functional use of language (CEF, 13) and include discourse competence, functional competence and schematic design competence. The "pragmatic language competence" descriptors deal with *"Flexibility", "Turn-taking", "Thematic development", "Coherence and cohesion", "Spoken fluency"* and *"Propositional precision"*. The total number of different descriptors in the CEF for communicative language competences is 113.

Table 2 shows the distribution of the abovementioned scales.

	Level:	***A1***	***A2***	***B1***	***B2***	***C1***	***C2***
Language competence / Linguistic	***LL1***	1	4	2	2	1	1
	LL2	1	3	1	1	1	1
	LL3	–*	1	1	1	1	1
	LL4	1	1	2	2	1	1
	LL5	1	1	1	1	1	1
	LL6	2	2	2	2	2	1
Language competence / Sociolinguistic	***LS***	1	3	3	4	3	3
Language competence / Pragmatic	***LP1***	–*	2	2	3	1	1
	LP2	–*	3	3	4	1	1
	LP3	–*	1	1	1	1	1
	LP4	1	2	1	2	1	1
	LP5	1	2	2	3	1	1
	LP6	–*	1	3	1	1	2

*– = no descriptors available

Table 2 Language competence in CEF

Of course, communicative competences of individuals differ due to a number of reasons.

When discussing communicative language competences we cannot overlook the general competences of a language user. The declarative knowledge, skills and know-how, existential competence and the ability to learn all play an important role in language acquisition and language use. Although the interrelatedness between an individual's general competences and the actual learning and/or use of language is of great importance, it shall not be included in this paper.

Adaptability of Scales in ELP for LSP

Stemming from the above overview, the question of which strategies and language competences descriptors to include in an individual portfolio arises. As there are far too many of them in the CEF, a selection is needed and it should primarily be based on the purpose of the portfolio and on its users. When deciding which ones to include and later on how to adapt them to best suit the purpose of a specific portfolio, a number of questions have to be answered. The rationale behind these questions is to analyse the concrete situation and the users of the portfolio since one must always stem from the profile of the portfolio user.

The primary question is concerned with the correlation between the adaptation and the language for specific purposes. If, in language, the aim is to achieve a particular purpose, we have to define what the purpose is. Language and its use exist only in definite domains and, within these domains, in particular specific situations. In individual professions, the users of language have to perform different tasks by applying different strategies in order to achieve particular and/or specific purposes. When choosing which descriptors to include, these facts should be well considered.

The portfolio development at the Faculty of Economics and Business (FEB), University of Maribor has been based on the needs and characteristics of the students of economics and business sciences in view of the language they will be required to use in their professional careers. From this aspect, the descriptors were adapted in order to create new ones characterised by the applicability for the users' needs.

Adaptations of descriptors in the FEB LSP portfolio were carried out mainly in order to tailor the descriptors to the occupational domain, comprising a person's activities and relations in his or her job or profession. We predominately considered *the events* in which our students will have to use the foreign language (e.g. meetings, interviews, receptions, conferences, trade fairs, consultations, etc.) and *the operations* they will be engaged in (e.g. business administration, management, office procedures, sales operations, selling, marketing, finance, etc.). In addition, we looked at the persons with whom they are likely to interact as well as the texts they will have to produce.

Unfortunately, due to the spatial limitations only a limited number of descriptors can be used in a portfolio. Therefore, the first issue that needed to be addressed when deciding on which descriptors for strategies and language competence to include was related to their relevance for the users. This fact also contributed to the selection of the most suitable ones.

As the development of our portfolio is in the final stages, new revisions might still be necessary and perhaps more omissions will have to be made.

For the adaptation of the CEF descriptors the methods of *combining two or more descriptors*, *specifying descriptors by indicating a context of use* and *supplementing a formulation by giving examples, linguistic simplification, dividing descriptors in which more tan one task or aspect is contained into two or more individual descriptors, adding a scale with gradations* were predominately used.

(a) Combining two or more descriptors

The slight differences between individual descriptors, especially the ones in the same category and sub-category enabled us to combine categories. Of course, the differences between individual descriptors are not there without a particular purpose. However, having the end users in mind, i.e. the students of economics and business sciences (students who are not language specialists), these differences were considered as not important enough to include all the descriptors.

The following example illustrates this approach.

CEF descriptor	***FEB LSP portfolio descriptor***
EXAMPLE 1 • *Can initiate, maintain and close simple, face-to-face conversation. (SI1 / A2)** • *Can use simple techniques to start, maintain or end a short conversation. (SI1 / A2)**	• *I know how to start, maintain and finish a simple, short, face-to-face or telephone conversation in work context and social context relevant to work. (SI1 / A2)**

*see the Notes at the end of the paper

(b) Specifying descriptors by indicating a context of use

The main idea behind this approach is to include the situation in which the language is used. It is a very simple way of adapting a descriptor and narrowing it to a specific context of use. It was the approach that was predominately used in the adaptation of descriptors for strategies and language competences.

CEF descriptor	*FEB LSP portfolio descriptor*
EXAMPLE 1 • *Can express him/herself clearly and without much sign of having to restrict what he/she wants to say. (LL1 / B2)**	• *I can express myself clearly and without much sign of having to restrict what I want to say in most work related contexts and in social contexts relevant to work. (LL1 / B2)**
EXAMPLE 2 • *Consistently correct and appropriate use of vocabulary. (LL3 / C2)**	• *I use general vocabulary and vocabulary related to my work and area of expertise consistently and appropriately. (LL3 / C2)**

*see the Notes at the end of the paper

As we can see from the first example, the method of adding a scale with gradations was also applied apart from the specification of context of use (i.e. "in most…") while in the second example we only specified the context of use.

(c) Supplementing a formulation by giving examples

CEF descriptor	*FEB LSP portfolio descriptor*
EXAMPLE 1 • *Can ask for attention. (SI1 / A2)**	• *I can ask for attention (e.g. "Excuse me!") (SI1 / A2)**

*see the Notes at the end of the paper

This is again a very suitable method for clarifying and focusing the portfolio user's attention on the specific knowledge or skills assessed by a particular descriptor.

(d) Linguistic simplification

CEF descriptor	*FEB LSP portfolio descriptor*
EXAMPLE 1 • *Has a very basic range of simple expressions about personal details and needs of a concrete type. (LL1 / A1)**	• *I know basic expressions to talk about personal details and concrete needs in work context and social context relevant to work (e.g. name, job, position). (LL1 / A1)**

*see the Notes at the end of the paper

This example shows a combination of various methods, i.e. linguistic simplification, specifying descriptors by indicating a context of use and supplementing a formulation by giving examples. It should also be noted here that linguistic simplification was applied mostly in descriptors for lower levels, i.e. A1 and A2.

(e) Dividing descriptors in which more than one task or aspect is contained into two or more individual descriptors

CEF descriptor	***FEB LSP portfolio descriptors***
EXAMPLE 1 • *Has enough language to get by, with sufficient vocabulary to express him/herself with some hesitation and circumlocutions on topics such as family, hobbies and interests, work, travel and current events, but lexical limitations cause repetition and even difficulty with formulation at times. (LL1 / B1)**	• *I have enough language to get by, with sufficient vocabulary to express myself with some hesitation and circumlocutions on work-related topics (e.g. workers, job description and job-related tasks and current events). (LL1 / B1)** • *My lexical limitations cause repetition and even difficulty with formulation at times. (LL1 / B1)**

*see the Notes at the end of the paper

It can occur that when expanding the descriptors by specifying the context of use, the descriptors themselves may become too long. For that reason it is advisable to divide them into two or more individual ones.

(f) deleting parts of descriptors

Sometimes descriptors are too wide for the purpose of a specific portfolio and thus one may omit certain parts. Of course, this is done not in isolation, but in context of other descriptors in the same category.

CEF descriptor	***FEB LSP portfolio descriptors***
EXAMPLE 1 • *Has a good command of a broad lexical repertoire allowing gaps to be readily overcome with circumlocutions; little obvious searching for expressions or avoidance strategies. Good command of idiomatic expressions and colloquialisms. (LL2 / C1)**	• *I have a good command of idiomatic expressions and colloquialisms used in work context and in the context related to my area of expertise as well as in social context related to my work. (LL2 / C1)**

EXAMPLE 2 • *Can interact with a degree of fluency and spontaneity that makes regular interaction with native speakers quite possible without imposing strain on either party. (LP5 / B2)**	• *I can interact in work-related contexts, in contexts related to my field of expertise and in social context relevant to work with a degree of fluency and spontaneity. (LP5 / B2)**

*see the Notes at the end of the paper

These examples show also the method of specifying *descriptors by indicating a context of use.*

The examples presented here show the applicability of different methods that may be utilised in adapting all CEF descriptors, not only the ones for strategies and language competence. We can conclude that the portfolio developers have a wide selection of methods to choose from, but what is even more significant is the fact that very often a combination of these methods is the most appropriate.

Scales in LSP Curriculum Development

The final part of this paper looks at the role of the discussed scales in a LSP curriculum development since the ultimate goal of developing the portfolio is its use by the students.

Once the descriptors are developed or adapted and portfolio created, it should be implemented in practice. As regards the adaptation of descriptors to the specific context the following can be observed. Here we see that this is an interrelated issue as the development of the curriculum can be based on the portfolio and the portfolio stems from the needs of students.

Within the Bologna process, a major review of curricula for business languages (business English and business German, as predominately taught languages) was carried out at our Faculty. In line with these changes, the new content was added or the existing one changed.

The introduction of the LSP portfolio is considered as one of the important components of language studies at FEB as it will serve as the tool for the students helping them raise awareness of different aspects of language as such and language use and as the guide in their studies. It will undoubtedly motivate the students to take a more active role in the acquisition of foreign languages. Since the users of LSP portfolios are young adults, the function of self-assessment is also of great importance.

As regards the teachers, a LSP portfolio should serve as an extremely useful tool in the following ways. It enables them to apply the descriptors more closely to the textbooks with the purpose of linking them more closely to the students' communicative needs and purpose of language learning. By applying the descriptors to the teaching material, the LSP portfolio is integrated into teaching.

In addition, it will enable them to more closely analyse the teaching material and, if needed, create new material to better facilitate the learning of individual aspects of language. This is of a great importance for the specialised courses for which not a lot of teaching material has been published or the existing material is no longer adequate.

Even if the portfolio is not created, the teachers may still use the descriptor scales in everyday practical work with their students.

Conclusion

In this paper we concentrated on the strategies and language competence descriptors in the CEF and their adaptability for a LSP portfolio. As there are too many different descriptors included in the CEF descriptor bank, a selection had to be made regarding the suitability of individual ones for a language portfolio for students of business and economics. Out of total 46 different descriptors for strategies and 113 for language competences only, approximately 60 per cent were used in the first draft of the portfolio. Of course, further selection will have to be made for its final version. Various methods were applied in the adaptation process and the decision about which one to apply was made for each individual descriptor. The most suitable one was the specification of the context of use with others be equally represented. This contribution, however, did not address the issue of deciding which particular descriptors to include in a portfolio and which ones to omit, as the process of revising and final editing is still underway. The analysis of the descriptors and their adaptation can prove extremely useful even if the actual portfolio is not developed as they provide a very helpful tool for the development of curricula and materials for language instruction.

References

Council of Europe: *Common European Framework of Reference for Languages: Learning, Teaching, Assessment*. Available at: http://www.coe.int/t/dg4/linguistic/Source/Framework_EN.pdf

Schneider, G., Lenz P. (2001) *European Language Portfolio: Guide for Developers*. Available at: http://www.coe.int/T/DG4/Portfolio/documents_intro/Eguide.pdf

*** Notes**

Abbreviations used in Table 1, Table 2 and the examples:

SP1	Planning
SP2	Compensating
SP3	Monitoring and repair
SR	Identifying cues and inferring (spoken and written)
SI1	Taking the floor (Turntaking)
SI2	Co-operating
SI3	Asking for clarification
LL1	General linguistic range
LL2	Vocabulary range
LL3	Vocabulary control
LL4	Grammatical accuracy
LL5	Phonological control
LL6	Orthographic control
LS	Sociolinguistic appropriateness
LP1	Flexibility
LP2	Turntaking
LP3	Thematic development
LP4	Coherence and cohesion
LP5	Spoken fluency
LP6	Propositional precision
A1-C2	CEF scales

DESIGNING A TASK-BASED ESP SYLLABUS

YASEMIN KIRKGOZ

Introduction

Turkey's desire to be a member of European community raises the need to redesign existing curricula, particularly at Higher Education institutions. This paper illustrates how an ESP curriculum has been redesigned for the first year freshmen learners in an English-medium department in Turkey in the light of Common European Framework (CEF). After a brief review of the literature, the next part of the paper sets out the stages involved in redesigning the curriculum and its components. The need to renew the curriculum is pointed out. This part also defines *general competence* and *academic competence* required of the learners in order for them to communicate successfully in their academic community. The level of academic competence, students are expected to have acquired, and the ways in which acquisition of corresponding skills and strategies can be facilitated is illustrated by means of sample tasks. The study provides a framework of categories representing a standard appropriate to freshman students' immediate and wider long-term goals of promoting effective language proficiency and personal development to enable them to act autonomously in social and educational contexts.

The CEF and the curriculum design

The CEF provides a common basis for curriculum guidelines. According to specification of the CEF, in an educational context a curriculum needs to be constructed within a "comprehensive", "transparent" and "coherent" framework having a harmonious relationship among its following six components:

1 The identification of learner needs
2 The determination of objectives
3 The definition of content
4 The selection of materials
5 The establishment of teaching/learning programmes

6 Evaluation, testing and assessment

Needs analysis is considered as the first component in the curriculum design process. As the next stage, the findings of the needs analysis have to be translated into appropriate course objectives (West, 1994). Course content needs to be specified and materials need to be selected in order to meet objectives. A comprehensive curriculum ends with testing and assessment of the learning process to ensure that the course objectives have been fulfilled. Within this guideline of the curriculum design process, tasks constitute central units of the learning experiences as will be described in the following section.

Task specification

Tasks are defined as actions that are performed by individuals strategically using their own specific competences to achieve a given result. According to CEF, tasks are a feature of everyday life in the personal, public, educational or occupational domains (Council of Europe, 2001: 157). Classroom tasks, such as problem solving, taking part in a discussion, giving a presentation, need to be chosen on the basis of learners' real-life educational needs. Successful accomplishment of a task by an individual involves the strategic activation of communicative language competences (linguistic, sociolinguistic and pragmatic knowledge and skills), in order to carry out a set of purposeful actions in a particular domain with a clearly defined goal and a specific outcome. For example, in the initial goal setting phase of a task, activation of learner's prior knowledge and appropriate schemata may facilitate successful task accomplishment.

Competences are the sum of knowledge, skills, and characteristics that allow a person to perform actions (9). *Academic competence* may comprise the necessary knowledge and skills students need to acquire so that they can function as effective members of their academic community.

Description of the study

This study was conducted in the Electrics-Electronics Department (EED) of Çukurova University. The EED is an English-medium department, which offers all its courses in English. Students start their freshman year after a one-year intensive English language teaching and their level of general English language proficiency corresponds to advanced level of proficiency.

Identification of learner's needs

As the initial stage of the course development, I carried out needs analysis to identify students' learning needs (Hutchinson, & Waters, 1987; West, 1994; Dudley Evans & St John, 1998) and difficulties they experienced in meeting those needs in their academic community, using a questionnaire and holding interviews with them. Analysis of the needs assessment revealed that students need to read up-to-date specialized texts and articles relevant to their academic discipline and learn corresponding lexical items; they needed to use English for written and spoken communication effectively; they were required to write projects and present them in class, which involved engaging in effective classroom discussion; they need to understand the essential meanings of these texts, and obtain information from specialized sources within their field.

Determination of objectives

The main objective of the study was to design a curriculum that would promote students' academic competence on the basis of the findings obtained from the needs analysis to enable the students to acquire the necessary knowledge and skills through carrying various academic tasks so that they can function as effective members of their academic community.

Course content and materials selection

In the previous course, the textbook entitled "English in Electrical Engineering and Electronics" by Eric H. Glendinning published in 1980, was used as the only source of information. However, my interview with the students revealed that the book did not meet students' needs in many ways: First, since the publication of this book, many changes had taken place in this particular scientific field. Second, it was not motivating for the students in terms of the content, topics, etc. Therefore, there was a need to redesign the curriculum.

The components of the curriculum, redesigned within the guidelines provided by the CEF, are as follows:

In the selection of appropriate texts, I maintained liaison with the lecturers. I identified the topics with the help of content lecturers as well as the students, which involved developing texts on such content area as "Fiber Optics, Robotics, The vacuum tube, Satellite, Air bags", etc. The course was administered once a week for 3 hours for 16 weeks, for a total of 48 hours instructional time. As there was a lack of appropriate ESP materials available in this specific field, I produced or adapted texts from various sources to be more closely aligned with the curriculum objectives.

The establishment of teaching/learning programmes

In order to promote students' academic competences, they were assigned particular tasks with a major focus on solving a particular problem within their field of study.

Applying problem-based tasks in the new curriculum

A particular task may involve several steps for its completion. In this study, I implemented philosophy of the problem-based tasks. The principal idea behind establishing problem-based tasks is that the starting point for learning is a problem, a query, or a puzzle that the learner wishes to solve." (Boud, 1985). As stated by (Duch et al., 2001), problem-based learning is an instructional method that challenges students to "learn to learn", working cooperatively in groups to seek solutions to real world problems. It has also been supported by John Dewey that "true learning is based on discovery, guided by mentoring rather than the transmission of knowledge".

Components of the tasks

In this instructional method students are encouraged to think, retrieve information for them, search for new ideas and debate them in a scholarly environment. This process differs from the traditional teacher-dominated approach. The process used in problem-based tasks is the following:

(a) Presenting a problem/case

First, students get together in small groups of 4-5. They identify a problem or scenario to investigate it. Since students are not handed content, learning becomes active in the sense that they discover and work with content that they determine to be necessary to solve the problem. Collaboration among the students gives students opportunities to work together in constructing knowledge.

(b) Explore the issues

In their groups, students organize their ideas, discuss their previous knowledge related to the problem. Throughout discussion, students determine what they know about the subject (the facts), by brainstorming their ideas and formulating hypotheses to form a foundation toward solving it. This enables them to gather information and learn new concepts, skills as they engage in the problem-solving process. In the present study, students worked on topics they identified in the needs analysis section I mentioned earlier in groups of 4-5. The learning needs they identify for themselves took them into: How plasma TV Works, history of air bags, debates about the pros and cons of mobile phones.

(c) Develop and write out the problem statement

A problem statement comes from the group's analysis of what they know, and what they will need to know to solve it. After a period of time in which students research their learning issues, they reconvene to discuss these issues and integrate their new knowledge into the context of the problem, as illustrated by a sample problem prepared by one of the group members, below:

Superconductivity and Superconductors

Superconductivity and superconductive materials are one of the most important working subjects for scientists in recent years when most energy source has been destroyed.
Too much energy is lost while it is carried one side of conductor to another. Superconductive materials are used for solution of this problem, and many scientists work on this because efficiency is very important in our life for using the energy.

General use of superconductors:

- In industry
- In daily life
- In business

Many people understood the importance of energy and one of the most important solutions for using the energy efficiently is using superconducting materials. My group and I are very interested in this subject and it is related with our department so we decided to search superconductivity and superconductors.

Setting a timeline

Students are assigned a schedule and set deadlines to complete the task. I collaborated with members of the EED who gained recognition for participating in the study. Students assume responsibility of completing the task outside of the class, or out-of-class meeting can be arranged.

Presenting and reporting findings

As part of closure, students are required to present their findings to classmates. This includes the problem statement, questions, data gathered, analysis of data, and solutions: in short, the process and outcome. Students are required to write a report or a project describing the research they have carried out. Appendix I shows the outline of two projects students have produced. As students participate in the project, learning becomes active in the sense that students discover and work with content that they determine to be necessary to solve the problem, stating clearly both the problem and the conclusion, summarizing the process they used, and difficulties encountered.

In the assessment of students' project report and presentation, I collaborated with content lecturers. The assessment involved assessing, product and process, group performance and individual contribution to the whole process. The use of these steps helps students fill the gaps in their own knowledge base, and use their newly acquired knowledge to refine their ideas thus generating a whole new set of "learning needs".

Assessment of the new curriculum

At the end of the course, students were requested to complete an evaluation form. This evaluation is used to determine to what extent the students' learning needs were met. Discussion with students (via structured focus groups) and questionnaire they completed offered further insights into students' learning experiences. Students indicated that the collaborative nature of the tasks with a focus on problem increased their level of inclusion in the learning process. In addition, students believed that their ability to evaluate information gathered from various sources increased; the new teaching/learning experiences made course content more interesting, and helped them become familiar with essential topics related vocabulary in their academic studies. It combined foreign language and professional subject knowledge. Students developed how to use information sources, report writing and presentation skills. Students also believed that their communication and interpersonal skills had improved as a result of participation in the course. With regard to language skills acquired students were able to learn professional and expanding general vocabulary; they promoted reading comprehension (dealing with longer texts, extracting information), academic writing skills (project reports), discussion and oral presentation skills. Incorporating problem-based tasks in the curriculum empowered students to take a responsible role in their own learning, helping them to develop into autonomous lifelong learners.

In addition, anecdotal information from the lecturers has been very positive about the usefulness of the course. According to the faculty lecturers, the new curriculum made significant improvements in students' communication skills.

Classroom implications

Although the present study has been conducted in a particular context, it has wider classroom implications due to the following advantages it offers:

- Students are actively involved in the learning process.
- Students construct knowledge through gathering and synthesizing information
- Students' critical thinking, and problem solving skills are expanded
- Emphasis is on using and communicating knowledge effectively to address issues and problems in real-life contexts.
- The role of the teacher is to guide, and support students' initiatives, rather than lecturing or providing easy solutions.

Conclusion

The results of the study showed that, the clear relevance of the curriculum to the learners' immediate needs has improved their motivation, changed their attitudes toward learning, and have thereby contributed to their learning better and faster. Our experience has shown that carefully identified needs, appropriate teaching materials, and creative employment of the right teaching methods has caused students to become efficient members of their business community. In addition, the revised curriculum has provided a comprehensive, dynamic and coherent frame of reference for language learning. Turkey's desire to be a member of European community raises the need to redesign existing curricula, not only at the level of primary and secondary education but at Higher

Education institutions as well. Therefore, it is expected that this study will provide a framework to be followed or adopted to similar situations in Turkish universities, which will consequently lead to standardization in curriculum issues.

References

Boud, D. J. (1985) Problem-Based Learning in *Education for the Professions*. Sydney: Higher Education Research and Development Society of Australasia.

Council of Europe (2001) Common European Framework of Reference for Languages: learning, teaching, assessment Cambridge: Cambridge University Press.

Duch, B. J., Groh S. E., & Allen D. E. (2001) *The Power of Problem-Based Learning*, Stylus: Sterling, VA.

Dudley-Evans, T., & St John, M. J. (1998) *Developments in ESP- a multidisciplinary approach.* Cambridge: Cambridge University Press.

Glendinning, E. H. (1980) *English in Electrical Engineering and Electronics*. Cambridge: Cambridge University Press

Hutchinson, T., & Waters, A. (1987). *English for specific purposes*: Cambridge: Cambridge University Press

West, R. (1994) Needs analysis in language teaching. *Language Teaching,* 1-19 January.

APPENDIX ONE

Project I

PROBLEM:
Disadvantages of today's government system.
SOLUTION:
Improving and applying electronic government system on people's daily life.

1 What's electronic government?
  - a The definition of e-government.
  - b Why do people need this system?

2 The problems while using this system
  - a Economical problems
  - b Educational problems

3 The countries which holds this system
  - a The improved countries
  - b E-Europe
  - c Turkey
    - i What's Turkey's point in the e-government world?
    - ii What we have to do to apply this project faster?
    - iii What's the importance for Turkey?

4 Conclusion

Project II

THE EFFECTS OF BASE STATIONS
Introduction
- a How do mobile phones work?
- b Base station and cells
- c What is electromagnetic energy?

1 Where the base stations are used

2 Problems
  - a Base stations in or near school
  - b In hospitals and aeroplanes
  - c At work
  - d Children and young people under 16
  - e SAR values

3 Mobile telecommunications and health researcher programme

4 Independent Assessment and Research

TEACHING PRINCIPLES AND TYPES OF WRITTEN AND SPOKEN COMMUNICATIONS IN ENGLISH FOR ACADEMIC/OCCUPATIONAL PURPOSES

NADEŽDA STOJKOVIĆ

Introduction

In today's highly competitive professional world, teaching principles of written and spoken communications is an especially relevant curriculum segment of English Language for Academic/Occupational Purposes. Broadly speaking, the types of communications most needed are: reports, spoken presentations, scientific argumentation, and correspondence. Depending on the exact profile of the target science/occupation, specific vocabulary, style, and organisational structure of presentation are elaborated. Mastery of these skills by far exceeds the knowledge of language as it subsumes thorough insight into related fields, such as psychology or sociology. Finally, it is the supreme proof of expertise.

Rationale of Presentation Principles Curriculum Segment

(a) The purpose of teaching presentation principles

Learning the principles of written and spoken presentations in English for Academic/Occupational Purposes is done with the ultimate purpose of better communicating scientific and professional knowledge to other professionals, but also non-specialists.

The goals in teaching this are:

- *to promote excellence in academic and professional communications;*
- *to advance awareness of the profession;*
- *to foster professional growth.*

Academic and professional communication skills are more important than ever in today's competitive world (Harty, 2005). For most professionals, writing reports, letters, memos, or speaking to various kinds of audience and in various situations, is an often task. For instance, getting a job demands an effective resume to promote the applicant well enough. After performing an analysis or a design, the practicing professional ought to communicate the results of their work to others. These "others" might be a supervisor, a fellow colleague, a client, a government agency, or general public. *Academic and professional communication involves gathering, analysing, and distributing the needed information efficiently and accurately to specific audiences* (Reinhart, 2005).

When advocating the importance of learning principles of written and spoken communications, students should be made fully aware that designing effective presentations requires insightful and well-trained thinking strategies that can produce clarity in communication without oversimplifying scientific/professional issues. The results are substantive, not merely cosmetic: *improving the quality of presentation actually improves the quality of thought and vice versa.*

(b) The correlation between scientific method and scientific presentations

The principles of presentation considered here are based on *the scientific method of research.* If the method of research and text structure are of the consistent organisational pattern, the scientific content that is presented will be better comprehended, analysed and critically examined (Stojković, 2005).

The scientific method is a process by which scientists endeavour to construct an accurate representation of the world. In order to achieve that, it is a must to avoid all possible personal and cultural influences in the interpretation of the phenomena in question. That is done by the use of standard procedures and criteria in developing a theory or an explanation. The same idea applies to both written and spoken presentations of those findings. The use of standard presentation structures ensures clarity, obvious rationale for the thesis, and is highly persuasive in the sense that the audience gets a strong impression that the author is a knowledgeable person, an expert.

Scientific and professional presentation communicates specific information about a specific subject to a specific audience for a specific purpose. Generally speaking, scientific and technical presentation often focuses on resolving some problem or delivery of information. The audience element is crucial for successful presentation. You have to make a precise judgment about who you write for or talk to, and according to that adapt your presentation to the audience's needs, expectations, levels of understanding, background. The purpose of scientific/professional presentation may be to inform and/or persuade the audience that your method of resolving a problem is effective and efficient. The achievement of the preset purpose proves the validity of your presentation.

(c) The interdependence of form and interpretation

The fundamental purpose of scientific discourse is not mere presentation of information and thought, but rather its actual communication (Hinder, 2005). The content that the author wants to convey is inseparable from the form they employ. With that as an aim we should always bear in mind that readers do not simply read/listen, they *interpret*. Information is interpreted more easily and more uniformly if placed where most readers expect to find it. Readers have relatively fixed expectations about where in the structure of prose they will encounter particular items. Writers aware of these locations can better control the degrees of recognition and emphasis audience will give to the various pieces of information being presented. For that reason teaching principles of academic and professional presentation *should focus on teaching the structure of various types of presentation.*

The illustration of this underlying concept of audience's expectation is perhaps most immediately evident at the level of the largest units of discourse. A research report, for example, is generally divided into recognisable sections, most often labelled Introduction, Experimental Methods, Results and Discussion. When the sections are confused, when too much experimental detail is found in the Results section, or when Discussion and Results intermingle, readers are confused. Readers have relatively definite expectations regarding the text presented and they search for certain information in particular places. Understanding the content of a passage is enhanced by its proper structuring. If these structural expectations are continually violated, readers are forced to divert energy from understanding the content of a passage to unravelling its structure.

(d) Types of communication

Hereby dealing with verbal communication only, professional/ academic communication can roughly be categorised into the following types:

Scientific communication mostly deals with ideas and research findings. It presents data, inferences and conclusions drawn from those. The information or the idea is the message. Most scientific information is communicated through articles in journals or in conference proceedings, and is almost exclusively aimed for experts.

Science communication is a kind of "popular writing". As technology is becoming more complex, there is an increasing need to "translate" information about science and technology to non-specialists. Science writing presents information for a general audience, such as readers of a newspaper or a magazine, newsletters, press release, TV and radio broadcast scripts.

Technical communication shares with science communication the primary objective to inform, yet is done for an even broader range of readers. The focus of the content is primarily on an operational level of how a product or system in question functions. It involves proposals, instructions, manuals, etc.

Procedure for Teaching Presentations in EAP/EOP

(a) Paragraph and essay

When teaching presentations it is convenient to start with the smallest organisational and logical units, paragraphs. A paragraph focuses on one idea which it develops and explains. The three, most common parts of a paragraph are: *topic sentence*, *supporting sentences*, and *a closing one.*

According to the content, paragraphs can be classified as following: definition, classification, description, compare and contrast, sequence, choice, explanation, and evaluation paragraphs. This, however, is not the only possible classification. The classes may differ according to various criteria employed.

The nucleus piece of writing is paragraph. If the logic of its organisation is comprehended, writing larger pieces will be easily mastered. The structure of an essay stems from, or is an enlarged, elaborate copy of paragraph organisation. The main parts of an essay are: title, the name and position of the author(s), introduction, supporting paragraphs, summary/concluding paragraph, references/literature cited.

Essays can be classified according to various criteria. It is very important to be aware that no piece of writing is purely a single type. Most often, the elements of many mix into a prevailing one.

The kinds of essays are:

1 Process analysis - describes a process;

2 Exploratory - the conclusion is not known in advance;
3 Argumentative - the goal of the argument is to persuade the reader of your thesis;
4 Cause and effect - gives reasons for an occurrence;
5 Compare and contrast - describes similarities and differences;
6 Classification - describes types or classes;
7 Definition - defines a term or a concept;
8 Narrative - a descriptive essay about one's personal experiences.

A classic format for compositions is the five-paragraph essay. It is not the only format for writing an essay, but a useful model when beginning to develop composition skills.

(b) Documentation of sources

Apart from the content presented, the expertise is also established with accurate documentation of sources that preceded and influenced the work. It proves authority to back up the ideas presented, and through it, appropriate credit is given to researchers and scientists on whose achievements one conceives their idea. The documentation of sources is the academic and professional writing practice of strengthening a scientific or intellectual argument by referring to work that other people have already produced. An author who wishes to prove a statement must demonstrate to the reader that the available evidence supports that statement. This evidence includes not only the data from the author's own research, but also the data and conclusions from other people's work. A well-documented paper is also more useful to a reader who wishes to investigate the subject more fully. Representative documentation formats are studied in relation to the kind of science they support.

(c) Report form

Reports are among most frequent forms of professional and academic writing. Regardless the actual type, which may be feasibility, proposal, progress, design, experiment report, etc., the main sections of a report are the following:

Title needs to be a kind of thesis statement, to introduce the main topic and the specific aspect of inquiring it.

Abstract has a special significance within a report. It is a 100-200 word summary of the project. An abstract needs to inform and persuade the readers of the validity of the work. It should include essential aspects of the work, statement of the problem and the purpose of the work, the scope and methods employed, and major results and conclusions drawn from those. Very often it is to stand alone, e.g., in journals or conference programmes, for which reason it has to be thoroughly concise and coherent.

Introduction should orient the reader as to the reasons for choosing to deal with a certain problem. It is to proceed with the background of the problem and its current relevance illustrated with an overview of relevant literature. The expected and achieved goals are precisely specified, as well as the employed approach and the criteria used.

Materials and Methods start with identification of equipment and materials needed for the project, review of the work progress, and the appropriateness of the applied method.

Results identify and elaborate the accomplishments. Whatever those may be, a detailed description should be given. In this section, graphs and tables can be used.

Discussion clearly specifies the achieved goals. Here, the expected and obtained results are to be compared. Very often the discussion and conclusion sections are merged into a single one which explains the results and their implications, significance. In light of all these, a personal viewpoint may be given, what one's experience is after completing the work and the recommendations for future or other investigators.

Appendices present supporting material, such as details of testing procedures, extended calculations, computer documentation, instructions, data tables, side issues, or large figures.

References are the section where all used sources of information - articles, books, interviews, etc., are to be listed in the appropriate style.

(d) Correspondence

Apart from actual expertise work, most professionals are often faced with the need to engage in some forms of correspondence. It has a significant place in promoting their work in diverse ways. The following topics are most common in academic/professional correspondence:

- cooperation;
- arranging visits abroad;
- arranging visits from abroad;
- professional training;
- requesting information;
- application letters;

- letters of recommendation;
- thank you letters;
- resume/CV;
- cover letters;
- memorandums;
- emails.

Teaching principles of appropriate correspondence would begin with the layout form of a standard letter, and then proceed to examine the structural specifics of each topic. Those are primarily matters of content and its segmentation, as well as adequate vocabulary and style.

(e) Spoken presentations

Spoken presentations are delivered in various situations and for diverse purposes. They may be in front of a convention or conference assembly, a class, management, government, fellow colleagues. Depending on the situation, the form of the presentation will vary, yet the principles of structuring the smallest logical units, paragraph and essay format, are copied onto the organisational structure of the spoken presentation. In other words, the logic of how ideas are structured and connected in paragraphs is the basis of all kinds of presentations.

Spoken presentation means public speaking. It is much more than a simple delivery of scientific and professional knowledge. The preconditions of an effective, but most importantly good spoken presentation are many. The success largely depends on judging all the specifics of the situation and responding to those properly, the impression one gives as a person, the way one stands, moves, articulates their words, looks at the audience (Reinhart, 2005).

The spoken presentation should not be a monologue, but a dialogue in which more than just verbal communication is involved (Stojković, 2005). To communicate means to understand, so students should be made to think of their audience and attentively look at them. Their reactions will direct them on the spot. The mastery of the subject topic and the good will to interact with others will allow students to actually enjoy sharing their knowledge in a constructive way both for their audience and themselves.

Audience assessment and the shaping of the presentation

In order to deliver a successful presentation it is of primary importance to *identify the audience* as precisely as possible. Different audiences require and are prepared for different amount and depths of information. It is customary to classify audience types as follows: experts, technicians, executives, non-specialists. Audience must also be analysed in terms of background, needs and interests, demographic characteristics.

In close connection to the audience type is the purpose of the presentation. The purpose may be informative, instructional, or persuasive. And according to the type, the shaping, organisation of the presentation, need to be such as to support it fully. The organisation of the presentation may be of one or more of the following categories: classification, partition or spatial division, segmentation, comparison, cause and effect, problem and solution, experimentation.

Spoken presentation is a dialogue with audience in which both verbal and nonverbal communications are equally important. Students need to become aware of structural and performative strategies that can add much to achieving the desired effect. Those are the high relevance of an attention grabbing introduction, or the importance of an effective summary, to name just two exemplary strategies. It needs to be sufficiently stressed that the entire delivery will largely depend on one's behaviour. *At this point, teaching spoken presentations by far exceeds language teaching.* Students should become conscious that literally every personal trait they exhibit will influence the meaning they try to convey. Therefore, it is important that they memorise that while presenting they need to: maintain eye contact with the audience, use natural hand gestures, keep body movement quiet and natural, maintain appropriate voice volume, avoid distracting personal styling, maintain a constant rate of speech, walk purposefully and confidently. Last but not least, the speaker is to respect the allotted time.

(f) Scientific discussion

Situations in which professionals finds themselves needing to discuss a specific issue are more than numerous. They may vary from most informal, a collegiate chat, to most formal ones, like conference discussions following the presentation of a research findings, for example. Whatever the case, structuring the content of the discussion would prove expertise, education and culture. For this reason, students should be taught how to develop and support their argumentation. That implies segmenting the delivery of argumentation in the following manner:

Introduction

Directing the audience's attention towards the problem, as to why it concerns them, of what relevance it is.

Credentials

Identifying precisely the source of your authority to speak on the subject. The reasons here may be infinitely varied, yet if stated clearly can be credited appropriately. You may be an expert in the field, or you may have seen something intriguing on television.

Advocated position

A brief summary of the thesis, the proposed solution to it, and reasons for advocating that particular solution.

Background of the issue

Before pointing to the complexity of the issue discussed, its background is to be presented

Arguments for the stated position

This is the central part of the discussion. Whereas the previous segments need not take up more than a sentence or two, this is the elaboration part. It is to be signalled by specifying minutely the judgement criterion. In as much detail as the situation, time and space allow, the thesis should be explained and supported with relevant and illustrative arguments and examples. Two supportive arguments are the basic standard.

Credit should be given to different options and opinions for the strengths they possess. Yet, prior argumentation should be sufficient to clearly defend the value of the option chosen on the outset.

Conclusion

Conclusion is in many respects a variation of the introduction, its summary. This repeating is in part done as a psychological manoeuvre intended to once again persuade the audience to confirm the validity of the thesis discussed.

Final argumentation

The overall aim of the subject of English Language for Specific Purposes is to enable students to better succeed in their profession by better communicating their expert knowledge. In today's fiercely competitive and demanding professional world possessing knowledge of the subject without knowledge and skills of transferring, advocating, promoting it, is insufficient for professional advancement. Therefore, teaching principles and types of written and spoken communications in English for Academic and Occupational Purposes is of utmost importance.

Here presented is an outline of the curriculum segment dealing with written and spoken communications. In practice, it needs to be elaborated and tailored according to the exact needs of the students being taught. This is highly demanding both for students and lecturers as it assumes profound insight into the characteristics, content, style, genre, of the science/field in question, yet also into psychological and sociological aspects that influence every presentation.

The presentation principles suggested here, make conscious for the students some of the interpretative clues audience derive from structures. Armed with this awareness, they can achieve far greater control (although never complete) of the reader's/listener's interpretative process. As a concomitant function, the principles simultaneously offer them a fresh re-entry to the thought process that produced science. *In real and important ways, the structure of the prose becomes the structure of the scientific argument. Improving either one will improve the other.*

References

Harty, K. J. (2005) *Strategies for Business and Technical Writing.* Pearson. Longman.

Hinder, D. E. (2005) *Building Arguments.* Eugene, Oregon. Wipf & Stock Publishers.

Reinhart, S. M. (2005) *Giving Academic Presentations.* University of Michigan Press.

Stojković, N. (2005) *Written and Spoken Presentations in English for Science and Technology.* Niš: Elektronski fakultet.

THE IMPORTANCE OF METADISCOURSE IN THE GENRE "PROMOTION OF TOURISTIC SERVICES AND PRODUCTS": DIFFERENCES IN ENGLISH AND SPANISH

FRANCISCA SUAU-JIMÉNEZ AND ROSANA DOLÓN-HERRERO

Introduction

The discourse of tourism is a language of speciality which displays across a series of genres, one of which is the *Promotion of Touristic Services or Products*, possibly the most well known and used genre within the field of tourism, usually promoting places, cities, natural regions or whole countries. Its communicative goal is always to persuade potential customers to visit those places and buy touristic services and/or products and it takes the form of printed leaflets, brochures or web pages. It contains a series of recurrent communicative functions working at the service of persuasion, such as explaining, describing, exemplifying, etc. which shape different grammatical structures. Specific vocabulary also plays a very important role since it carries all the semantic and conceptual burden. However, the study of this language of speciality would be incomplete if we did not take into account its metadiscourse.

Metadiscourse has been defined as the linguistic material, spoken or written, which does not add anything from the propositional or content viewpoint, but helps the reader to organize, interpret and evaluate the given information (Vande Kopple, 1985; Crismore et al., 1993). In the same vein, some recent new approaches to discourse analysis have revisited the concept of genre and have introduced that of social construct (Fairclough, 1992, 1995), suggesting that texts are part of social events or the linguistic form in which people act and interact socially. Both authors of texts and their audiences are seen as agents whose actions are not free, but socially delimited or constrained. Therefore, metadiscourse is especially important in certain genres with a performative purpose, as happens with the one we have analyzed in this research, where the reader does not only decode a message but, as a result of it, also acts. Besides, metadiscourse coincides with the function of language that Halliday (1978, 1994) describes as *interpersonal*, that is to say, the function which explains how the author addresses the tenor by means of different linguistic elements like personal pronouns, imperatives, certain adjectives or epistemic verbs which contain part of the author's beliefs, opinions or hints that try to influence the reader's interpretation of the text.

If we compare the amount of language that metadiscourse needs to be displayed with the propositional content of a text, it holds a very small percentage of words or structures. However, its importance is considerable in certain genres where the interpersonal relationship with the reader is important, as happens in touristic ones.

When metadiscourse in academic and scientific genres (Moreno, 1998; Salager-Meyer, 1994; Hyland, 1998) has been the object of multiple studies and research, we have not found that touristic genres have been analyzed from this viewpoint. And yet, we find that metadiscourse plays an important role in touristic genres, since they have a relevant performative function. Readers are highly influenced by the propositional and metadiscursive elements that touristic texts contain, and, thus, their communicative goal to persuade potential customers is carried out in this way.

Also, from a research carried out recently (Suau, 2006) we have observed that the discourse of this typical genre of tourism has different characteristics in different languages, in this case, English and Spanish. Its specific communicative functions are basically the same, such as historic, geographical or cultural description, exemplification or explanation. It usually does not contain any quotation or direct speech and its register can vary from being highly technical to colloquial. Metadiscourse, however, may differ from one language to the other, since the interpersonal function responds to different cultural patterns and filters. In the field of tourism (Suau, 2006) the Spanish metadiscourse, for instance, usually displays abundant qualifying adjectives and adverbs of a positive tone, where English metadiscourse contains very little of these elements, but abounds in hedges, references to the tenor in the form of personal pronouns and self-mention.

Examples:

> "If ***you*** have limited time ***we recommend you*** follow this list or take our ***recommended*** itinerary to visit London. Some of the information here ***you'll probably*** know, but ***it's worth reading it*** all at your leisure."
>
> www.londontourist.org

> "¿Qué hacer en Castellón? Llegar por una **emocionante** ruta al Santuario de la Balma en Zorita. Ir a la vecina población de Castellfort, desde donde se contempla una **magnífica** panorámica de la zona. Conocer la **serena** belleza de los parques naturales del Prat de Cabanes."
>
> www.comunitatvalenciana.com

Method

Hyland & Tse (2004) suggest that metadiscourse is a functional category within discourse that is important to be taken into account. Through metadiscourse an autor can transform a hard and difficult text into friendly prose of a much nicer reading, and at the same time s/he establishes an important link with the reader. These two authors propose a framework of analysis for academic metadiscourse which can serve as a basis for analysing other specific languages. We are particularly interested in what they propose as Interactional Framework, involving the reader in the argument. This is the method we have followed in the current research. However, this framework is the result of research carried out over English texts and, as far as we know, has also been applied to academic English Texts. Our purpose now is to apply it to both English and Spanish texts of tourism. Therefore, this framework will serve us as a basis but will surely provide new metadiscursive elements since it is the product of a very typified and specific genre, the promotion of touristic products and services, as well as of a different cultural filter, that of Spanish.

Framework for analysis: Hyland & Tse (2004)

Interactional Metadiscourse: involving the reader in the argument.

Category	*Function*	*Examples*
Hedges	withhold writer's full commitment to proposition	might/perhaps/about
Boosters	emphasize force or writer's certainty in proposition	in fact/definitely/it is clear that
Attitude markers	express writer's attitude to proposition	unfortunately/I agree/ surprisingly
Engagement markers	explicitly refer to or build relationship with reader	consider/note that/ you can see that
Self-mentions	explicit reference to author	I/we/my/our

Our corpus is made of around 12000 words of both Spanish and English texts of the mentioned touristic genre.
Our research questions are:

1 Is the framework for metadiscourse analysis provided by Hyland & Tse (2004) valid to be applied to the genre "Promotion of Touristic Services and Products"?
2 Are both types of metadiscourse, English and Spanish different in this genre and, if so, does this difference need to be taught at higher education?

Analysis and results

Table 1 Metadiscourse in English texts of tourism

Total words	***Hedges***	***Boosters***	***Attitude markers***	***Engagement markers***	***Self-mention***
5870	29	41	10	143	59
	0.50%	0.70%	0.17%	2.46%	1.01%

Remark: all the categories of Hyland & Tse's framework have been found.

Examples:

Hedges
"Or you ***can*** take a boat out to Greenwich." "***It'd be*** a crime to visit London and not take in a show." "The atmosphere on the late tubes ***can be*** a bit rowdy, but it's never dangerous." "This ***can cause*** amusement when somebody asks you if they can borrow you rubber." "At any moment trouble ***can brew up*** in the Atlantic and lead to cold weather." "Alcohol ***can be bought*** off licence." "Dinner is usually at about 20:00 – though it ***may be*** much later."
Boosters
"London is still a huge ***bewildering*** place if it's your first visit." "Regent's has ***excellent*** cultivated gardens." "The view from the bridge in St James Park towards Whitehall is ***stunning***." "What's ***amazing*** is the consistent high quality of all the works displayed." "At other times the debates can be ***soporific***." "It has the ***most beautiful*** youth hostel in the country." "The post and telephone services in the UK are ***superb***."
Attitude Markers
"Many visitors waste large amounts of money ***simply*** because…" "Some of the information here you'll ***probably*** already know…" "You'll ***probably*** want to visit both, the Tower of London and Hampton Court." "These are moveable feasts – ***especially*** the spring holiday."
Engagement Markers
"If it's ***your*** first visit, …" "We ***recommend you*** to follow this list." "***You***'ll get to see such treasures as King Charles I." "***You*** can bathe naked on Hampstead Heath." "For money withdrawals ***you*** will need to produce ***your*** passport." "***You*** can buy a ticket to attractions like the Tower, …" "***Don't miss*** the Museo de Bellas Artes." "***Head*** for the Playa de la Malvarrosa."
Self-mention
"This is walk two in ***our*** itinerary page." "***Our*** colonial past has made the city more cosmopolitan." "***We*** are proud of our national football." "***We*** don't clearly have defined seasons like in central Europe." "***We***'ve included the websites of all the attractions here." "***We***'ve got details of all London sights and attractions."

Table 2 Metadiscourse in Spanish texts of tourism

Total words	***Hedges***	***Boosters***	***Attitude markers***	***Engagement markers***	***Self-mention***
5865	14	84	3	2	2
	0.24%	1.41%	0.03%	0.02%	0.02%

Remark: categories are represented in a very different way to those of the English texts. The number of boosters is here very high and it has to be mentioned that attitude markers, engagement markers and self-mention elements are very low.

Examples:

Hedges
"Valencia ***puede ser*** una ciudad de tópicos." "Son claves para ***tratar de explicar*** lo que no se puede explicar con palabras." "***Aconsejamos*** al amigo lector que seleccione si opta por visitar todo un barrio, o…" "Todo esto ***se puede complementar*** con la visita a la Ciudad de las Ciencias." "Y no deje de ***tener en cuenta*** la Lonja de la Seda."
Boosters
"Valencia ha experimentado una ***significativa*** transformación en los últimos años." "El nuevo Palacio de Congresos....representativa de la arquitectura más ***vanguardista***..." "Llegar por una ***emocionante*** ruta al Santuario de la Balma en Zorita…" "Conocer la ***serena*** belleza de los parques naturales del Prat de Cabanes…" "…en el ***magnífico*** entorno natural del balneario de Montanejos." "… las ***espectaculares*** huellas de los dinosaurios de Alpuente." "…con unas ***espléndidas*** vistas del Rincón de Ademuz." "… acercarse a la ***imponente*** Cartuja de Porta Coeli." "Degustar una ***excelente*** paella en los restaurantes del paseo marítimo."
Attitude markers
"Se caracteriza por un clima suave, ***típicamente*** mediterráneo." "… claves para tratar de explicar lo que, ***en realidad***, no se puede contar con palabras." "…están transformando ***definitivamente*** el perfil urbano."
Engagement markers
"… no ***deje*** de tener en cuenta la Lonja de la Seda." "… al amigo lector que ***seleccione***."

Self-mention
"***Aconsejamos*** al amigo lector que seleccione..."
"***Vamos a sugerirles*** unos cuantos de los museos y monumentos..."

Discussion and conclusion

Metadiscourse as a tool for linguistic analysis has proved to have well defined and powerful elements as well as others of a weaker nature. There elements have basically been studied in academic and scientific discourse in English (Hyland, 1998; Hyland & Tse, 2004; Suau, 2005, 2005), where *hedges* have shown by and large to be the most frequent and relevant ones. They are displayed through conditionals, modals and epistemic verbs and also a key aspect of scientific prose, where the convention of non-imposition is crucial for the scientific community to accept academic articles reporting new findings or theories. Also, Hyland & Tse (2004) propose *boosters* in their framework, as a means to confirm the certainty of a statement through adverbs or frozen expressions.

However, we think that qualifying adjectives of a positive or superlative tone, very frequent in the Spanish metadiscourse of tourism are also used in order to emphasize or modulate the propositional content of a statement and would, therefore, assist in the task of hooking the reader and establishing a link between author and reader. *Attitude markers* have, in our opinion, a similar function to that of *boosters,* with adverbs and frozen expressions such as ***in fact, really, absolutely, without doubt***. *Engagement markers* do not admit any doubt and are radically different in number in English and Spanish. These direct references to the reader are typical of the English metadiscourse and very rare in the Spanish. Finally, the self-mention or pronominalization in the first person singular or plural is also very frequent in English and rare in Spanish.

In order to answer both research questions we should say that, first, this metadiscourse framework by Hyland & Tse has proved useful to analyze the genre "Promotion of Touristic Services and Products" as a launching platform. However, several differences have been observed is compared with scientific and academic discourse. These differences can make us conclude that, possibly, a different kind of metadiscourse framework would be necessary for touristic genres. Secondly, it has proved more useful to analyze English metadiscourse than Spanish, where it has needed to be adapted and new elements have been found which would shape a different framework for Spanish texts. The results that match this second research question could lead us to think tentatively that each cultural filter establishes linguistic constraints that influence genre writing, as has been demonstrated when comparing English and Spanish metadiscourse.

From all the previous data we could probably conclude that these differences have important implications for teaching specific languages and, in particular, for teaching genre writing to higher education students of tourism both in English and Spanish. Very possibly, as has been suggested in Suau (2006a), differences in metadiscourse from one language to another must be taken into account when, for example, translating this kind of touristic genres. Otherwise, readers may not feel at ease when reading a touristic leaflet that does not reproduce metadiscourse as their cultural filter prescribes. To sum up, these differences in metadiscourse are surely important when making text books or when teaching genre writing seminars or specialized language courses in higher education.

References

Crismore, A., Markkanen, R., Steffensen, M. (1993) "Metadiscourse in persuasive writing", *Written Communication 10* (1): 39-71.

Fairclough, N. (1992) *Discourse and Social Change.* Cambridge: Polity Press.

—. (1995) *Critical Discourse Analysis.* Harlow: Longman.

Halliday, M. A. K. (1978) *Language as Social Semiotic.* London: Arnold.

—. (1978) Language as Social Semiotics. London: Edward Arnold.

—. (1994) An Introduction to Functional Grammar, 2nd edition. London: Edward Arnold.

Hyland, K. & Tse, P. (2004) "Metadiscourse in Academic Writing: A Reappraisal". *Applied Linguistics 25/2*: 156-177.

Moreno, A. I. (1998) *"The explicit signalling of premise-conclusion sequences in research articles: a contrastive framework"*. Text, 18 (4): 545-585.

Pickett, D. (1989) "The sleeping giant: investigations in business English". *Language International* 1, 1, 5-11.

Salager-Meyer, F. (1994) Hedges and Textual Communicative Function in medical English written discourse. *English for Specific Purposes,* 13 (2), 149-70.

Suau Jiménez, F. (2006a) "El metadiscurso en el género "Promoción de Servicios y Productos Turísticos" en inglés y español: importancia de su traducción y uso adecuado como recurso para la persuasión del cliente." *Paper given at the I Congreso Internacional de Traducción*

Especializada, organized by Colegio de Traductores Públicos. Buenos Aires, July 2006.

—. (2001) "El género y el registro en la traducción del discurso profesional: un enfoque funcional aplicable a cualquier lengua de especialidad" *Culturele.* Barcelona: Universitat de Barcelona. Available at www.ub.es/filhis/culturele/tinasuau.html.

—. (2005) "Matizadores discursivos frente a elementos apelativos y fáticos o la importancia de gustar a la audiencia: comparación entre artículos de investigación y de divulgación científica en inglés desde el metadiscurso*".* *Revista Española de Lingüística Aplicada (ReSLA),* Volumen Monográfico sobre Lenguas de Especialidad en España, editado por Aguado de Cea, G. y Gil Salom, L.

—. (2005) "The difficult balance between author's and scientific community's power over research articles in applied linguistics". *LSP & Professional Communication,* Vol. 5, No. 2, 59-72.

Vande Kopple, W. J. (1985) "Some exploratory discourse on metadiscourse". *College Composition and Communication 36*: 82-93.

A Language Competences Project and its Application in Training Doctoral Students

Božena Zavadilová

Introduction

The outcome of the language competences project entitled Writing Professional English and developed under Leonardo da Vinci programme offers rapid and flexible solutions to writing problems of professionals in engineering, technology and science who need to write professional texts in English and want to improve their writing skills.

Reference Handbook versions covering eight branches present examples of selected subject areas. Each section is connected with interactive task-based exercises related to two parts: science and technology. The core exercises cover selected topics of the chapters involved in the Reference Handbook. The optional exercises arise from specific problems and needs of particular nationalities involved in the project including Czech. The Czech exercises are highlighted at the grammatical items that are different from English, such as using correct articles, word order and punctuation. The exercises are equipped with self-assessment keys, immediate feedback and comments. The materials are computer-based with access through the internet. They are open and flexible and they can be used both as a self-study resource and in taught courses.

The objective of the doctoral study programme is to prepare highly qualified specialists in particular scientific branches. Doctoral students like other professionals encounter requirements to present the results of their research at conferences and in scientific journals. Therefore they need to write effectively in English in order to become more competitive.

Needs of doctoral students

One of the most required types of writing for doctoral students is a research paper. Generally, the students can read papers in scientific journals without problems, but they do not know how to write their actual papers properly. They usually know very little about the composition of a research paper, professional style, and language functions. In addition, they often make mistakes in grammar and in using correspondent vocabulary.

The materials contained in Reference Handbook and focused on the areas of engineering such as physical and materials engineering, medical engineering, process engineering, or electrical engineering and informatics can be especially applicable and helpful for their needs.

In the classroom courses, or tutorials, the students mostly use printed versions of the Reference handbook, and are provided with the explanations of the recommended sections important for their writing. In particular, some linguistic terms are made clear. They can also follow the electronic versions interactive with exercises. The task-based exercises which relate to particular topics are recommended especially as a self-study resource.

Before starting their work, the students are provided with necessary information on writing paragraphs, titles, types of abstracts, introductions and conclusions. Concerning the main body of the paper, some possibilities are offered, but they are not compulsory, and the students can decide how to make up the main body independently.

Writing a paragraph

The first subject that the students encounter in their writing is a paragraph. Since paragraphs appear as separate block of texts on the printed page, they provide the reader with visual help in following the writer's argument which progresses by moving from the main idea in one paragraph to the main idea in the text. The principal items practised in writing paragraphs are:

- length of a paragraph;
- number of ideas in one paragraph;
- placing the main idea;
- structure of a paragraph.

The doctoral students first select appropriate examples of paragraphs in research papers presented in journals or at conferences and analyze them. They identify the "topic sentence" (the main idea in a paragraph) and the functions of the other sentences. See the example below.

Sample paragraph

The following paragraph[1] can be analyzed to show its structure and the functions of the 8 sentences. (The numbers are inserted only to identify the sentences)

Sample paragraph	Analysis
(1) Residual stresses are defined as stresses that exist in materials or structures in the absence of any external loads. (2) They could arise due to non - linear plastic flow of material during load/unload, coefficient of thermal expansion (CTE) mismatch during thermal contraction or phase transformations. (3) We can distinguish two scales of stress i nature: macrostress and microstress. (4)The former is at significantly larger scale compared to the microstructure and varies with position inside a structure. (5) Microstress is generated at the microstructural level e.g. inside metal-ceramic composites upon cooling from the processing temperature. (6) These stresses usually vary from grain to grain or between different phases. (7) The study of residual stresses in metal-ceramic composites is important for several reasons. (8) It affects the micromechanical behaviour in the plastic region as well as fracture characteristics.	*(1) is the topic sentence - defining residual stresses in materials or structures in the absence of any external loads* *(2) describes conditions of their origin* *(3) - (6) distinguishing features of the two scales of stress* *(7) and (8) provide an overall conclusion - importance and effects of stresses in practice*

The next part of the training is practicing interactive exercises that refer to the studied topic. The exercises are aimed at dividing a long paragraph, structuring a paragraph and points to include in a paragraph. After that, the students write their actual paragraphs. Finally, they check and amend them following the recommendations in the Reference Handbook.

---

[1] Agrawal, P. et al. (2003) Thermal residual stresses in co-continuous composites, Acta Materialia, Volume 51, Issue 4, February ed. (adapted)

Points to check in your own writing

Here are some simple tasks for you to see if you are constructing paragraphs properly.

- *Take one or two pages of your academic writing. Do a 'visual' check on the length of paragraphs – does the text look too heavy or too 'bitty' or about right?*
- *Check whether the average length of the paragraphs is between 7 and 14 lines (3 to 7 sentences).*
- *Count the number of words in randomly selected sentences. Does the average number of words come to between 15 and 25? If so, this is about right.*
- *Do the 'skim' test: read through the first sentences only of your whole text and see if you can follow the gist of your argument. If you can, you are writing your topic sentences well.*

This activity can be implemented individually, or in pairs where the students compare their pieces of writing and mutually correct them.

Writing a research paper

(a) Abstracts

After composing the title of the research paper based on the instructions given in the Handbook, the students work on abstracts.

Firstly, they are provided with necessary information on types of abstracts following the printed versions of the Reference Handbook and materials on the internet. Then they select examples of abstracts in scientific journals or proceedings of conferences that refer to their specialization. They try to distinguish descriptive, informative, or mixed types of abstracts. After that, in pairs or small groups, they present their chosen examples to the other students and compare them. Before writing their actual abstracts, the students practise the topic using the interactive exercises with immediate feedback and comments. They may choose from a number of exercises focused on differentiating between descriptive and informative abstracts, identifying keywords in abstracts, adding sentences into a text, words with similar meaning, linking words and phrases, or structuring an abstract. A sample exercise with the instructions, correct answers, and feedback is demonstrated in Appendix 1.

In the next step, the doctoral students write their individual abstracts and explain their ideas and choice of the particular type of the abstract.

Finally, in pairs, they study the abstracts of their partners, reciprocally check the texts and help to amend them, or correct mistakes if it is needed.

(b) Introductions and conclusions

The same or similar procedure as mentioned above is used in writing introductions and conclusions of research papers. Additionally, the Handbook offers a number of sample phrases that can be used in introductions, such as stating the purpose of the paper, relating the paper to current work, or indicating the structure of the paper. Similarly, the users may select convenient phrases for stating their conclusions. See below.

Sample phrases you can use in conclusions:

- **Summarising what you have done**

In conclusion, we can say that ... *In this paper, we have seen that ...* *This research paper has clearly shown that ...* *The discussion in this article has given an overview of ...* *This paper has provided a systematic study of ...* *From the research that has been carried out, we can conclude that ...* *The aim of the present paper was to examine whether ... and this has now been achieved.* *Finally, it is worth pointing out that ...*

- **Indicating the limitations of your own work**

This article has only been able to touch on the most general features of ... *Even a preliminary study, such as the one reported here, has highlighted the need for ...*

- **Looking to the future and further research**

Clearly, further studies are needed to understand / prove ... *In order to validate the work we have carried out, a more in-depth investigation into ... is needed.* *The results of this research could assist policy makers to ...*

The interactive exercises provide the users with the possibility to practise important items contained in the Reference handbook. In Appendix 2, see a sample exercise aimed at identifying various functions in an analysis of a conclusion.

After finishing their research papers, the doctoral students read through their pieces of writing, check and amend them according to the following suggestions.

Points to check in your own writing
▪ *Can the reader understand the gist of your paper by reading only the introduction and the conclusion? If not, re-write them.*
▪ *Have you merely re-stated what you said in the introduction? If so, think how you might present it somewhat differently in the light of the supporting evidence in the main body.*
▪ *Do you conclude with an emphatic finish? Do you leave the reader with a strong impression?*

Abreast with their writing, the doctoral students acquaint themselves with the style and language functions. The general rules which have become accepted as the norm in technical and scientific communication include objectivity, clarity, formality, hedging techniques and signposting.

Grammatical items that make difficulties in professional writing are explained in the Reference Handbook in the section on Grammar. In training doctoral students, the main attention is paid to using correct articles, word order and punctuation. Again, most of these topics are covered in the interactive exercises. For Czech users, in addition to the core exercises, there are extra optional exercises targeted at their problems and tailored to their specific needs.

Conclusion

The aim of the current paper was to present some experience in the practical application of the language competences project entitled Writing Professional English for training doctoral students. The particular concern was focused on writing a technical research paper. The procedure in writing was demonstrated in accordance with the materials included in the Reference Handbook and interactive exercises. The materials are highly convenient and helpful in writing professional research papers namely in that they are based on authentic texts and examples related to the particular branches of engineering.

The Reference Handbook covers many problem areas faced by doctoral students when writing in English and offers ways of solving them. The information contained in the sections of the Handbook is supported in the interactive exercises with instant answers and feedback. The exercises give users the opportunity to carry out practical tasks in areas that they have difficulty with, so as to deepen their understanding and improve their writing skills. These interactive computer-based exercises are preferred primarily as a self-study resource although they can be used in taught-courses especially in classrooms fully equipped with computers.

The model materials included in the project Writing Professional English are extremely useful for professionals who need to write in English more effectively. Moreover, the materials offered can be further extended, modified and tailored to the specific application in classroom courses and self-study purposes.

References

Writing Professional English, A Language Competences Project – Leonardo da Vinci Programme CZ/02/B/F/LA/134043, 2003-2005

A Handbook for Physical and Materials Engineering, Leonardo da Vinci Programme, CZ/02/B/F/LA/134043, 2005

Zavadilová, B. (2005) Writing Professional English – Training Materials for Engineering and Chemistry, Teaching Professional Language at Non-Linguistic Universities, Brno: University of Defence, 137-140.

APPENDIX ONE

The interactive exercises provide the users with the possibility to practise important items contained in the Reference handbook. See below.

2.11 Exercise 7: Structuring an abstract

The abstract below has been jumbled. Read carefully the jumbled sentences, then put them into correct sequence. Use the arrow buttons to move blocks of sentences backward/forward.

◀▶ A finite element model has been made of a spline coupling between a shaft and a sleeve. The stress concentration factor is calculated and compared to analytical calculations. An analytical model for the load distribution in the axial direction and the torque transfer between shaft and sleeve is presented and compared to finite element results. ◀▶ For the future, it is probably possible to extend the fatigue life at least two times for this spline, by uniforming the load distribution. ◀▶ The analytical model also shows that the best way to make the load uniform is to vary the thickness of the spline tooth in the axial direction. Different shapes and sizes of the tooth thickness variation are also investigated. ◀▶ This analytical model is used to test methods of making the load distribution uniform and thereby decreasing the stress concentration factor. The induction hardened shafts with splines are fatigue tested and the lives are presented. The residual stress on the shaft surface is measured.

[Check] [Answer]

The correct sequence of the sentences in the abstract:

A finite element model has been made of a spline coupling between a shaft and a sleeve. The stress concentration factor is calculated and compared to analytical calculations. An analytical model for the load distribution in the axial direction and the torque transfer between shaft and sleeve is presented and compared to finite element results. This analytical model is used to test methods of making the load distribution uniform and thereby decreasing the stress concentration factor. The induction hardened shafts with splines are fatigue tested and the lives are presented. The residual stress on the shaft surface is measured. The analytical model also shows that the best way to make the load uniform is to vary the thickness of the spline tooth in the axial direction. Different shapes and sizes of the tooth thickness variation are also investigated. For the future, it is probably possible to extend the fatigue life at least two times for this spline, by uniforming the load distribution.

Comment:
If you had any problems with completing this task correctly, please refer to Section 2.11 in the Reference Handbook.

Appendix Two

2.6 Exercise 1: Analysis of a conclusion - identifying various functions
Match the numbered sentences of a conclusion with functions. Choose from the list below.

1 proposes a solution to the problem (as part of the conclusion)
2 summarises what was done
3 suggests further investigations into the topic
4 draws conclusions about the work done

> The high temperature mechanical response of YTZP nanocrystals doped with different amounts of amorphous phases has been reported. [2 ▾] ✔ Constant strain rate tests as well as the microstructural characterization of the deformed and as-received by means of TEM and AFM have been carried out. [2 ▾] ✔
> The analysis of all the experimental outputs have permitted us to conclude that no threshold stress exists in these materials, and the softening effect of the glassy phase has been assessed [4 ▾] ✔
> Grain boundary sliding seems clearly to be the deformation mechanism for all the cases studied. [1 ▾] ✔ Future work must be devoted to the explanation of the high activation energy and the non-existence of a threshold stress in this system. [3 ▾] ✔

Comment:
If you had any problems with completing this task correctly, please refer to Section 2.6 Conclusions in the Reference Handbook.

CHAPTER II:

ICT IN LANGUAGE TEACHING

INTRODUCTION

DAVID BRETT

The field of second or foreign language learning is one of the disciplines that stands most to gain from the extraordinary developments in Information and Communications Technology (ICT) that have taken place in recent years. Operators within the field have not been slow to realise this potential – to the contrary, they numbered amongst the pioneers of technology-based education even at its earliest stages. Furthermore, the use of New Technologies (NTs) offers great potential to the sector of Languages for Special Purposes (LSP) in particular, especially in relation to the large quantities of authentic material that these make readily available.

When one thinks of technology and language learning the image immediately springs to mind of a student or group of students gazing at a computer screen, intent upon carrying out some exercise or other on the web. Rarely do we reflect on how greatly technology has changed, undeniably for the better, the process of preparation of materials to be used in class. Gone are the felt-tip pens, the scissors, the glue and the mountains of old newspapers of yesteryear – today, by using NTs, teachers are able to produce exercises based on authentic materials, of a quality that could be offered only by publishers just a short time ago. Hence, from this backstage perspective, technology's permeation of the LSP sector reaches very high levels, and has doubtlessly contributed, at some stage or other, to all the works in the preceding section.

However, this section will focus mainly on contexts in which technology is used directly by learners, as well as by those facilitating the learning. In adopting this slightly narrower perspective, we enter an area in which there are still many open questions and many solutions to be arrived at before we can claim that we are exploiting to the full "the dizzying array of technologically feasible options" (Doughty & Long, 2003).

The emergence of Computer Assisted Language Learning (CALL) as a field of studies in its own right has been warranted by the realization of the fundamental differences that exist between learning experiences in technology-enhanced contexts and those in more traditional scenarios. Indeed, due to the shifting nature of the terrain, the history of CALL is rich in unexpected turns: from an initial focus on autonomous student–computer interaction, attention has moved on to encompass the use of Computer Mediated Communication (CMC) provided by such technologies as Moos, email, chat rooms and videoconferencing. As a result of the swift developments that are taking place, nomenclature itself is also an issue, as the term CALL is stretched to include ever more frequently utilized technologies such as cell-phones and handheld devices (see Chinnery, 2006 for discussion of the latter).

The role of the teacher in the creation of interactive language learning material has been an issue from the very start. In the early stages optimism was commonplace: Weible (1983) writes that "teachers must not become too remote from the actual programming effort" and therefore should learn to script their own exercises. However, events have proven that only a small minority of language teachers are willing, or able, to do so, perhaps due to the fact that most members of the category have a background in the humanities, furthermore, as the creators of the highly successful Hot Potatoes program note, "few working teachers have the time to do formal programming courses, and most would think that any kind of programming is therefore beyond them" (Arneil & Holmes, 2004). Nevertheless, most training courses for language teachers now include some components on the use of NTs (see Hegelheimer et al, 2004, for a realistic appraisal of the possibilities).

Therefore, while some teachers can and do create their own materials thanks to the use of the aforementioned Hot Potatoes program and other authoring tools, the presence of technical support is essential in large scale projects. This, however, often gives rise to another problem, expressed in a rather extreme way by Felix (2003) as: "There is no dialogue between teachers and technologists about what kind of technological innovation learners need: neither side knows how to begin the dialogue." A similar and recurrent theme is that of language teaching professionals underestimating the extent to which NTs can realise their "wish lists", or conversely, of the technologists underestimating the importance of seeking solutions to what they may see as trivial requests. In fact, it is technology that must serve education, not the other way round – programmers generally need to be prodded a little, as John Allison (2006) candidly puts it: "Don't let the geeks decide!".

This brief discussion of just a few of the issues surrounding the use of NTs in CALL, with particular reference to the LSP sector, aims to provide the reader with some points to be borne in mind when reading the following papers. In fact, these works refer both to teachers creating materials autonomously and to larger projects, involving teams of language teaching professionals and ICT experts, in some cases crossing national boundaries. Of particular note are two papers dealing with an application of technology to language teaching that has turned out to be especially fruitful in the case of LSP: that of corpora and data-driven learning. Examples and discussion are provided with reference to two such diverse fields as business studies and oral implantology.

References

Allison, J. (2006) Plenary talk at "Languages for Special Purposes in Higher Education – Searching for Common Solutions" conference held at Brno (Faculty of Mechanical Engineering, Brno University of Technology, Czech Republic), 24-25.11.2006.

Arneil, S. & Holmes, M. (2004) 'Hacking in Hot Potatoes - A little knowledge brings a lot of power', TEL&CAL, 2, 45-49.

Chinnery, G. M. (2006) Going to the MALL: Mobile-assisted language learning. *Language Learning & Technology,* 10 (1), 9-16.

Doughty, C., Long, M. H. (2003) Optimal psycholinguistic environments for distance foreign language learning. Language Learning and Technology, 7(3), 50-80.

Felix, U. (ed.) (2003) Language Learning Online: Towards Best Practice, Lisse, Netherlands: Swets and Zeitlinger.

Hegelheimer, V., Reppert, K, Borberg, M., Daisy, B., Grgurovic, M., Middlebrooks, K. & Liu, S. (2004) 'Preparing the new generation of CALL researchers and practitioners: What nine months in an MA program can (or cannot) do', ReCALL, 16:2, 432–447.

Lamy, M.N., Jørgen Klarskov Mortensen, H. (2007) ICT4LT Module 2.4 – Using concordance programs in the Modern Foreign Languages classroom, available online at: http://www.ict4lt.org/en/en_mod2-4.htm

Sinclair J. (ed.) (2004) How to use corpora in language teaching, Amsterdam: John Benjamins.

Weible, D. (1983) 'The foreign language teacher as courseware author', CALICO Vol. 1 (1).

E-LEARNING IN ESP TEACHING

NINA BEXAEVA

Introduction

Saratov State Technical University (SSTU) being a participant of TEMPUS Joint European Project (JEP) has started the programme promoting effective foreign language learning in technical university. The knowledge of English has become an objective social need because for millions of people the English language is now a tool of their trade. Businessmen, tradesmen, engineers, scientists and scholars all over the world must know English and other major languages because it is the international means of exchanging information and experience. The dominance of English serves to facilitate globalization. In situations where English dominates, non-English-speaking people are inevitably disadvantaged. They cannot fully participate in communication. In contrast, speakers of English are in a position to control communication to their own advantage, while those who cannot speak English fluently may be seen as incompetent or even inferior.

Background

Reduction of classroom hours, changes in learners' lifestyles and work patterns, the concept of lifelong learning and new possibilities of e-learning facilities have given a new impulse to self-access learning. It has been given more attention, more resources in recent years.

It is assumed that educators the world wide, need to be more proficient in educational technology, more aware of the theoretical and practical aspects of foreign and second language teaching, as well as increase recognizing the need to build further awareness of how teaching methodologies, learning strategies, and learning may be changed based on this new medium of e-learning.

The situation with foreign language learning in Russian Universities is in some ways different from that of many European countries. In Russia, students in all specialties have foreign languages on the curriculum as an obligatory subject for two years (170 academic hours) out of the average five years of the full course. Thus, Russian students not only want to learn foreign languages, but students from all disciplines must learn a foreign language as part of their syllabus. A three year gap within the learning programme minimizes language acquisition and the graduates' possibility to find a well-paid and interesting job as many job requirements demand "a good working knowledge" of a foreign language. The statistics shows that 83.7 % graduates' resumes are rejected because in the heading "Foreign language" they write "poor". Thus, though the potential of technical graduates is very high, it is not used fully at the interface between learning and work.

The need for a network of fully resourced Language Centres in the Volga region through which the teachers can have a continuous professional development in training programme for languages and through which students and business partners will be able to access language learning is evident. There the university teachers can coordinate language training programmes. Its establishment would assist in exchanging experience and solving problems of continuous professional language education with high acquisition of language and cross-cultural skills.

The wider long-term objective of the language education in technical universities is to develop a retraining system for specialized language teaching in professional communication in Volga region appealing to the European Union experience in this field. Research has shown that Language aqusition is a high priority for small and medium sized industries which are the future economic drivers of the region. Russia needs to reach a full potential in this respect. Consequently the Centres will encourage exchange of information, obtained experience and know-how in LSP teaching and provide supported self-study materials for staff, students and businesses on the regional and national levels which can be accredited to EU standards and thus enhance global communication and regional economy. A dissemination network scheme will increase the awareness of LSP teaching in every technical university on the Volga by access to the project Web site.

The JEP activities focus on foreign language curricula development in technical universities and the development of an operational network of foreign language centres within the Volga Region technical universities, incorporating a continuous scheme of language education and curricula design of LSP courses and supported self study materials.

The purpose of the Centre will be to help bridge the gap between the first two years of a degree programme where some launguage is taught and entry to employment three years later. The graduates of the Technical Universities within the partnership will therefore be able to maintain and enhance their language learning through open access to the centres and through supported self-study and tutorial support continue to learn. The packages developed for the centres will also be available for employees in local businesses who recognise the need for lauguage training in order to enable their businesses to grow. The technical expertise available within the cohort of graduates seeking employment in the global community will therefore be enhanced as will the skills output from the univerities in the partnership.

The new LSP courses based on modern computer and communicational teaching technologies (e-learning) are being designed now using the problem-based approach which is new in the Russian higher educational system. This will make the educational process more intensive and effective, and give students real practical language skills while studying at the university.

Needs analysis

The learning environment provided by the institution for independent study (e.g. a Self-Access Centre) should be conducive to effective study as well as the materials and the distribution of space.

While pedagogical goals and the specific needs of individual learners are the most important factors in considering self-access learning materials and milieus, we made a survey of students' needs and wants.

Eighty five second-year students from the school of electronics took part in the survey directed to find out the students' aims, expectations, needs and wants while learning at the Self-Access Centre. The questionnaire consisted of 14 questions. Having analyzed the students' answers we got very interesting results, which make the true picture of students' needs.

The first motive to continue foreign language education for the most part of students (64.4%) was their career or their future professional activity. 45.7% are planning to travel abroad. 22% want to develop their communication skills, 20% need practice to maintain their language level.

Half of the students (49%) consider technical facilities (e.g. DVD, video, audio, and computers) to be widely used in their learning. 35.5 % are of the opinion that technical equipment should be used at classes sometimes. 51% of the students have never learnt a foreign language using CD programmes or multimedia. Some students know such programmes as "Professor Higgins", "Talk to me", "Bridge to English", "Lingua",

"Oxford Dictionary". 66% of the students consider computer assisted language learning helpful and useful. Some students suggest using the programs providing a dictionary section, a communication section, and tests. Also the students suggest using Cambridge textbooks, authentic newspapers, magazines, different dictionaries, grammar materials, fiction. 47% attach more importance to teachers' activity at classes than to the choice of the learning materials.

Materials

The crucial point for SAC sustainability is a stock of self-access language learning materials. We have analyzed the advantages and disadvantages of different kinds of materials and the sources from which materials can be obtained and issues of materials production. We have to decide which materials best suit the language learning needs of our students and are appropriate to the contexts in which the students are learning. The availability of language resource facilities (books and cassettes, multimedia, satellite TV, guides and worksheets, Internet, borrowing arrangements, useful Web links – including course materials, SAC software database) is a useful part of training process.

Unfortunately not all the materials are appropriate to students' needs and interests. In this case the materials must be specially produced.

The advantages of tailor-made materials are obvious. David Gardner and Lindsay Miller (2005) mention twelve reasons for special production of self-access materials.

	Reason	Comments
1	Specific learning	Some self-access language learners may have specific goals, like particular examinations or specific language functions, which are not addressed by other materials.
2	Learning styles	Learners are individuals. They approach learning in different ways. This diversity of approaches is not always met in available materials.
3	Culture	Materials which are specially produced can meet the requirements of specific cultures in a way that other materials cannot.
4	Variety	In-house production allows a large number of small pieces of work with great variety in style and content.
5	Cross referencing	Materials can make references to other self-access materials

6	Pathways	Specially produced materials can include a variety of pathways to suit different learners' needs.
7	Manageability	Individual pieces of material can be short and thus easily managed.
8	Motivation	Specially produced materials demonstrate to learners their teachers' interest in helping them.
9	Cost	In some circumstances in-house production may be cheaper than purchasing published materials, for example when: teacher time has been allocated to it; teachers volunteer to do it; published materials are expensive relative to teacher time; many copies are required; one set of in-house materials replaces the need for a number of published materials.
10	Teacher development	While engaged in materials production teachers learn more about the needs of self-access learners.
11	Teacher commitment	When teachers become involved in self-access materials development they may he more committed to the success of self-access learning.
12	Up-to-date	Materials can be updated on a regular basis so that they are always about current issues.

We agree with each point and try to establish a system for production tailor-made materials in SSTU in spite of the fact that such work is very time-consuming and needs a lot of organizing coordinating production efforts. Particular emphasis is placed on independent learning, the aim being to assist students in their attempts to engage in effective language learning outside the classroom teaching environment. The language CD-program is intended to prepare the learner for real-life situations. One of the main purposes is to help the learner to develop strategies for dealing with the new language. Quite often the learner can function without understanding every word, picking up clues from the context and using his previous experience in similar situations. The learner can also make himself understood even if his language is far from perfect. With CD-programme the learner can choose to "drift" in the new language like at a pace he wishes. He can try to guess and check his guesses against the translation. He can learn phrases without analyzing them word by word, just as he does in a new country. Or he can watch videos and other materials and follow the story of the main characters. But the learner can also check the meanings of individual words or have the grammatical points explained to him by a language consultant. In Self-access centre he can also find some cultural notes.

We assume that every component of this programme must be assessed as well as every stage of the process (from goal-setting to the final evaluation).

For both formative and summative purposes we use the following criteria for assessing our learning programmes:

(a) Goal setting
Are the goals relevant to the learner's needs?
Are they realistic and achievable?
Are they sufficiently demanding on the learner's ability?

(b) Choice of material
Are the chosen materials relevant to the goals?
Are the chosen materials suitable for the strategies that are intended?
Are the materials suitably varied?

(c) Strategies used
Are the strategies relevant to the goals?
Do the strategies suit the learner's personal learning style?
Do the strategies suit the materials chosen?
Are they suitably varied?

Assessment of progress made:

(a) Validity
Is the assessment procedure relevant to the goals?
Is the assessment procedure related to the materials used?
Is the assessment procedure related to the strategies used?

(b) Reliability
Are the assessment criteria sufficiently explicit to ensure that similar performances would obtain similar scores?
Would any trained marker using the same criteria give a similar score for the same performance?

(c) Response to assessment
Is there an accurate diagnostic of strengths and weaknesses revealed through assessment?

Is there an adequate evaluation of the effectiveness of materials and strategies that were used?
Is there a suggested course of action to meet the needs revealed through assessment?

Conclusion

One of the challenges in training and supporting self-access learners is to help the students to develop the skills they need without overwhelming them with theory or paperwork. The trick is to get the balance right.

The establishing and functioning of Self-Access Centres is one of the possible solutions that can help Russian higher education institutions to adapt to the needs of both the changing student population and employers.

The successful work of any SAC depends on the provided materials. They can take a variety of forms in technical universities, e.g. skills-based (with a syllabus structured around strategies for developing skills such as reading, listening, speaking, writing, grammar and vocabulary), project-based (written file, poster or spoken presentation); customised (tailored to the individual needs of each student); or blended (combining different approaches, possibly within a conventional course). At the moment we are developing CD programmes meeting the needs of technical students.

References

Gardner, D., Miller, L. (2005) Establishing Self-Access. From theory to practice. Cambridge University Press.

Carvalho D. (1993) Self-Access: Appropriate Materials. Manchester.

Canning-Wilson, C (2000) E-learning with the E-teacher: Considerations for On-line Course Design.

Long-Term Retention and Reuse of E-Learning Objects and Materials (2004): Report Commissioned by the Joint Information Systems Committee (JISC).

FROM BOTH SIDES NOW: ONLINE LISTENING AND RECORDING FOR SECOND LANGUAGE LEARNING

DAVID BRETT

1 Introduction

Second or foreign language learning is one of the sectors that has most to gain from the recent technological revolution, as New Technologies (NTs) allow seamless integration of static media such as text and images on one hand, and dynamic elements, such as audio and video, on the other. This opens up possibilities for both the creation and diffusion of materials that were simply not feasible a relatively short time ago: Ariew (1987) notes that "CALL... is ill-suited for work in listening since, without additional expensive software, the medium cannot provide any audio". Today's scenario is very different, as audio reproduction is a standard feature of even the most modest computer, and digital recording can be carried out not only using computers, but also a number of common and relatively inexpensive handheld devices, such as mobile phones and mp3 players. The appearance of the latter devices has also boosted the potential for the diffusion of such material (see Chinnery, 2006, for a discussion of their applications to second language learning). Mp3 players in particular are a resource to be tapped, as they have become extremely economical and a large proportion of students in higher education already possess them.

This paper will argue that this vast potential has not been sufficiently exploited, and will proceed to discuss best practice for the presentation of sound in online CALL materials, and then continue to illustrate: advanced features that can be incorporated through the synchronisation of sound and text; interactive exercises involving the manipulation of sound clips; and possibilities for exercises in which the learner records his/her voice in an online environment.

Rather than clutter this paper with figures and screenshots of the exercises being discussed, the author has decided to direct the reader to a

series of web pages in which working examples of the exercises can be tried out. These pages can be found at:
<http://davidbrett.uniss.it/brno2006/>

1.1 The production of CALL materials: the audio v. video debate

In the design phase of CALL materials one must weigh up the relative merits of the two dynamic media, video and audio, in order to make decisions regarding which to use, on the basis of utility versus expenditure of time, energy and funding. While video is obviously preferable in that it provides settings that are closer to the majority of real world interactions, it is far more complicated to produce high quality materials. The production of audio requires no more than a computer with a sound card, a microphone and speakers, and a suitable program (see <http://audacity.sourceforge.net/> for a freeware sound editor); video, on the other hand, requires at least one actor, one camera operator and a set. In fact, the production of high quality, professional-looking video may indeed be rather costly. For example, for reasons relating to expenditure, the developers of *Longman English Interactive* recycled video clips presented during a course, for the final tests, rather than creating new material, while admitting that the latter would have been more desirable (Jamieson et al, 2004). Another consideration concerns accessibility, if the materials created are to be published on the web, even low quality video clips are of particularly large dimensions, and may operate as a discriminating factor against users who do not have broadband connections (see Egbert & Yang, 2004, for a discussion of the Digital Divide in relation to CALL). As a result, albeit offering less complete input (e.g. the lack of non-verbal communication), concentrating on the production of audio materials may be deemed more productive in many contexts.

2 The web as a silent place

In a previous paper (Brett, 2005b) the author underlines the considerable lack of audio in web-based CALL materials. This dearth is caused by several factors:

1) An information gap: foreign language teachers, the Subject Matter Experts (SMEs), are often unaware of how easy it actually is to produce such material. Others are unaware of the fact that expensive hardware and software are not necessary.

2) Traditional solutions for the presentation of sound on the web been developed for fields such as commercial music, online radio etc. and do not cater to the specific needs of language learning. Knocking the corners off the proverbial square peg requires considerable technical knowledge before it can be placed in the round hole – knowledge that goes beyond that possessed by most would-be users – as the creators of the highly successful *Hot Potatoes* program note: "few working teachers have the time to do formal programming courses, and most would think that any kind of programming is therefore beyond them" (Arneil & Holmes, 2004).
3) Courses that prepare teachers to use NTs may not pay enough attention to this aspect of CALL materials development. Hegelheimer et al (2004) describe state-of-the-art training given to future language teachers/researchers in a postgraduate course, yet make only fleeting reference to the fundamental skill of sound recording.

2.1 Digital v. analogical audio: the potential for CALL

The advantages that digital, as opposed to analogical, audio offers the CALL field are indeed obvious, yet are here reiterated to allow further discussion below:

1) Given its non-linear nature any segment of a digital audio file may be accessed with equal ease, hence the user is freed from the necessity to spend considerable time and energy rewinding, fast forwarding etc. in order to find a particular part of a passage.
2) Digital audio can be presented in a single format together with other media such as static and dynamic text, images etc., therefore, the distraction that results from switching from textbook to tape recorder and back, for example, is eliminated.

These considerations are self-evident, yet, as noted above, the potential offered by digital audio is far from having been exhausted by the community at large. In short, effective solutions, that are easy to exploit and are free for all to use, have only partially been enacted. This paper will illustrate working solutions that aim to explore and tap the potential of both the advantages outlined above, while adhering to three underlying principles:

1) Output must be in a format that guarantees maximum diffusion – in the current scenario this is represented by browser-based material, that can be viewed both on- and offline.
2) Any tools that are produced must be user-friendly from an authoring point of view – aimed at the majority of operators in the sector, rather than the technically-gifted few.
3) Materials that are created must be in a format that guarantees maximum compatibility, with both:
    a) Future technological developments – while nobody can predict what direction these may take, steps can be taken to avoid technological dead-ends, i.e. situations whereby materials become obsolete in a short period of time.
    b) Other systems – well-designed authoring tools should store output so as to allow *pooling*, the possibility for materials to be used by applications based on different systems (Cushion, 2004).

2.2 Macromedia Flash

The program that allows the creation of a system that best complies with the three criteria outlined above is Macromedia Flash, the latest version of which is Flash 8 (although the materials described in the current paper were developed using an earlier version: Flash MX). A list of its main features follows:

1) Extremely high accessibility (97% of web users have the Flash player)
2) It is cross platform/cross browser
3) Flash material is ideal for the web, being of far smaller dimensions than Java-based solutions
4) It supports Unicode – so-called "special" characters can be visualised
5) Excellent handling of audio (.mp3) and graphics (.jpg, .swf)
6) Excellent handling of XML
7) PHP posting to allow online storage of user interaction

Points 1 to 3 satisfy the first mandate in section 2.1, in that, in the vast majority of cases, materials can be accessed without the necessity to download and install additional software. The second mandate, that regarding ease of materials production, is met by points 5 and 6, as the media referred to, audio and graphics in the first point, and text in the second, can all be stored externally. Therefore systems can be created whereby templates are developed using Flash that upload content at runtime – in this way, there is a clear division between form and content. Materials writers do not have to enter the rather challenging Flash program and wade through hundreds of lines of script, but instead create new exercises by editing text in an XML file, and placing files containing other resources (images, video, animations and sound) within a given directory with given names (e.g. "imageFile.jpg", "soundFile1.mp3" etc.). Apart from making life easier for materials writers, this system also complies with the third mandate, that regarding compatibility, as XML has emerged in recent years as a standard format for the storage of text variables, and as such can be read by a large array of scripting languages (see Ward, 2002 and Tamburini, 2004, for other applications in CALL); the same applies to JPEG and MP3, that represent standards for their respective media types, and thereby are likely to be catered for by major software developers in the foreseeable future.

3 Audio on the web: moving towards optimum solutions

3.1 The presentation of audio on the web

Brett (2005c) reviews options relating to the presentation of audio on the web for use in CALL, identifying three main practices:

1) Inserting a link that opens up a media player such as Real Player, QuickTime or Windows Media Player.
2) Embedding a media player plug-in in the Web page.
3) Using Flash buttons.

The first is deemed to be ill-advised as media players act as a distraction in that they open up above the page being viewed, thereby blocking as much as 25% its content. The second does not create this problem, but entails a certain amount of knowledge of scripting. Furthermore, visualisation depends on what media player is defined as default on the end user's computer, the variations that result may be aesthetically displeasing, or in the worst of cases compromise functionality. The third option is recommended as being the most suitable, in that players can be tailor-made to the specific necessities of language learning: players with full functionality (PLAY, STOP, FF, REW etc.) can be presented for long passages, whereas simple PLAY buttons can be presented for single word/short phrase files. Further features that can be incorporated include:

1) Preloaders that inform the user of download progress, avoiding the frustration that stems from having to wait for data for an indeterminate period of time, in keeping with the findings of Myers (1985) regarding the necessity to keep users informed of the progress of processes that last more than 10 seconds.
2) Keyboard hotkeys for PLAY, PAUSE, REW and FF (e.g. the UP, DOWN, LEFT and RIGHT arrow keys, respectively).
3) The possibility to access segments of an audio file that has been previously downloaded: "there is no need to create a new file containing only the utterance of interest, as Flash players can be coded to access a given file from 6 sec. to 10 sec, for example." (Brett, in press).

The recommendation to propose Flash players as being the most suitable means for the presentation of audio in web pages dealing with CALL is borne out by recent trends which have displayed notable adoption of this system for materials created both within the commercial and educational domains (see the *Hot Potatoes* forum, <http://groups.yahoo.com/group/ hotpotatoesusers/>, for extensive discussion of issues relating to audio and video in interactive exercises). However, some of the more advanced features described above are not always incorporated.

In order to render the process of creating web pages with Flash buttons swifter and easier, the author has developed a helper application called *soundItOut* (see <http://davidbrett.uniss.it/software>), whereby the materials creator need merely decide what kind of players are required on the basis of the sound files to be inserted (long and short, only long, or only short), and then select the sound files to be presented. The program then proceeds with the creation of a HTML page containing all the necessary code, and copies the sound files and Flash mp3 players to the destination folder. The HTML file can then be edited using the materials writer's preferred web editor.

3.2 Advanced features: the synchronisation of sound and text

Recent work undertaken by the author concerns the exploration of possibilities to exploit the two features of digital audio referred to in section 2.1. Essentially this involves the synchronisation of sound and text in order to provide elaboration of input with enhanced functionality. CALL materials often attempt to make a closer connection between transcriptions and listening exercises than that which exists in the traditional textbook and cassette scenario. Two examples of note are: the *Longman English Interactive* course (Jamieson et al, 2004), in which learners click on a hyperlink to visualise the transcription; and Randall's ESL Lab (<www.esl-lab.com>), which offers dynamic enhancement of transcriptions by way of glossed items.

Creating features such as the synchronisation of sound and text is a method which is not new to CALL: Hulstijn (2003) describes an application called "123Listen" for tagging sound and video files for successive use in the language learning class, however, the output does not seem to be web-compatible. The author has developed an application, prosaically called *synchroniseSoundAndText* (see <http://davidbrett.uniss.it/software>), by means of which association is made between chunks of text and time intervals in a sound file merely by clicking to place the cursor at the end of each chunk of text as it is heard. If necessary, in a successive phase, the time intervals for each chunk can be fine-tuned to the range of 1/10 sec. The text and time interval data that are defined are then stored in an XML file, and can be used for a series of different activity types, examples of which are outlined below.

3.2.1 Karaoke players

A "karaoke" player is one that visualises the segments of transcription as they are heard. By default the transcription is not visualised, but is expanded when the user clicks on a speech bubble. Showing the transcription of only the part of the sound file that is currently being heard has several advantages: first and foremost, the presence of the transcription is more discreet than a pop-up window *cf.* the solution offered by *Longman English Interactive* (Jamieson et al, 2004); the learner is encouraged not to read all the transcription, but only to access parts that are not comprehended; difficult vocabulary items can be hyperlinked to a web page using HTML formatting within the XML tags; finally, the transcription, if visualised, changes as REWIND/FF are pressed, enabling users to search the audio file for the position of a given utterance.

3.2.2 Clickable texts

A second way of presenting a transcription is as a "clickable text", typically to be used after the main listening exercise. In this case the whole transcription is visualised together with an mp3 player with full functions. As the user listens to the file, sections of the transcription are highlighted using enhanced formatting: e.g. underlining and/or changes in text colour.

If the user clicks on a part of the text, the sound file (if playing) is paused, and the segment of the file corresponding to the chunk of text is played. This encourages learners to concentrate on parts of the input that were not understood via listening alone.

3.2.3 Dictation

Dictation is a notoriously difficult exercise to present efficiently in CALL activities. Essentially the problem regards how to provide effective feedback for a large body of text input. By "effective feedback" we do not mean "Very Good!" and "Try again" with associated gleeful or gloomy sound effects, but rather feedback that is *intrinsic*, defined by Bangs (2003) as that which should "mimic a good teacher offering helpful advice and encouragement". Appropriate scripting can go beyond the Boolean right/wrong response by parsing an input string character-by-character and colour-coding (and/or underlining) segments that do not correspond to the model. This type of operation is feasible only for short segments of input text, as the huge variations in learner input presented by long texts will compromise the effectiveness of the script. Therefore, when developing dictation exercises, it is far easier to handle an audio file that is divided into short segments, the input for each of which is corrected on a one-to-one basis. Furthermore, working on a segment by segment basis may render the exercise less tedious, and also more effective, as the learner receives immediate feedback, rather than having to type out a long passage before receiving any evaluation.

3.2.4 Annotation of comprehension/non-comprehension

Synchronising text with sound files also allows the creation of a system whereby the learner, when listening to a sound file, can interact with the interface to mark passages which are not understood, e.g. by clicking on a "???" button. Once the listening file has finished, the learner may then visualise the transcription which has altered formatting (colour-coding and/or underlining) in the segments of the transcription corresponding to the times when difficulty was signalled. As in section 3.2.2 the learner may then click on any segment of the text to listen to the corresponding part of the sound file.

4 Interactive exercises using digital audio

A type of interaction that is extremely under-exploited in CALL exercises is that of drag'n'drop (Brett, 2005a). Practically non-existent are exercises that involve dragging sound clips, even though these can be created with relative ease using programs such as *Hot Potatoes*. The author has developed several Flash-based templates to explore possibilities to create exercises of the following types (note that in all these types "Check", "Reset" and "Key" buttons are provided, as is optional visualisation of the transcription of sound items):

1) Matching exercises – the learner must associate sound clips in one column with those in another. Association may be made by moving the sound clips in one column, or by moving arrows to link the items in the two columns, a type of interaction more reminiscent of exercises in textbooks.
2) Jigsaw listening, whereby the learner listens to scrambled segments of a single passage, and must move the sound clips into the correct order.
3) Grouping exercises – in this exercise the learner listens to a certain number of sound clips and assigns them to two or more groups on the basis of phonological, semantic or other factors.

An element common to these three exercise types is the possibility to directly manipulate the order of sound objects – in this way learners' interactions are represented graphically on the screen providing a far more tangible result than in traditional tape and textbook scenarios, where letters or numbers are used to assign a given order, or group, yielding a result that is rather abstract. Incorporating the drag'n'drop function means that, at the end of the exercise, learners have "physically" recomposed orders and groups.

5 Online recording and CALL

Features that allow users to record their own voices and make comparisons with models are common in CALL software that is to be run locally, e.g. from a CD-ROM, desktop application etc. Providing such a feature in an online environment is quite a different matter as it involves granting access to local resources (sound card, local memory, microphone etc.) that may well pose security risks. For this reason such features are rare in web-based exercises. However, it may be argued that online learner voice recording is an important function as it is basically the only way in which we can actually get learners to speak and therefore practise one of the fundamental skills in second, or foreign language learning.

Learner voice recording activities can be divided into two typologies, depending on the destination of the material produced:

1) Recordings are sent via e-mail, or are saved to server, so that the instructor can then access and/or download the learners' production for correction.
2) Learners record their own voices in order to practice pronunciation, sentence formulation etc. and compare their production with given models. In this scenario, the instructor does not necessarily have access to the production.

The first scenario is essentially voice-mail, for which a number of free and well-established websites exist (see <http://odeo.com/> for one example). The second regards a function which is far less common, of use to CALL and few other fields. Hence, the following discussion will focus on systems for the latter and evaluate three options, discussing their respective merits and drawbacks. It is to be borne in mind that, in order to develop CALL activities with an online recording function, existing applications must be enhanced considerably and any solution developed should comply with the criteria outlined in section 2.1.

5.1 Online recording exercise typologies

Apart from the traditional "record and compare" activities, online recording can also be used for exercises in which learners must formulate input before recording. Examples may include activities in which the learner is provided with an answer and must formulate the question that was asked, or, conversely, answer questions relating to a reading or listening passage (i.e. based on specific content). After recording, the learner can then access model input composed of sound files with optional visualisation of transcriptions. It may be argued that this type of exercise is not truly interactive, in that, given the absence of evaluation of input, feedback is not provided and it is up to the learner to make judgements based on comparison with the model answers. While evaluation of input via speech recognition is perfectly feasible in the desktop environment and is used in several CALL packages, online, server-side running of such functions is perhaps beyond our current possibilities, at least in the authoring scenarios envisaged in this paper.

5.2 Applications for online recording activities

5.2.1 Flash

In section 2.2 Macromedia Flash was identified as being an excellent tool for the creation of interactive CALL exercises, however, online recording cannot not be carried out using Flash alone. While Flash can access the user's microphone, it acts as a mere interface and cannot capture and replay the input without resorting to another, rather expensive, component, Flash Communication Server. Hence, two notable disadvantages emerge: first, setting up the system from the author's point of view is quite complicated and costly; second, the activities created can only be used in an online, and not offline, environment. See <http://duber.com/blog/archives/00000023.html> for an example of a Flash interface for a voice-mail application.

Dennie Hoopingarner has carried out admirable adaptation of this system to the CALL field, see: <http://www.audioportfolios.com/>

5.2.2 Java applets

To the contrary of Flash, Java applets can access the local computer's sound card and microphone to capture and replay sound input. See <http://www.vimas.com/ve_record_applet_sdk.htm> for an example of such a device designed for use in voice-mail applications. The author has developed an interface in Flash which communicates, via JavaScript, with the applet used in the above example. The learner clicks on a "play" button to hear a phrase (the transcription of which can be optionally visualised), and then clicks on a "record" button and repeats the phrase. Clicking on a third button plays both model and then learner input. When satisfied with his/her production, the learner clicks on a "next" button, whereby a new phrase is presented.

This system presents both advantages and disadvantages, the former include:

1) The Java applet is quite small and loads quickly.
2) Authoring is easy, based on the system of external data in XML and MP3 outlined in section 2.2
3) The system can work offline.
4) Since it is based on software for voice-mail, learner input can be saved on the server, although setting this up does require some technical knowledge.

Drawbacks include the following:

1) The applet does not appear to work reliably on Netscape-type browsers.
2) The system may be hampered by security settings – when used offline the Flash Player settings may need to be modified in order to allow cross-script communication. Note that this problem is not inherent to the applet, but rather to the interface developed by the author.
3) The licence fee for the applet amounts to $199, *cf.* a similar applet produced by JavaSonics <http://www.javasonics.com>. This is made available with a more restrictive licensing scheme based on user activity: e.g. 5,000 credits are offered for US $200 (a "credit" is consumed each time a user uploads or downloads a file to server, though not if sound is recorded and played locally).

5.2.3 Shockwave

Macromedia Director is a program developed by the same company as Flash (Macromedia products are now distributed by Adobe). While under some aspects the two products are similar, Director is used more for the creation of multimedia CD-ROMs and desktop applications and hence offers some functions that are absent from Flash (e.g. access to local files, the possibility to save files locally etc.). Audio Xtra is a component that allows online recording using Director – a working example of this system can be viewed at: < http://xtras.tabuleiro.com/products/audio/sample_ movie.htm>

Since Director allows similar levels of interactivity to Flash, this component can be integrated into a application to allow easy creation of CALL activities.

Yet again this system has its pros and cons – in comparison to the Java applet described above, advantages include the following:

1) The output appears to be more accessible as the application works reliably on all browsers and systems.
2) All interaction takes place within a single application, hence security restrictions relating to cross-system scripting do not apply.
3) The Audio Xtra component allows greater functionality as users can define input source and sampling rate, as well as maximum recording time.
4) Projectors can be made for local use in which all the necessary components are packaged, thereby avoiding the necessity to connect to the Internet to change settings, or download

components. Furthermore, in this context sound material may be an encoded and saved to disc as mp3 files.

5) The licensing agreement for the Audio Xtra component foresees free use for non-commercial enterprises such as schools and universities.
6) Director's programming language, Lingo, caters for interfacing with speech recognition programs (see section 5.1).

The main disadvantage relating to this system regards the fact that, unless a projector application is used, the Shockwave Player is needed to run it. Recent surveys regarding the diffusion of server applications (see <http://www.adobe.com/products/player_census/flashplayer/>) display that 97% of web users have the Macromedia Flash Player, while the material to be viewed using the Shockwave Player is immediately accessible to 57% of Internet-enabled desktops. Download of both players is extremely straightforward, albeit somewhat long for users with slow connections (c. 6 min for the Shockwave Player) bearing in mind the finding that "[secondary school pupils] disliked having to download helper applications" (Hughes & McAvinia, 2004).

6 Conclusion

This paper has attempted to outline some of the possibilities that New Technologies offer the CALL field, and in particular to identify problem areas to which more attention need be paid. Many of the solutions proposed, such as the use of Flash for the presentation of sound on the web, are widely adopted in the commercial field, unfortunately, however, these well-designed systems are usually unavailable to those in the educational sector. A standard, open-source method for presenting sound in on- and offline courses would be a boon to the CALL sector – and it is only a matter of time before such an application emerges from the several strong candidates that currently exist. On the other hand, online recording is a sector that requires considerable work before optimum solutions will be arrived at. Of the three options discussed, Shockwave with the Audio Xtra component does seem to be that which offers greatest reliability and functionality, however, developments in the field are rapid and alternative contenders are sure to appear in the near future.

Acknowledgements

The work reported herein was funded by a research grant from Banco di Sardegna to the Faculty of Foreign Languages and Literature, University of Sassari, Italy. The author would like to thank Yvan Baptiste of Lycée Jean Lurçat, Perpignan, for initiating and discussing the online recording issue in the HotPotatoesUsers forum, and Sergey Kuchma of Vimas software for allowing free evalution of his audio applet.

References

Ariew, R. (1987) "Integrating Video and CALL in the Curriculum: The Role of the ACTFL Guidelines", in *Modern Median Foreign Language Education: Theory and Implementation*, W. Flint Smith (ed.), Lincolnwood, IL: National Textbook Company.

Arneil, S. & Holmes, M. (2004) "Hacking in Hot Potatoes – A little knowledge brings a lot of power", TEL&CAL, 2: 45-49.

Bangs, P. (2003) "Engaging the learner: how to author for best feedback" in Uschi, F. (ed.) (2003), *Language Learning Online: Towards Best Practice*, Lisse, Netherlands: Swets and Zeitlinger.

Brett, D. (2005a) "Drag'n'drop Exercises and 2nd Language Learning", *Atti del 3° Convegno AICLU: "I Centri Linguistici: approcci, progetti e strumenti per l'apprendimento e la valutazione"*, Trieste: University of Trieste.

—. (2005b) "Why is the web such a silent place?", *Proceedings of the 8th CercleS Conference*, Bratislava: University of Bratislava.

—. (2005c) "The Use of Sound in CALL Web Pages and Interactive Exercises", *Annali della Facoltà di Lingue e Letterature Straniere (Vol. 2)*, Sassari: University of Sassari.

—. (in press) "*Conductor*: Flash-based creation of CALL material", Proceedings of IATEFL Conference: "Learning Technologies In The Language Classroom: A Step Closer To The Future" University of Cyprus, Nicosia. May 26th – 28th, 2006.

Chinnery, G. M. (2006) "Going to the MALL: Mobile Assisted Language Learning", *Language Learning & Technology*, Volume 10(1): 9-16. Available online at: <http://llt.msu.edu/vol10num1/emerging/>

Cushion, S. (2004) "Increasing accessibility by pooling digital resources", *ReCALL,* 16(1): 41-50.

Egbert, J. and Yang, Y. F. (2004) "Mediating the digital divide in CALL classrooms: Promoting effective language tasks in limited technology contexts", *ReCall* 16(2): 280–291.

Hegelheimer, V., Reppert, K, Borberg, M., Daisy, B., Grgurovic, M., Middlebrooks, K. & Liu, S. (2004) "Preparing the new generation of CALL researchers and practitioners: What nine months in an MA program can (or cannot) do", *ReCALL,* 16(2): 432–447.

Hughes, J. & McAvinia, C. (2004) "What Really Makes Students Like a Web Site? What are the Implications for Designing Web-based Language Learning Sites?", *ReCALL,* 16: 85-102.

Hulstijn, J. H. (2003) "Connectionist models of language processing and the training of listening skills with the aid of multimedia software", *Computer Assisted Language Learning*, Vol. 16, No. 5, 413–425.

Jamieson, J., Chapelle, C.A., & Preiss, S. (2004) "Putting principles into practice", *ReCALL*, 16(2): 396–415.

Myers, B. A. (1985) "The importance of percent-done progress indicators for computer-human interfaces". *Proc. ACM CHI '85 Conf.* (San Francisco, CA, 14-18 April), 11-17.

Tamburini, F (2004) "Dynamic generation of web-based multimedia language learning materials through on line templates", *Proceedings of the 7th CercleS Conference*. Paris, September 2002.

Ward, M. (2002) "Reusable XML technologies and the development of language learning materials", *ReCALL,* 14: 285-294.

METHODOLOGY OF E-LEARNING IN LSP AND DESIGNING LEARNING ACTIVITIES IN TECHNOLOGY-RICH CONTEXT

SVETLANA FEDYUNINA

Introduction

Since 2005 the Linguistic Centre of Saratov State Technical University (SSTU), participating in TEMPUS Joint European Project 25020-2004 "Foreign Language Education for Russian Technical Universities on the Volga», has been developing e-learning and specific self-access learning strategies in LSP for technical students. We are going to focus on the following problems of LSP: (1) aims, components of self-access learning, (2) changing roles of teachers and learners in self-access centre (SAC), (3) perspectives and strategies of self-access e-learning as components of effective methodology of ESP.

Background of the problem

For more than 15 years the Linguistic centre of Saratov State Technical University has been creating the integrated multilevel system of linguistic and lingua-rhetoric education in SSTU. It includes: teaching foreign languages (English, German, and French) at different levels, Russian language and culture of speech, interdisciplinary elective courses (e.g. Computer linguistics, Intercultural rhetoric for students of humanities, etc.), and pedagogical rhetoric for teachers and post-graduates. In accordance with this approach a graduate of technical university should be not only a specialist in his field of knowledge but also possess creative skills of linguistic and rhetoric dialogue as the bases of humanitarian culture.

The *main aim* of the system is the formation of *linguistic personality* of a learner possessing the following skills:

- the ability to transform information in native and foreign languages in different ways;

- the ability to behave adequately in different professional communicative situations using appropriate communicative styles and ethic norms;

Communicative competence is defined as a certain level of language mastery, social and cultural knowledge and skills that allows a communicant to vary speech behaviour depending on the functional factor of speaking, creating a basis for communicative multicultural development.

For achievements of the main goal *structural components of the system* have been determined. They are:

- learning outcomes at each educational level;
- content of learning (material component –variants of learning programs and functional component – learning process at each level);
- methods of teaching and types of activities;
- teaching aids and facilities;
- Assessment and feedback.

The multilevel linguistic and lingua-rhetoric training was defined by the programs of learning.

(a) Foreign languages

- The first level – basic course (two years), developing elements of cultural, linguistic and communicative competence);
- The second level – further development of cultural and communicative competence, necessary for business and professional communication (bachelor level);
- The third level – development of creative language skills in scientific and partnership communication (postgraduate level)

(b) Native language (Russian) and interdisciplinary learning

- The first level – Russian language and culture of speech (one year). Students study and learn styles of speaking, such as scientific, business, the language of mass-media; generals of modern rhetoric (development of communicative and linguistic skills) ;
- Elective courses for technical students and integrative cross-cultural courses for students of humanities (further development of communicative skills and development of pragmatic skills) ;
- Pedagogical rhetoric for teachers and post-graduates (mastering all types of competences)

In 1998 the Linguistic Centre licensed the 5-th year program of applied education "The translator in professional communication" for students of SSTU and in 2006 has celebrated the fifth generation of its graduates. Important dimension in the development of the Linguistic Centre has been participation of its teachers in different international projects in 1996 – 2005.

In 2004 the Linguistic Centre of SSTU together with partner universities (Surrey University (GB), Oldenburg University (Germany), Volgograd Technical University and Samara Technical University in Russia) became the winner of the TEMPUS project "Foreign Language Education for Russian Technical Universities on the Volga" which gave the staff opportunity to develop new trends in LSP. It is the theory and practice of self-access language learning (SALL) and e-learning as the main element of self-access. The main aim of the project has been setting up of self-access centres of LSP in 3 Universities of the Volga region. The purpose of the centres is to help bridge the gap between the first two years of a degree language programmes (that are parts of Russian educational standards) and entry to employment three years later. Graduates will be involved in developing language skills through open access to learning and through tutorial (counsellor) support.

Aims and components of self-access learning

Self-access has been applied as an effective way of learning all over the world. In different parts of the world there have been different focuses in the way this focus has been implemented. But as a recognized term it is used to denote pedagogical approach to encouraging learners' autonomy. Learners' autonomy involves: the responsibility to learning, working without a teacher, the choice dimension. Self-access language learning is an approach to *language learning*, not to *language teaching*. It is the integration of elements which provides a learning self-access environment. They are:

- resources (learning and authentic materials, technologies, activities, access to users)
- people (teachers and learners, performing different functions)
- management
- system (organization of SALL facilities)
- Individualization (learning strategies, styles, time, space, content of learning etc.)
- needs/wants analysis
- learner reflection (consideration of language ability and progress in

learning, goal setting, suitability of SALL for self)
- counselling
- staff training
- learner training
- materials development
- assessment (kinds and purposes)
- evaluation (See in detail: D. Gardner & L. Miller, 2005).

Setting up a self-access centre requires changes in understanding traditional meanings of some above mentioned elements. Workshops in Surrey and Oldenburg universities, in which Russian teachers have participated as well as further cascade trainings in Russia, have been good practice for the members of the project to discuss and realize the differences of traditional and learner-centred approaches in LSP. First of all the project members have to get accustomed to new roles of learners and teachers in SAC and realize e-learning perspectives.

Learners and teachers in self-access centre

In learners-centred pedagogy learners become central figures in learning process, they must be aware of their responsibility for planning and evaluating learning activities, they become self-assessors and self-motivators. It means that the learner determines his *interactive learning paradigm* with specific goals and interests.

The function of the teacher is radically changed in self-access. The teacher in self-access can perform familiar roles, such as assessor or material developer, but he can be administrator, manager, organizer, evaluator, counsellor (in other terms – tutor, language advisor, consultant). The learner is to be highly motivated to self-access learning and the enthusiastic language teacher, proving advantages of continuous self-education, is an important "influence" factor. (Peers, educational establishment and modern society which needs linguistic personality at the labour market, are other factors of influence). By discussing and demonstrating self-access approaches, the teacher can motivate and encourage students to autonomous learning.

Managing learners and counselling in self-access centre are rather new roles for teacher and need separate description. We should only mention that the challenge for the self-access manager is to help self-access learners define their aims and outcomes. It depends upon the managing strategy but the main constraints of it are needs analysis, assessments, providing workshops, counselling services and access to all kinds of materials. Counselling in self-access requires special pedagogical skills when interacting with learners and accumulates the focus of new teaching roles.

D.Gardner & L.Miller investigated the roles of traditional classroom teaches and self-access counsellors. They showed difficulties the teachers experienced in changing their roles in self-access and using different methodologies. They found that the work of language counsellors requires training of specific pedagogic skills, among them are: initiating – introducing new directions and options, goal-setting – helping the learner to formulate specific goals, guarding – offering advice and information, modelling – demonstrating target behaviour, supporting, giving feedback, evaluating, linking – connecting the learners' goals and tasks to wider issucs, concluding (D. Gardner & L. Miller, 2005: 183).

So the learners in self-access must be confident that they get help and advice, feel comfortable in their learning, will be free from stress , and be aware of their learning aims. The teachers, which are going to be counsellors, should be aware of changing attitudes to language learning, promoting innovations, encouraging reflective independent learning. To above mentioned teaching skills it is necessary to add: the ability to work in a team and the ability to understand what e-learning is.

E-learning perspectives

E-learning (electronic learning) is the "heart" of self-access language learning. Universities make investments in e-learning because they realize that it is: competition for students at the global education market, "borderless" education and demand from students. Establishing computer-based language environment and using innovation technologies is the mainstream in language education. The potential of e-learning revolutionizes language learning in six key dimensions:

- Connectivity – access to information is available on a global scale
- Flexibility – learning can take place any time, any place
- Interactivity – assessment of learning can be immediate and autonomous
- Collaboration – use of discussion tools can support collaborative learning beyond the classroom
- Extended opportunity – e-content can reinforce and extend classroom-based learning
- Motivation – multimedia resources can make learning fun (See: Effective practice with e-learning, 2004)

E-learning is defined as facilitated and supported through the use of information and communications technology learning. It may involve the use of different technologies.

SAC in SSTU involves the following:

- 13 desktop and 2 laptop computers
- software, including assistive software
- interactive whiteboard
- electronic communication tools, including e-mail, discussion board, chat facilities.
- internet

There are different forms of activities where e-learning can be used. In SSTU SAC we are developing the following activities in e-learning: *supporting (enhancing)* learning for existing courses where e-learning was not a required element; *blended learning* as a combination of traditional and electronic practices (replacement of some elements of traditional learning) and *fully on-line* – using e-learning component as primary course mechanism.

We realize that effective learning is a complex process and the core of it is special pedagogic approach to learning. The well known traditional components of teaching technologies (aims and objectives, content of teaching, methods, teaching aids, assessment, outcomes) acquire another meaning in e-learning. Designing learning activities in technology-rich context required solving some urgent problems beforehand, among them are the following:

- What are the learners' needs and motives for sell-access learning?
- What are the learners' prior experiences of learning, their social and interpersonal skills?
- What styles of learning have the learners experienced beforehand?
- What is the level of learners' linguistic and communicative competence?
- What are goals and intended outcomes?
- How will the learner interact with the environment to achieve the planned outcomes?
- What kind of learning environment is the most effective for achieving the goals?
- What resources and technologies are available?
- How will the learner be able to assess himself and develop further skills?
- What kind of feedback will the teacher (counsellor, tutor) use?

The answers to these questions we tried to receive through questionnaires that were given to more than 400 students of 3 universities, through intensive workshops in Surrey, Oldenburg, Saratov, Samara and Volgograd, in discussions at scientific conferences and experimental work in SACs.

Electronic EL educational programmes (modules) for students of Electronic faculty have been developed by the teachers of SSTU, EL modules for students of Machine-building faculty have been developed by SSTU partners from Samara and EL modules for students of Ecology have been worked out by the partners from Volgograd. In September 2007 all the programmes are to be piloted in 3 Universities as well as electronic programme for students of Machine–building faculty, studying German.

Conclusion

Self-access to language learning is a very flexible and innovative approach to learning in modern society. It is a combination of a wide range of human and technological resources. It allows individualization but gives way to communication throughout the global world. It widens participation in lifelong learning. It changes teachers' and student' roles and the learner becomes the main figure in education process. E-learning exploits interactive technologies, it occupies the central position in self-access. It can cover a spectrum of activities from supporting learning to blended learning and fully on-line learning. Designing for learning must take place in the context of innovative pedagogical approach where all teaching-learning components and technological resources are clearly defined and taken into consideration.

References

Effective practice with e-learning. JISC e-learning Programme (2004), www.jisc.ac.uk/elearning

Gardner, D. & Miller, L. (2005) Establishing Sell-Access from Theory to Practice, Cambridge University Press.

NEW TECHNOLOGIES APPLIED FOR PRACTISING ESP/EAP SKILLS: PROFESSIONAL WRITING

DITA GÁLOVÁ

Introduction

Competence in a number of languages is of central importance in the process of European integration and in the creation of a European knowledge-based society – one of the principal aims of the Lisbon Process. This is why there are efforts being made to promote and professionalize language teaching and learning in the education systems. Language skills play an important role in the social, cultural and economic integration of Europe, and support academic mobility, as well as employability.

In the 21st century, language teaching is characterized by change and rapid development. Change is accelerated by the application and recognized potential of information and communication technologies. They apply to the delivery of teaching and learning and improve the whole learning process. The new forms of delivery and methodology may help make the language learning more attractive, and effective, too.

Information and communication technologies present solutions to many traditional challenges in modern language teaching and learning. A diverse range of skills and associated activities can be mixed and blended effectively via technological applications in (1) CALL classes, multimedia classrooms, or (2) via virtual environments such as Moodle or other on-line products. The latter group offers efficient and economic solutions to many issues in language learning, and addresses a number of key issues encountered by learners. They can be delivered to large number of students on-line, without necessity of buying books, providing tailor-made materials corresponding to students' professional needs. Moreover, students may get the feedback immediately, can practise various skills through activities of different types (audio, video, quizzes, and the like). A. Stevens suggests that

> "this form of language learning, as technology and online links become more widely available, will no doubt be a major influence on future provision, with learners having immediate access to learning support and resources on demand."
>
> (Stevens, 2005)

The new approach to language learning may be encountered not only within the instruction at schools and universities. It also plays an important role in the course of the lifelong acquisition of the language skills required. However, these two areas should not be separated, but – in particular with English for Specific Purposes (ESP) and/or English for Occupational Purposes (EOP) – related to enable closer connection of professional education and the real requirements of the professional practice.

Blended learning as a part of teaching foreign languages

When the language is being taught for general purposes (English for general purposes – EGP), the course design reflects the input level of learners and the group is more or less homogeneous. Specialized courses, on the other hand, usually require prior L2 knowledge which is used to develop specifically oriented skills. Here, the L2 students often have different input knowledge in general, and their language skills vary, too. In traditional courses the level and speed of progress cannot be adjusted to individual students too much, and that is why using new technologies may be a good solution for ESP/EOP courses, as well as in courses of English for Academic Purposes (EAP). Students can be provided with extra tools and sources to practise their language skills with respect to different professional areas. The electronic support may facilitate managing this specificity offering tailor-made materials addressing individual needs.

Purely online tutoring and courses (e-learning) possibly cannot fulfil the requirements of successful and effective L2 learning since it misses personal communication and interaction. Consequently, a combination of face-to-face teaching and interactive (frequently electronic) practice activity could result in a more motivated, efficient and effective teaching-learning process. New technologies can contribute to the creation of varied learning conditions needed to cope with limited number of contact hours with the teacher whose role in the language learning cannot be substituted for. Hence, great emphasis shall be put on blended learning[1]. According to

[1] The term is understood here as combination of contact hours and the use of web-based approaches although some authors warn of the existence of contrasting

McCormick (2005) "blended learning can prepare students to speak more in class and become fluent faster" because they can prepare individually according to their own needs and knowledge.

Blended learning provides students with extra activities and reference materials related to the teaching materials used in the classes. A few language teachers have necessary technical skills to create own web sites, but everybody can use on-line products already available, or a virtual learning environment such as "Moodle". This is a course management system that enables teachers to create effective online learning courses, including educational websites, assignments, dictionaries, and quizzes to be done outside the lessons. It is possible to record students' attempts, monitor their self-study, and fix the terms for completing the quizzes. The language learning can therefore be supported by a systematic work that is reflected in the end-of-semester assessment. Apart from grammar and pronunciation guides intended for self-study especially, the Moodle environment can provide students with a wide range of quizzes that cover the material learned at lessons, including morphological, lexical and semantic exercises for individual course book units or individual weeks of instruction. They may be open for limited period only, which makes students work on them systematically. With respect to ESP courses there may be a selection of professional texts for practising reading skills and reading comprehension, thus students work individually on developing their terminology having the necessary feedback provided either by the system itself (checking of correct answers) or by the teacher at the following lesson or via forums.

Writing as one of the key ESP skills

According to Dudley–Evans & St John (1998) ESP is based on needs analysis, course and syllabus design, materials selection and production, teaching and learning, and evaluation. It should be student-centred, and focused on adults, either university students or professionals from various fields (Robinson, 1991). Students are supposed to have sufficient level of L2 (at least intermediate) and have specific goals to achieve, i.e. to master language competences and skills related to their specialization or professional fields.

---

definitions, cf. Oliver, M. & Trigwell, K. (2005): "The term 'blended learning' has gained considerable currency in recent years as a description of particular forms of teaching with technology. However, like so many terms within this field it remains ill-defined." In fact, there is still quite a bit of ambiguity about what is meant when the term is used.

ESP taught at universities very often requires covering two areas: English for Occupational Purposes (EOP), example of which is English for Science and Technology or English for Business Purposes, and English for Academic Purposes (EAP). The goals are therefore different from those of General English courses and the methodology has to take these requirements into consideration.

The most typical ESP learners are tertiary students, researchers, engineers and corporate students. Writing represents one of the key skills they need with regard to ESP. It is quite understandable because both the students and the specialists have to write research papers, reports, journal articles and the like. In order to learn language effectively, some experts suggest using of authentic texts (Feez, 1998; Holiday, 1994; Dudley-Evans & St John, 1998) as models to learn lexical, morphological, stylistic and other characteristics of the language. This method is known as a product approach. Robinson (1991) identifies the following stages: familiarizing with a model text → comprehension/analysis/manipulation with the model text → creating new input → obtaining a parallel text as an output. The product approach of course cannot be applied in isolation as it could lead to a mechanical copying of the model text. However, this method may still be useful especially at the beginning stages of learning academic/scientific writing which then may be used as a basis for more independent strategy referred to as a process based approach (Flower, 1985). It requires more creative work "emphasising the idea of writing as problem-solving" (Dudley–Evans & St John, 1998: 177). The concept of blended learning can be successfully adopted for these purposes, since it offers possibility to explore and analyse texts, as well as check understanding of e.g. composition and stylistic features via on-line interactive activities (see the project description below).

Professional writing = professional English writing?

The 21st century is often characterised as the "information age". There is growing evidence that English has become the lingua franca of today's knowledge-based society and most professional publications and academic journals with international readership are therefore published in English (Crystal, 1997; Swales, 2000, 2004; Belcher, 2007). The dominance of English is by no means restricted to science. It is the language of trade, business, international politics, etc. Some linguists have argued for the importance of linguistic diversity within the scientific community (Salager-Meyer, 1997), others warn of

> "the spread of English as a 'language problem' threatening to engulf and replace ingenious European languages, as reflected in European policy statements."
>
> (Rogerson-Revell, 2007: 106)

or of "linguistic imperialism" (Phillipson, 1992). Nevertheless, it is commonly accepted that international and cross-cultural communication may be facilitated by use of a common language (Tardy, 2004), so the use of English as lingua franca or international language is rather pragmatic.

Writing Professional English project

In order to ensure better position of researchers and professionals who need to write professional texts or improve their writing skills, the Institute of Foreign Languages, Faculty of Mechanical Engineering, Brno University of Technology (CZ), in cooperation with four partners has developed the project entitled *Writing Professional English*[2] (for more information see http://www.kj.fme.vutbr.cz/leon2/index.html). Since we highly agree with the idea that there has to be a dialogue between the language specialists and ICT experts, the project group did not consist of professionals with linguistic skills in the area of ESP only, but multimedia experts from educational institutions and translation agencies, too. In the course of the project development, a team of material developers approached the end-users (testing partners) from colleges, universities, research institutes, and industrial enterprises with the aim to validate the outcome of the project.

The project *Writing Professional English* addresses professional writers in the fields of science and engineering and provides them with guidance and support in their needs to write more effectively in English. In engineering education, the development of writing skills is often completely neglected or reduced to lower-level writing that does not reflect the needs of up-to-date science and technology. The acquisition and mastering of advanced writing skills in English is a necessity for any engineer who wishes to succeed at the common European labour market.

Together with the needs analysis which is regarded as the necessary prerequisite for designing an ESP course (Hutchison, 1987; Waters, 1994; Strevens, 1988; Robinson, 1991; Dudley-Evans & St John, 1998), an

---

[2] WPE is a language project developing the results of the previous project *Writing in English – A Practical Guide for Technical and Scientific Writes*. The project and its outcomes have been co-financed by the European Commission from the programme Leonardo da Vinci.

informative research of national markets was conducted in the countries of the project partnership. The research has revealed a lack of comprehensive material on professional writing. Commercial publications and course books dealing with writing problems in English concentrate on academic writing in general, without paying a special attention to practical problems of writers in the workplace or to specific linguistic problems of the nationals from the targeted professional fields.

The presented reference and instructional modules contain self-study training modules (reference handbooks and exercises) for professional writers in English. The expected impact of the project's outcome is to enhance professional writing skills of the end-users in industrial enterprises, research and educational institutions from various engineering fields (see Fig. 1). These newly acquired competences will give the professionals a greater confidence in performing their working tasks in the internationally competitive working environment. Being able to write more effectively in English will help technicians, engineers, managers, etc., to apply professional knowledge to European working environments where the writing skills in English are required. A competence-based and self-study oriented approach is user-friendly and therefore attractive for professionals who seek a quick access to the problems they face in their everyday routine at the workplace.

An innovative aspect of the handbook for materials engineering can be seen in the methodology applied through all the phases of the material development, testing and evaluating. A diverse partnership, both in terms of transnationality and in terms of subjects involved (technical universities and colleges, industrial enterprises, research institutes, and chamber of commerce and industry) facilitates cooperation between material developers and target groups (needs analysis, testing draft products, evaluating, and dissemination). Thus, from the very beginning, there was a feedback on what had been produced. The interaction between linguists from educational institutions and technicians/scientists from industry gathered in one team proved to be highly effective. The result is a flexible product where the end-users can choose a material suited to their linguistic and professional needs.

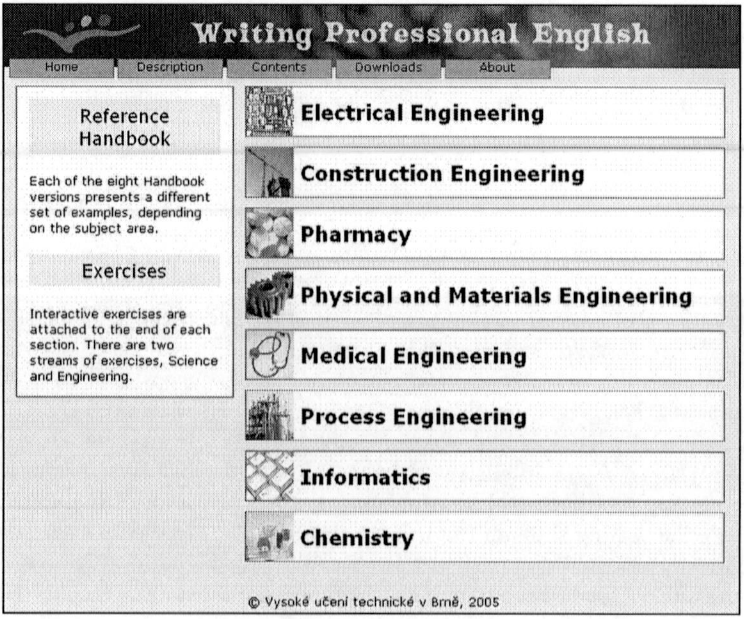

Fig. 1 Writing Professional English

Another innovative aspect of the product can be seen in its versatile approach to the practical needs of professionals in the workplace. At the present time, the on-line version is being used in the partners' institutions. At the Faculty of Mechanical Engineering, Brno University of Technology, it is employed within English courses for graduate students (for practical application of the product in Ph.D. courses see Zavadilová in Chapter I of this book), as well as academic staff from different institutes. Besides this, the end-product is being prepared for commercialization to enable professionals from various universities, institutions, companies, etc. to make full use of the training modules. Another aim is to create a basis for further adaptations of the materials to meet the changing needs of the professional writers through adding new problem areas and extending glossaries of operative expressions and synonyms used in science/ technology texts.

The reference handbooks provide the learner with authentic examples and extracts of texts from the selected professional area. The main objective is to make the general descriptions of writing problems more directly relevant to the writers from particular fields. This approach seems to be very convenient for the end-users because authentic examples and texts related to their field offer the terminology that they can easily understand.

The Reference Modules (see Fig. 2) include six chapters plus glossaries. The first chapter Types of Writing represents an introduction to science/technology writing in general as it describes the individual types of

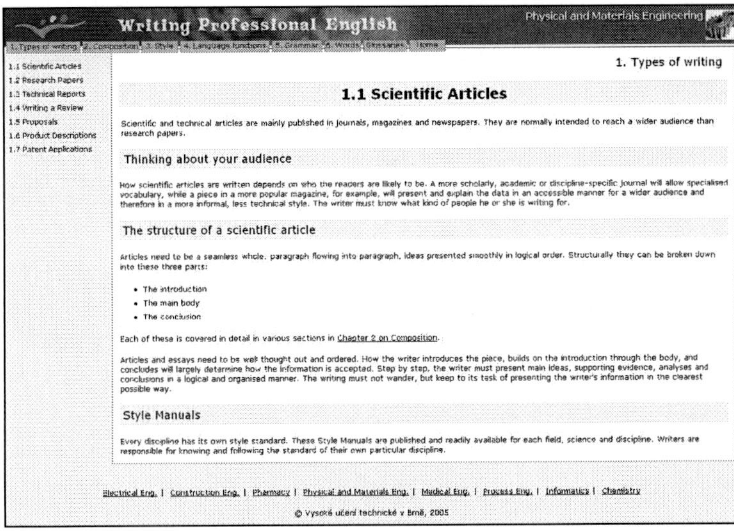

Fig. 2 Types of writing

writing – scientific articles, research papers, technical reports, reviews, proposals, product description, and patent application. The following five chapters offer short explanatory notes on previously identified problem areas followed by authentic examples related to materials engineering. The second chapter Composition is devoted to the structure of a piece of writing and contains the following sections: Titles, Planning your Writing, Paragraph Writing, Introductions, Writing the Main Body, Conclusions, Referencing, Plagiarism, Abstracts, Summary Writing, Acknowledgements, and Appendices. The third chapter provides information on Style (Objectivity, Clarity, Formality, Hedging, and Signposting). Chapter four deals with Language functions (Agreeing and Disagreeing, Classifying, Comparing and Contrasting, Defining, Describing a Process, Emphasizing, Generalizing, Paraphrasing, and Quoting). Chapter five – Grammar – focuses on selected grammatical difficulties that frequently occur in science/technology writing (Writing Numbers, Articles, Using Nouns, Verb Tenses, Using the Passive, Word

Order, and Punctuation). The last chapter Words contains sections on Abbreviations, Words of Latin and Greek Origin, Prefixes and Suffixes, and Confusing Words. Glossaries include terms frequently used in professional writing with their national equivalents (Czech, Icelandic, Italian, and Slovene).

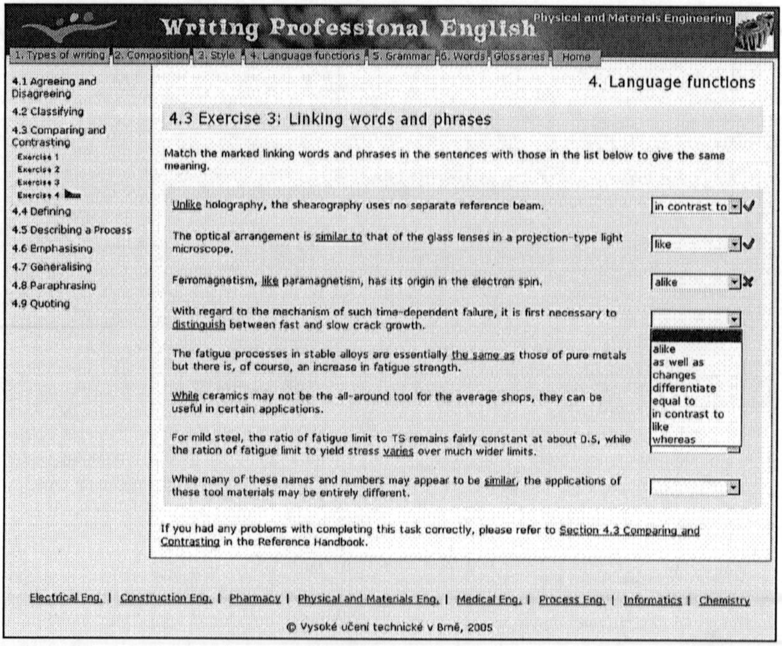

Fig. 3 Exercise – matching

The Exercises (Fig. 3 and 4) take form of a web application that can be used on-line. They include interactive exercises related to the chapters of the Reference Handbook. They are split into core and optional exercises highlighting nationally-specific writing problems for Czech, Icelandic Italian, and Slovene nationals (indicated by flags). The activities are of various types (e.g. matching exercises, true/false statements and the like) with authentic examples, i.e. model texts, from the selected area. The student is provided with correct answer enabling quick self-assessment, as well as with comments and links to the reference material. Therefore, the Exercises may be used for self-study.

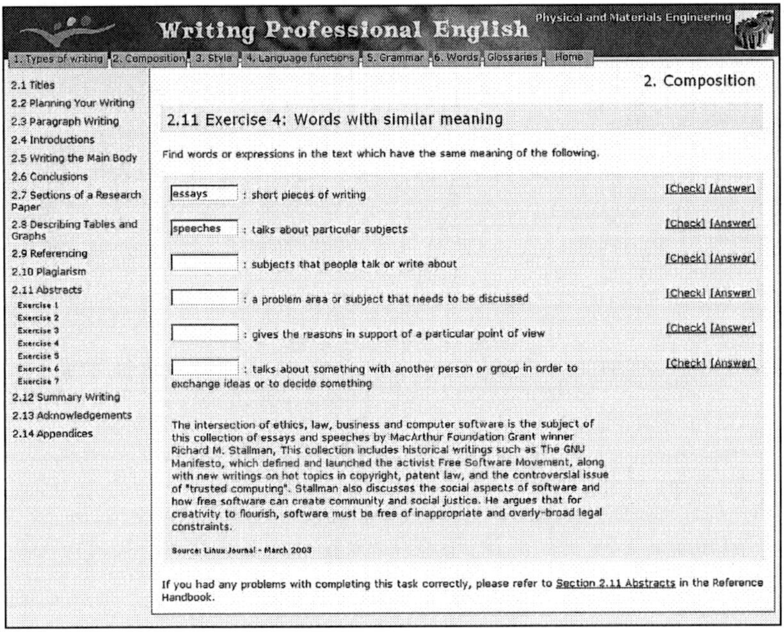

Fig. 4 Exercises – cloze test

Conclusion

Information technologies represent a great challenge for teachers of foreign languages, as well as for learners. Should these be open software such as Moodle enabling teachers to create interactive materials and courses without specific technical knowledge or skills, or specially developed products such as WPE, it always brings about best use of time, space and resources. Depending on the goals and requirements of the learner, these tools can be used effectively both for self-study supporting the idea of learner's autonomy, within lifelong-learning, and can employed as a basis for taught courses, i.e. to be blended with contact hours.

References

Belcher, D. (2007) *Seeking Acceptance in an English-Only Research World.* In Journal of Second Language Writing, 16, pp. 11-22.

Feez, S. (1998) *Text-based Syllabus Design.* Sydney : NCELTR.

Flower, L. (1985) *Problem Solving Strategies for Writing.* 2nd edition. San Diego: Harcourt Brace Jovanovich.

Holiday, A. (1994) *Appropriate Methodology and Social Context.* Cambridge: CUP.

McCormic, C. (2005) *An introduction to 'blended learning' for the teaching of languages.* EF On-Line Lecture. Available at http://www.ef.com.

Oliver, M. & Trigwell, K. (2005) *Can 'Blended Learning' Be Redeemed?* In E-Learning, Vol. 2, No. 1, pp. 17-26.

Phillipson, R. (1998) *Linguistic Imperialism.* Oxford: Oxford University Press.

Promoting Language Learning and Linguistic Diversity: An Action Plan 2004-2006. Commission of the European Communities. Communication from the Commission to the Council, the European Parliament, the Economic and Social Committee and the Committee of the Regions -. COM(2003) 449 final.

Rogerson-Revell, P. (2007) *Using English for International Business: A European case study.* In English for Specific Purposes 26, pp. 103-120.

Robinson, P. (1991) *ESP Today: a Practitioner's Guide.* Hemel Hempstead: Prentice Hall International.

Salager-Meyer, F. (1997) *Scientific multilingualism and ''lesser languages''.* Interciencia, 22, pp. 197–201.

Stevens, A. (2005) ENLU – The use of distance education and e-learning for language learning among undergraduates. In *European Network for the Promotion of Language Learning among All Undergraduates - Report of the task group 3.* Available at http://web.fu-berlin.de/enlu/

Svobodová, Z. (2003): Psaní v angličtině – Writing in English. In *Strojní inženýři pro XXI. století*, Brno.

Svobodová Z., Gálová D. (2004) Effective Communication in Technical/Scientific Writing in English. In *RAAD'04 – 13th International Workshop on Robotics in Alpe-Adria-Danube Region,* Brno.

Tardy, C. *The role of English in scientific communication: lingua franca or Tyrannosaurus rex?* In Journal of English for Academic Purposes. 3 (2004), pp. 247–269.

Writing in English – A Practical Guide for Technical and Scientific Writers, Leonardo da Vinci Project, 1998 – 2001.

IMPLEMENTING A USER-FRIENDLY APPROACH IN LSP COURSES

DANA HANESOVÁ

The context of the UFA project

Living in the 21st century inherently involves the weakening of traditional educational structures and a marked acceleration of changes in the way adolescents and adults learn. These rapidly modernizing circumstances require that the learners should be able to solve effectively a wider range of problems with a greater degree of reliance on ICT and their own resources than ever before.

Internationally oriented educational organizations are giving a high priority to the use of ICT for more equitable and pluralistic development in education, in all study fields (including LSP – languages for specific purposes), aiming to a) expand the knowledge base about the educational issues, b) create networks of partners and to establish principles and guidance for good practice, c) give policy advice, and where appropriate d) engage in specific development co-operation.

ICT has become an important means by which we think and communicate. As far as foreign language teaching and learning is concerned, computers have long been accepted not only as a tool for successful LSP, but also as a wealthy source of specialized material (the Internet), and more recently, as a more sophisticated and inevitable form of communication with which each student has to become familiar. The LSP learner can now "interact with the computer using it not only as a tool for furthering his/her language competence but also for developing active communication" (Mansfield, 2005: 123). The aim of such communicative competence is to prepare students for international students' exchanges and for success on the international labour market.

Nowadays in most European countries the accredited university study programmes offer two alternative courses: daily (full-time) study and external (part-time) study. Thus the university students, logically, fall into two categories: full-time students and part-time (distance) students. The vast majority of present distance courses function on the basis of using various forms of ICT.

This is also the case of our institution, the Faculty of Education, University of Matej Bel (PF UMB) in Banska Bystrica, Slovak Republic. Since the academic year 2005/2006 all distance courses have been accomplished via e-learning. Thus, on the one hand, the school responds to the present trends in education in the EU, as it comes under the category of schools with a highly pro-active attitude toward computer-assisted distance learning in courses such as education, psychology, social work, theology, missiology as well as LSP. On the other hand, the organization and methodology of full-time study is still being built primarily on the traditional compulsory contact time with the teacher in the classroom, providing lectures and discussions in groups as the basic methods of the courses. With the exception of several courses at the departments of mathematics, theology and missiology, art and music, until recently the full-time students at PF UMB have not been given many opportunities to experience a more flexible teaching approach, allowing them the enjoyment and the advantages of distance learning. Neither could they face its challenges or start to develop their skills of more independent study though it might become a skill of crucial importance for them at the time as well as in the future, and not only that. Considering their present life situations a more flexible way of study might be for them the most effective way of learning.

This was the reason why the project of combined instruction called the "User-friendly approach" (UFA) was designed for the courses at PF UMB. In order to support teaching and enhance learning, this offers a flexible, and supportive approach through the integration of classroom teaching and on-line learning. It takes into account students', teachers' and institutional constraints and desires and to find innovative answers.

The authors of the UFA decided to base it on the combination of methods that were authorized by the Educational Act about universities No. 131/2002, § 60 in 2002. According to this document, both full-time and part-time courses may use any of the following methods of study:

(a) face to face attendance of students (direct contact with the teacher);
(b) distance study (compensation for the direct contact: communication via ICT);
(c) a combination of (a) and (b).

It means that - when necessary - even the full-time courses have a legitimate right to implement some elements from distance methodology (e-learning via ICT) and to combine them with vis-à-vis contact lessons. We envisage that this applies efficiently to LSP too because, as "Hardisty and Windeatt went on to suggest already in 1989, all of the interactional patterns typically seen in non-computer classrooms are also possible with computers" (from Nunan, 1996: 197).

The philosophy of the UFA project

The UFA project is based on the philosophy of open education that shifts the control of the learning process towards the student. It represents such an educational approach that focuses on the individual needs of individual subjects involved in education. It allows a maximum level of individual study even for full-time students (for more see e.g. Lojová, 2005: 28-38). It is the individual student-oriented approach that caters not only for different learning skills and strategies but which suits individual needs and interests of learners and teachers. To some extent, the philosophy of the UFA project is similar to the one of the Cambridge University Language Programme (CULP) that also strives to "put learners in the centre of the learning process" (King, Radic, 2004: 83). CULP authors believe that learner support through a rich, flexible and supportive environment is the best way to support language learning. With this in mind they state – similarly to the authors of the UFA - that "the best way forward is to integrate classroom teaching and on-line learning." (p. 74.)

The basic principles of this open education philosophy are a) the improvement of access to education and b) the elimination of educational barriers. These barriers may be geographic, financial and (in case of further education of adult people) the obstacles connected with complex family commitments, etc. If circumstances change, students can use e-learning instead of physically attending the class with the teacher.

A major factor in the success of the UFA project is its flexibility. The language training programme has to be very flexible if students with various needs are to progress and achieve their full potential. Flexibility of life-long language learning is always essential for adults who have to balance a range of commitments. Being adults these learners need to be able to learn, and also have their learning assessed, at times and places to suit them. Learner support and encouragement, and ongoing recognition of progress and achievement are needed to maintain motivation and commitment. It means the UFA should operate within the constraints of its students' interests, duties and responsibilities, and the time which they can devote to their studies.

In case of LSP, the UFA creates an open environment, within which language learners can encounter and use various ways of learning languages, prepared by the teacher but also by their own invention. This is possible as the philosophy of the course involves the idea of self - production where less teacher's control of materials is required. The emphasis is on providing a wide range of open-ended learning opportunities rather than specifying materials which focus on specific linguistic contents and sub-skills. The UFA project for LSP is thus vitally based on the use of two macro-strategies. The first one concerns creating alternative learning opportunities for students learning in and/or out of a physical classroom – it should be the result of a joint production by participants engaged in the classroom. Thus, learning opportunities can be created by the teacher. The second strategy could be described as the utilization of learning opportunities created by learners. So the premise is that teachers and learners are co-participants in the generation of classroom discourse. The teacher's role becomes that of the role of a tutor, manager and facilitator of the learning process (see teacher's roles in Homolová, 2003: 28-29; Thurzová, 1998). With the assistance of ICT the students can access the tutor for preparation or even for revision purposes.

If this user-friendly and flexible way of language learning is to be functional, it has to focus on the following two basic principles:

– Students desire to study. They are intrinsically motivated so the teacher may trust that they do not make up excuses and they tell the truth about the reason of learning other than a direct form of study. Hopefully

> "the very fact that students today are using ICT as tools that are very familiar to them is certainly a point in favour of … motivation and feeling at ease while learning. Indeed, technology has now become a consolidated means of exploiting teacher-student, student-student and student-computer interaction."
>
> (Mansfield, 2005: 125)

– The students are willingly accepting the basic rules of these courses, so that it is not an open door to laziness but it makes their work real.

Integrating advanced technology into LSP courses is a complex process that involves several changes (personal, group, organisational, institutional and cultural). Under the standard circumstances, the ICT can help students to improve their foreign language skills. The UFA values highly the use of ICT in LSP as it supplements the direct teacher-student and student-student contacts in certain times of need. Therefore though the UFA project considers the direct vis-a`-vis contacts between teachers and full-time students to be essential it is open to other kinds of contacts, typical to distance methodology, via ICT. As a few authors envisaged already in 1991, the ICT could handle a very large volume of interaction and could deliver to the student feedback of some subtlety in cases that often happen when students cannot attend a class (because of illness, timetable clashes, and other problems).

> "The ICT can help to solve these problems. The students can use the ICT to benefit from the course. The use of ICT accommodates different speeds of learning etc. Distance language teaching is eminently feasible by computer."
>
> (Ahmad, Corbett et al., 1991: 4)

Thus the use of ICT expands the study opportunities for full-time LSP students in many dimensions.

To support the idea of the UFA, there are a lot of supportive examples describing the efficient use of ICT in the classroom (e. g. the use of the internet encyclopaedia Wikipedia in the course by Rošteková, 2006). As Nunan and Lamb (1996) say, the use of ICT in language courses helps to carry out tasks which are impossible in other media. According to them some of the most successful lessons they have observed are those "in which the computer is used for interactive group work involving problem solving and simulations" (p. 198). A computer-assisted project offers a great deal of power and responsibility to the learner. It also prepares the teachers for the collaboration strategies/IT alliances between teacher training institutions and schools as the future workplaces of the students.

There are some similarities of the UFA with Mansfield's on-line language programme (2005: 134). The UFA project of computer assisted learning reinforces interactive language learning by:

- taking the pressure off "institutional" learning by arranging learning outside the formal classroom (as Manfsfield suggests, especially via setting a Tandem partnership with an on-line native speaker as a partner) and thus creating an ideal opportunity for learning authentic language;
- keeping the teacher as a facilitator not the main speaker;
- arranging various collaborative forms of asynchronous and synchronous communication among students;
- giving students opportunities to learn in their own way, intra and/or interpersonally.

To summarize, the final form of this project should be an application of an *eclectic approach* to User-friendly study. That means the effective combination of the present forms of study (direct contact) with the e-learning methodology via the internet, Skype, Moodle (or any other e-learning study management software) and various assessment techniques.

Methodology of user-friendly approach in LSP

There are several specific circumstances where the UFA might be especially advantageous. Methodological considerations of the UFA are shaped by several aspects of the programme but the most important of them is the following one: the students who can attend the lesson "only" from places other then the school building/the given classroom. Here are examples of such specific problem situations in LSP courses:

- The need for a native speaker. There might be a person who is not able to be physically present at the specific school but who is willing to assist the learning process by consultations via Skype and email (more or less regularly).
- There is a native speaker teaching in the specific course but he/she is at the same time a consultant/committee member/conference speaker, etc., somewhere else. So he/she is often travelling and cannot participate directly in all the scheduled lessons. But he/she might be ready to contribute to students' learning via Skype consultations (conversation classes) even then or at least chat through Skype or Moodle.
- The same may be applied to any teacher of an LSP course who for various reasons cannot be physically present at the lessons, but along with that he/she might be prepared at least to explain study instructions to students or check the results of their work, etc. The e-learning software may be useful especially if there are tests scheduled for a special time but there are obstacles in carrying them out. The teacher might participate in the lessons, e. g., from abroad through Skype and e-mailing.
- In the case of electives (for example the LSP courses at PF UMB) there might exist some objective obstacles to finding a suitable time and space in the schedule (because of the number of course programmes and their combinations, shortage of classrooms, setting aside days for teachers practice in primary schools). So in situations like these the e-learning study and Skype consultations might be the only way to manage the course during the semester.

- There is a potential to make the lessons even more open and user-friendly by allowing the students who cannot attend the class for serious reasons (lengthy infectious illness, fractures, pollinosis, taking care of a sick child, natural calamities, strikes etc.) to take part in them again, e.g., through Skype or Moodle.

To create the UFA in LSP courses expects students and teachers to implement several necessary steps.

(a) For the students, the following phases of creating the UFA are necessary:
   - Presentation of the UFA philosophy and of the aims of such an LSP course by the teacher, discussion with the students.
   - The training of students so that they would get the introductory information and skills for e-learning.
   - Precise instructions as to the course expectations and assignments by the teacher.
   - Co-operative scheduling (both teacher and students) and planning of activities. As Nunan and Lamb suggest, the methodology should include interactive discussion. Students should be given the opportunity of working on the programmes in pairs or small groups as well as individually.
   - The fulfilling of the plan substituting for the expected contact lesson via e-learning and Skype version of completing the task by any participant of the course (in justified situations).
   - The participants are expected to work regularly on all the assignments given by the teacher and send them to the teacher's e-mail address by the set time. The teacher has to give a full assessment, both summative and formative, and send it back to the student via email.

(b) The role of the teachers is to try to apply the various specific teaching methods and techniques which best match the dynamics of all learners with various learning needs. So for the teachers (and the management team of the school), the procedure in the UFA might be following:
   - Getting informed about the required changes for this type of education on their part.
   - Developing the methodology for improving the e-learning and Skype skills of full-time students.
   - Producing the characteristics (aims, contents and assignments) of all the UFA – LSP courses.

- Preparation for the new way of teaching: know-how – methodology for starting and running the course, assessing the students' assignments, preparing e-tests and the ways of their assessment (probably in co-operation with the supervisor).
- Consistently preparing necessary study materials and adequate software.

The implementation of the UFA project should be based on the needs analysis done among the specific students. Some learners have specific needs and this language project should respond to these. It must also cater for a variety of different levels of students' language competence and enable them to be involved in planning of the UFA course in their group.

If the data from the needs analysis show a positive need and there is an interest in this way of learning, all the following phases of setting the aims, teaching materials and assignment design, assessment of assignments as well as course evaluation should reflect the openness of the UFA (see Hanesová, 2003). The choice of specific activities depends upon the LSP thematic areas chosen according to the student's profile. The problem of testing requires special sensitivity of the course manager. The choice of tests, the way of their administration in co-operation with a supervisor and their assessment should by compensated for by the overall requirements for valid communicative testing (Bérešová, 2004).

It is important to note that the lack of direct contact requires a valuable substitution in the form of well-prepared methodology and ideas for study material. To some extent, the success of the UFA - similarly to CULP - depends upon setting a rich learning environment that would offer a wide range of different resources to learners.

> "If successful language learning depends on interaction with a large and varied diet of textual materials and the development within the learner of a capacity to take decisive initiatives, then we must provide the learner with resources that he or she can draw on as an individual. According to this view all language learning turns out to have a self-instructional component, and the self-access system is seen not as an alternative to the teacher but as a necessary resource for all language learners."
>
> (Singleton, Little, 1989: 32-33)

The flexibility of the environment does not refer only to the on-line material, but also to the methodological concepts and approach.

> "It is a model based on blending the choice of appropriate technologies with aspects of campus-based delivery, open learning systems and distance education."

(King, Radic, 2004: 74)

In case we need to use the UFA (for various reasons), we can still pursue the communicative competence but do it in a different way – via dealing more with the authentic texts. According to several authors, including Feez (1998), people do learn language best through working with whole authentic texts. We found a great deal of support for this approach in Holiday's strong version of teaching language as communication. This version of LSP can be almost entirely culture-sensitive.

> "Whereas in the weak version the term 'communicative' relates to more students communicating with the teacher and with each other to practise the language forms which have been presented, in the strong version, 'communicative' relates more to the way in which the student communicates with the text."
>
> (Holiday, 1994: 171-174)

So this approach allows less dependency on the traditional presentation, practice and lesson production format. Here the students communicate primarily with the text. This focus is pursued by text unlocking activities, solving language problems and producing new text. The lesson input could be a piece of writing, found on the Internet, or a recording of speech. These activities do not have to be carried out in the classroom, in groups or pairs, as individual students can communicate themselves with the text. The output – their new text – could vary in its language forms, e.g. an essay or analysis or a report from individual student's activity. Holiday's idea is that the student produces a hypothesis about the language which might well be the subject of later discussion (direct or via email, Skype, etc.), but "it might be internalised and not produce any new external language until much later, possibly outside the classroom". This is feasible if the tasks are authentic and meaningful to the real world of the students.

Conclusion

The intent of the UFA project at PF UMB is to relieve the participants of LSP courses from the stress of how to deal with several very common problems at many schools. The project puts a bigger emphasis on the content of the actual interaction than on its form (e.g. that everybody should sit at the desk in the same classroom). It can be viewed as teaching without borders - without space limits.

In the academic year 2005/2006, a combination of direct lectures, instructions in Moodle and Skype seminars has been piloted in several chosen subjects taught partially in a foreign language (CLIL) and in ESP at PF UMB. The reason for doing so was that its teacher, a native speaker, was finishing his PhD. studies in the USA. These courses offered seminar assignments in Moodle and individual e-learning consultations as well as assessment through Skype and supervisors. If it had not been for the UFA, the courses would not have been feasible and successful as they actually were.

As can be concluded so far from the existing experience, it seems that though the most effective form of learning in the full-time programmes is the regular direct contact time with the teachers, in the case of various real needs it is useful to combine it with e-learning and Skyping (or any similar software methodology). Thus several insolvable situations could be overcome with the assistance of ICT without too much extra effort and finances.

If the piloted UFA project proves to be efficient from a longer perspective, the following objectives will be pursued at PF UMB in the future:

- Enlarging the choice of the subjects that are built on this User-friendly philosophy (to all LSP and CLIL courses at PF UMB).
- Increasing the number of teaching/learning phases that would implement ICT for creating a holistic user-friendly course: not just in the initial phases, such as the production of the outline of the course, the introduction of instructions and assignments, but also during the actual lessons, seminars, tutorials and consultations via Skype and Moodle along the whole term.
- Applying the UFA even to the assessment and evaluation process during and after the term by the combination of Moodle, Skype and human supervisors.

We hope that the UFA project proves useful in enhancing both the communicative competence of our LSP students and their preparation in a more realistic way for the international academic and professional setting.

References

Ahmad, K., Corbett, G., Rogers, M., Sussex, R. (1991) *Computers, Language Learning and Language Teaching*. Cambridge: CUP (4th ed.).

Bérešová, J. (2004) *Komunikatívne testovanie cudzích jazykov v súlade s požiadavkami Rady Európy*. Trnava: TU.

Brown, H. D. (1994) *Teaching by Principles: An Interactive Approach to Language Pedagogy*. London: Prentice Hall Int.

Feez, S. (1998) *Text-based Syllabus Design*. Sydney: NCELTR.

Hanesová, D. (2003) *Odborná angličtina na pedagogických fakultách*. Banská Bystrica: Trian, 2003.

Hardisty, D., Windeatt, S. (1989) *CALL*. Oxford: OUP. In Nunan, D., Lamb, C. (1996) *The Self-Directed Teacher: Managing the Learning Process*. Cambridge: CUP.

Holiday, A. (1994) *Appropriate Methodology and Social Context*. Cambridge: CUP.

Homolová, E. (2003) *Uplatňovanie princípov komunikatívneho vyučovania prostredníctvom učiteľských rol*. Banská Bystrica: FHV UMB.

King, A., Radic, N. (2004) A Rich, Flexible and Supportive Language-learning Environment – the Cambridge University Language Programme (CULP). In Sewell, Ch. (ed.) (2004) *Language Learning for Work in a Multilingual World*. London: CILT, pp. 73-84.

Lojová, G. (2005) *Individuálne osobitosti pri učení sa cudzích jazykov*. Bratislava: PF UK.

Mansfield, G. (2005) Humanising Online Language Learning – Some reflections. In *University Language Centres: Broadening Horizons, Expanding Networks*. Bratislava: CercleS, pp. 123-136.

Nunan, D., Lamb, C. (1996) *The Self-directed Teacher: Managing the Learning Process*. Cambridge: CUP.

Rošteková, M. (2006) Using internet in Language Teaching and Learning. In *Multimedia in Foreign Language Teaching III*. Nitra: SPU, 2006. [CD]

Singleton, D., Little, D. (1989) *Setting the Context*. In Hedge, T., Whitney, N. (ed.) (1996) *Power, Pedagogy and Practice*. Oxford: OUP.

Thurzová, M (1998) Úloha tútora v procese rozvoja študentov dištančného vzdelávania. In *Vzdelávanie dospelých*, No. 4, pp. 48-52.

http://portal.unesco.org/ci/en/ev.php-URL_ID=2929&URL_DO=DO_TOPIC &URL_SECTION=201.html

EXPLOITING LSP CORPORA IN THE STUDY OF FOREIGN LANGUAGES

ANTONIO PINNA

Corpus linguistics can be defined as an approach for studying language in use that is based on principled electronic collections of texts, specific software applications for information retrieval and related techniques of data analysis. As a method of computer-assisted language study, it has contributed to the fields of language description, language learning and translation. The purpose of the present paper is to show how corpus linguistics resources and techniques can be exploited by learners and teachers to explore LSPs (Languages for Specific Purposes). In particular, real examples of language use will be retrieved and analyzed from specialized corpora in order to promote learners' communicative competence in those LSPs.

Corpus linguistics has become a useful approach to study language in use which combines the analyst's intuition and competence with direct evidence of linguistic facts extracted from electronic collections of texts. Corpora are examined by means of special software tools which corpus linguists use in various investigative techniques and has given rise to an ever increasing bibliography showing the central role of this method of language study (e.g. Sinclair, 2004; Gavioli, 2005; Scott and Tribble, 2006). Foreign language education has particularly benefited from it as corpora provide additional resources for language teaching and learning. In a didactic context, teachers can employ them to build their syllabuses, while students can use them as reliable information sources. In particular, LSP corpora can be a fundamental resource in the identification of specialized terms, the study of how they are typically associated with their co-texts, and the description of recurring stylistic features characterizing the text-types which are used to convey the contents of a specific subject matter. The objectives of the present paper are to introduce corpus linguistics resources, tools and investigative techniques which could be exploited within a corpus-driven approach and to demonstrate how they can be used to investigate the specialized vocabulary of oral implantology (a subfield of dentistry) in order to improve learners' communicative competence in this LSP.

1 Corpus linguistics: an approach to the study of language

This section focuses on the central issues of defining corpus linguistics and describing the corpus-driven approach to the study of language.

1.1 Corpus linguistics: quantitative and qualitative approaches

Corpus linguistics can be defined as a method of language study which combines human intuition with the efficiency of computer technology. The ease and reliability with which computers and their networks facilitate the finding, storage and retrieval of large amounts of data have contributed extensively to the quantitative and qualitative examination of language in use. As an empirical method, corpus linguistics can be used to study the occurrence and contextual behaviour of different language phenomena, from lexis to syntax to pragmatics. A quantitative approach is useful in determining the proportions with which certain predefined classes of phenomena are present in specific groups of texts. For example, Biber's studies (e.g. 1988, 1995) demonstrate that difference among genres in English, as well as in other languages, can be described in terms of varying combinations of sets of co-occurring language features realizing some key dimensions of variation. An approach to qualitative analysis necessarily takes the contextual behaviour of language phenomena into account. These can be explored with reference to their typical associations with their linguistic context. In this respect, Sinclair (1991, 1996, and 1998) has demonstrated the widespread tendency of words to co-occur within limited co-texts. In his model of language performance, the principle of co-selection has been critical in delineating a set of meaningful syntagmatic relationships between words at increasing levels of abstractions.

1.2 Corpus-driven linguistics: exploring contextual associations

Corpus-driven linguistics, in Tognini-Bonelli's (2001: 84) definition, is based on the study of the contextual use of language elements free of received theories. In this approach the analyst follows an inductive procedure which results in the formulation of theoretical statements as the conclusive step in a series of repeated cycles of data observations, specification of hypotheses and their empirical validation. The resulting statements describe language phenomena on the basis of their recurrent associations with their contexts. According to Sinclair (1991: 110) the principle of co-selection can account for the tendency of words to co-occur in a short span of text. Every language user has at his or her disposal a large set of semi-preconstructed chunks that are chosen as a single unit. These can be described as co-occurring words at the lexical level, i.e. collocations, the grammatical level, i.e. colligations, the semantic level, i.e. semantic preferences, and the pragmatic level, i.e. discourse prosody.

Sinclair's definition of co-selection is textual, since it operates, together with morphosyntax, as a key mechanism in the organization of discourse. Partington (1998: 18) and Hoey (2005) hypothesize a psycholinguistic dimension of the phenomenon. Partington (1998: 18) suggests that the principle may be at work in text production and interpretation, so that it must be integrated in the system of communicative competence, specifically in relation to performance and context-related tasks. Hoey's (2005) theory of *lexical priming* considers it the most important mechanism in text cohesion. He maintains that competence is the result of a speaker's knowledge of the typical linguistic and pragmatic associations of lexical items.

This approach stresses the importance of lexis and its fundamental connection with grammar and meaning. From the perspective of language learning, it points to the necessity for the learner to be aware of and know the most typical associations between words and their co-texts. This is also true in the field of LSP where learners must become acquainted with the preferred ways of expressing content and organizing discourse by subject matter experts.

2 Corpora, corpus tools and techniques: a brief survey

In this section LSP corpora are defined and a typical design framework is illustrated. This is followed by a brief introduction to the most typical corpus tools and techniques used in linguistic analysis. Their presentation is also helpful from a didactic point of view in that the same resources can be exploited by LSP learners in their exploration of authentic language usage following a corpus-driven approach.

2.1 Corpora for LSP

A corpus is a principled collection of texts or text samples in an electronic format. Corpora are compiled with the objective of representing a language or a subset of a language on the basis of explicitly stated characteristics. Corpus designers must make important decisions concerning the content of a corpus in terms of language(s), size, medium, subject matter(s), text types, authorship and date of publication. These and other specific design criteria are listed and illustrated by Pearson (1998: 58-62). Setting aside considerations of language and subject matter, which are obviously dictated by the type of LSP under investigation, the particular purpose for which a certain corpus is being created will be of the utmost importance in determining the other criteria. For example, an LSP corpus designed for language learning with the limited aims of highlighting key language features, terms and phraseology at work in a given subject matter may not be as big as a corpus designed for a full-blown scientific study of that special language. The choice in text types may also be limited to those which are actually needed by the students, a consideration that frees the compiler from the need to identify all the text types which are actually used to convey aspects of that subject matter. In particular, the corpus of oral implantology (a subfield of dentistry) which has been used for the analyses provided in Section 4 was designed and compiled by the author of this paper as a language learning resource for students of dentistry specializing in that subfield. It consists of approximately 50,000 words and includes two written text types (research articles and clinical articles) extracted from relevant international journals published in 2003 and authored by acknowledged professionals and researchers.

2.2 Corpus tools and techniques

A number of computer software resources and techniques enable the linguistic analysis of corpora. Information is usually displayed in the form of word lists and concordance lines.

One of the most common types of corpus tools compiles word lists on the basis of how frequent each word-form in a corpus is. A common characteristic of this type of lists is that function words are usually on top as a consequence of their closed-class membership. Content words, on the contrary, are usually down in the lists and their presence and relative positions reflect the topics and subject matters of the texts. Since the frequency of content words is linked to topic and register, an analysis of their list constitutes an initial analytical practice in the study of the vocabulary of an LSP corpus, especially if the identification of specialized terms is necessary.

A second type of word list is obtained by the automatic comparison of the word lists from two corpora. In the *Wordsmith Tools* package (Scott,

1996) this procedure is carried out by the software programme *Keywords* which produces a list of words on the basis of how outstanding their frequency in a given text or corpus is when compared with their frequency in a reference corpus. Scott (2000) defines this characteristic as a word's *keyness* and discusses its importance in determining what a given text is about. In language learning and glossary compilation this can be a useful resource in determining the most important terms of a specific LSP.

A collocate tree is another type of word list in which only those words that typically co-occur with a node-word are listed. This is based on the concept of "collocation", i.e. the association of lexical words within a short span of text, usually constituted by four intervening words (Sinclair, 1991: 170). The procedure for identifying collocations is usually a built-in facility in various concordance programs and takes as a starting point the series of concordance lines for a given word or phrase that are retrieved from a corpus. As a second step it calculates a frequency list of the words that co-occur with the node-word. A statistical algorithm (e.g. Barnbrook, 1996: 87-101) may be needed to reveal those words whose co-occurrence is particularly significant.

A fourth critical tool that can be used to search, retrieve and display information in a corpus is a concordancer. Concordance lines usually display a list of occurrences of a given word or phrase in a corpus together with its surrounding co-text. As far as language study is concerned, information retrieved from these lines shows what is typical and central in language use. This highlights the communicative dimension of language, that is, "the social practice retrievable in the repeated patterns of co-selection" (Tognini-Bonelli, 2001: 3). The close association between a word and its co-text can be explored at various levels. Recurrent lexical and grammatical associations may reveal the preferred contextual uses of a word. In LSP this may be relevant in refining the identification of specialized terms, but it can also prove important in establishing the conceptual framework of a discipline. Also, concordance lines yield more details in the behaviour of lexical items. In particular, contextual clues can point to how words are typically combined for functional purposes in the construction of discourse, an aspect which is particularly relevant in the LSP field as its learners must also acquire this specific skill in order to become fully proficient users of a specialized language. Finally, concordance lines can reveal whether a word or phrase is connotated. This phenomenon has been called "semantic prosody" by Sinclair (1991: 74), who described the typical behaviour of the phrasal verb *set in*, usually associated with subjects that refer to unpleasant states of affairs. In a certain sense, the typical association of this phrasal verb with such negatively loaded subjects has determined its acquisition of a "negative aura", so that its negative connotation is usually expected. Exploring this aspect may show an important, sometimes unsuspected, level of communicative competence which is required by a competent user of an LSP.

3 Corpora in LSP learning

Following Aston's (1997: 54-56) suggestion of corpora exploitation in the communicative approach, corpus linguistics can be integrated into LSP learning both in syllabus design and guided individual learning. First of all, corpus linguistics can facilitate the creation of a syllabus of relevant aspects of an LSP, including an inventory of the most important terms, their definitions and use. In this respect, an LSP teacher addressing semi-expert learners has the primary task of identifying the key features of a specialized language and its fundamental conceptual frameworks. Bowker and Pearson (2003: 31-39) point to the use of LSP corpora to extract specialized terms, identify their typical contextual associations, specify the stylistic characteristics of the genres used in a given LSP, clarify aspects of conceptual knowledge. These activities may be carried out by the teacher before class and their results can be used to substantiate the content of the course, for example by directly pointing to the problematic aspects of using a specific word in a certain LSP context.

However, these same activities may be combined with problem-solving tasks to stimulate learner participation in communicative activities where non-linguistic goals are to be achieved. As Aston contends (1997: 56), corpora can be both the source of such problem-solving tasks and the source of opportunities for analysis and reflection on language that is important for learners' discourse participation. In this second approach, learners must also be taught how best to exploit corpora through corpus tools and techniques. In the context of English for Science, for example, teachers asking learners to report on an experiment may set up the appropriate environment for task-based learning in which they are required to work out the terms for the concepts they are going to deal with, use them appropriately in context, and produce an experiment report following its typical genre specifications. Once learners have mastered how to use corpus tools and techniques for LSP exploration, they could also proceed autonomously along their discovery paths. The teacher could then act both as facilitator, helping learners with corpus tools and techniques, and as language expert, as she can give advice and guide learners in dealing with difficult aspects of the second language.

4 Exploiting corpora in LSP learning: some examples

This section provides examples of how an LSP corpus can be autonomously exploited by foreign language learners who want to improve their knowledge of its specialized vocabulary and the ways in which this is typically used. Learners of an LSP may need to have explicit knowledge of the terms in use in order to transpose the conceptual framework of a given subject matter in the foreign language. This is typically achieved by producing a glossary of the LSP terms in the source and target languages. Due to reasons of space, the objective of this section is limited to showing how corpus tools and techniques can be used to search the English corpus of oral implantology described in Section 2.1 in order to identify term candidates, refine and expand the list of terms, describe their phraseological characteristics and their potential implied meanings.

4.1 Three ways of identifying term candidates

In a given subject matter, terms are words with a clearly defined meaning. The identification of term candidates can be carried out semi-automatically by means of corpus tools and techniques. The following sections illustrate various search and retrieval techniques which can be used to identify potential terms in a specialized corpus.

4.1.1 Abbreviations and acronyms

Some specialized terms are typically introduced in a text as abbreviations or acronyms, usually within brackets, and are conventionally accompanied by their full form. Therefore, one way to retrieve term candidates with a concordancer is by using the search pattern (*). Table 1 illustrates a random series of concordance lines for this pattern.

An analysis of the concordance lines in Table 1 yields more than just a list of candidate terms, though these are clearly the main search objective in a study of the vocabulary of a particular LSP. Indeed, since brackets include numerals, letters, abbreviations and acronyms, chemistry symbols and words, they provide material for reflecting on some of the stylistic features of research and clinical articles. In particular, Table 1 shows that, besides reporting measurements in statistical terms, numerals are used to enumerate a sequence of activities, list the component parts of a device, refer to elements shown in a picture or table. While letters could also be employed to perform these functions, they are exclusively used as an alternative way of illustrating the legends of figures. Some words (e.g. *arrows*) can also be used as a way of connecting text and pictures. At the level of LSP terminology, abbreviations and acronyms in Table 1 point to potentially specialized terms at work in the field of oral implantology. This technique is rather straightforward in identifying term candidates as they are spelt in their full form beside their abbreviations or acronyms. A complete list of their full and abbreviated forms would then be the first step in order to build a glossary. Significantly, most of the abbreviated terms in Table 1 refer to substances or processes of critical importance in oral implantology. Since students possessing semi-expert knowledge of the specialized terminology of a certain subject matter in a foreign language often make great use of abbreviations and acronyms without the necessary awareness of what they stand for, an exercise on their full form could also be an introduction to this particular LSP.

4.1.2 Frequency lists

Since only some term candidates are typically abbreviated, other techniques are needed for their identification. One of these is the creation of word lists based on their raw frequency, with the caveat that function words will probably have to be discarded. Word lists may include single words or, following the results discussed above, clusters of word forms. Tab. 2 includes the top 10 results drawn from the frequency lists of single words, 2-word and 3-word clusters in the oral implantology corpus. Function words have not been included.

A cursory examination of Table 2 reveals that this technique does not automatically yield candidate terms. As a matter of fact, in the single-word column one can immediately identify *figure* as the likely reference to a picture or diagram in a text. In the 2-word and 3-word cluster columns, students with some knowledge of the register of scientific English will probably exclude *original magnification* and *materials and methods* from the list of candidate terms for the specialized field of oral implantology. In particular, they may recall that the former is typically used in the captions printed underneath a picture to provide information about the degree to which the object portrayed has been increased, while the latter refers to one element of the typical structure of research articles. However, confirming these intuitions and, moreover, producing an accurate list of specialized terms require further exploration of words and clusters in their contexts of use by means of concordance lines, as illustrated in Section 4.2.1.

1	FIGURE 5. Key:	(1)	External carotid artery; (2) maxillary artery; (3)
2	ver a broad range of functional activities:	(1)	signaling transduction, (2) translation, (3) cell c
3	when compared with nonperforated sites	(100%)	(P .0146). The study demonstrated that perforat
4	The device comprises (1) the guide magnet,	(2)	a sensor array supported by a facebow, and (3)
5	FIGURE 8. The cross-sectional slice	(a)	shows the buccolingual irregularities of the cre
6	of P-15 and natural anorganic bone mineral	(ABM)	was examined. ABM/P-15 is a synthetic, collag
7	the pocket a few osteoblasts and osteoclasts	(arrows)	are present. Toluidine blue and basic fuchsin,
8	ion of purified bone morphogenetic protein	(BMP)	in cranio-maxillo-facial surgery: BMP in comp
9	d spectra for as-sputtered calcium phosphate	(CaP)	coatings, 4008C heat-treated CaP coatings, and
10	s been advocated. Guided bone regeneration	(GBR)	is a technique often used to augment the
11	insulin-like growth factor binding proteins	(IGFBPs):	characterization of connective tissue growth fa
12	crovessels to evaluate microvessel density	(MVD).	The aim of the present study was to conduct a co
13	er of a new class of protein-tyrosine kinases	(PTK),	is characterized by the presence of a second
14	y. Plain glass (PG), tissue culture plastic	(TCP),	amino phased glass (APG), peptides 1 through

Tab. 1 A series of concordance lines for the pattern (*)

N	Single words	2-word clusters	3-word clusters
1	bone	Dental implants	Cross-sectional slice
2	implant	Implant surface	Bone-implant contact
3	implants	Oral implantology	Implant contact percentage
4	oral	Subperiosteal implants	Marrow stromal cells
5	surface	Original magnification	Bone-implant interface
6	titanium	Surface roughness	Bone morphogenetic protein
7	figure	Titanium implants	Bone-to-implant
8	study	Lingual artery	Inferior alveolar artery
9	tissue	Subperiosteal implant	Materials and methods
10	dental	Oral implant	Guided bone regeneration

Tab. 2 Frequency lists of single words, 2-word and 3-word clusters

4.1.3 Keyword lists

Another helpful technique in the identification of candidate terms is the creation of keyword lists. These are the result of a statistical comparison between frequency lists extracted from the corpus under investigation and a reference corpus, usually a larger one, representative of a specific general language. For the purpose of illustrating this technique, I have chosen to compare the frequency list of the oral implantology corpus with that obtained from the FLOB corpus, a 1-million-word representative corpus of general written British English produced in 1991. The procedure, automatically carried out by one of the software programmes included in *Wordsmith Tools*, recognized those words in the implantology corpus whose frequencies are particularly relevant with respect to FLOB. Table 3 presents the top ten items in the single-word, 2-word-cluster and 3-word-cluster keyword lists.

N	Single words	2-word clusters	3-word clusters
1	implant	Dental implants	Osseointegrated dental implants
2	bone	Implant surface	Newly formed bone
3	implants	Bone formation	Dental implant placement
4	oral	Dental implant	Bone-implant contact
5	titanium	Original magnification	Bone morphogenetic protein
6	figure	Titanium implants	The present study
7	tissue	Surface roughness	Periodontal osseous defects
8	dental	Bone resorption	Implant contact
9	surface	Bone regeneration	Cross-sectional slice
10	clinical	Lingual artery	An experimental study

Tab. 3 Keyword lists of single words, 2-word and 3-word clusters

Each column in Table 3 shows a number of terms which are characteristic of the field of oral implantology. Though perhaps more reliable than raw frequency lists, keyword lists do not automatically yield specialized terms and still require the analyst's exploration of the co-text of a certain word or cluster via the production of concordance lines to decide whether it can be considered a specialized term of that subject matter.

4.2 Studying LSP vocabulary

In this section I will illustrate how concordance lines can be exploited to study the vocabulary of oral implantology research and clinical articles. For reasons of space the analyses will concentrate on the word *bone*, the importance of which has been signalled in the word lists above. First of all, concordances are used to identify specialized terms comprising the word *bone*. Secondly, the most frequent lexical and grammatical associations of the word are highlighted and explained. Finally, some aspects of implied meaning conventionally associated with some verbs of causation are exemplified.

4.2.1 Identifying specialized terms by means of concordance lines

Tables 2 and 3 demonstrate the high frequency and relevance of words such as *implant*, *implants*, *dental* and *oral* which are obviously related to the field of oral implantology. However, one cannot fail to notice the importance in the same tables of the more general word *bone*, whose analysis is now carried out in order to see if it is used in specialized ways. Table 4 shows a series of random concordance lines for *bone*, which is actually present with 1,328 instances in the corpus under investigation.

The reading of these lines indicates a tendency for *bone* to co-occur with other words as part of specialized terms, some of which are easily identifiable by means of following abbreviations or because they denote specific entities or processes. This is the case, for example, of terms such as *bone graft*(*ing*), *cortical bone*, *cancellous bone*, *demineralized allogeneic bone*. Interestingly, other specialized terms can be identified in the proximity of the node word.

The same procedure should be repeated for each candidate term identified in section 4.1. A thorough analysis of their concordance lines could clarify whether these are actual specialized terms and could also point to additional terms worth including in a glossary.

1	mplant placement has been advocated. Guided	bone	regeneration (GBR) is a technique often used to au
2	nsisted of HA and demineralized freeze-dried	bone	allograft (DFDB) mixtures with or without strut re
3	le membrane are used to cover the autologous	bone.	The mesh is fixed with microscrews. FIGURE 4. R
4	cribe our experience with performing the tibial	bone	graft procurement procedure under intravenous se
5	s good cancellous bone surrounded by cortical	bone	of adequate thickness on both sides. Most polym
6	procedures. In this case, fracture of the basal	bone	occurred in the postdistraction period. This compl
7	oinductive properties of DFDBA. Some donor	bone	has shown no activity at all and simply provided a
8	ing size, the surgeon harvested the cancellous	bone	medially and inferiorly down the tibial shaft until
9	ent posts or struts, surgical pocket elimination,	bone	grafting, or revisional sectioning of any portion of
10	All of the patients in this study had significant	bone	atrophy that would have required bone grafting p
11	ilable. The ability of demineralized allogeneic	bone	to promote bony ingrowth has been well documen
12	d subperiosteal implants using both the direct	bone	impression technique and CT-generated subperios

Tab. 4 A series of concordance lines for *bone*

4.2.2 Collocations and colligations of specialized terms

Analysing the concordance lines for a given term will yield other important information concerning the ways in which it is typically used in a specialized field. The notions of collocation, i.e. the co-occurrence of lexical words within a given span of text, and colligation, i.e. the preferred grammatical associations of a word, are thus particularly useful. Table 5 shows the top 10 collocates of *bone* in terms of their t-scores, i.e. a statistical algorithm that measures the strength of the association between a collocate and its node word.

N	Word	t-score	N	Word	t-score
1	implant	12.7	6	autogenous	4.9
2	formation	10.4	7	regeneration	4.3
3	implants	9.7	8	resorption	4.0
4	contact	7.6	9	induce	3.9
5	graft	5.1	10	cause	2.7

Tab. 5 Top ten collocates of *bone*

An analysis of the contexts in which these words co-occur with *bone* shows that there are specific collocations which are in relation to the main concerns of the scholars in the field of oral implantology. One of these is the evaluation of patients' reactions to implants, an assessment which is carried out at the point of connection between bone and implant. Therefore, it is not surprising that the strongest associations are between these words, as is also testified by such frequent clusters as *bone-implant contact*, *bone-implant complex*, *bone-implant interface* and *bone-to-implant contact*. Other common collocations refer to processes undergone by the patients' osseous structure after an implant (i.e. *formation*, *regeneration* and *resorption*). The only two verbs collocating extensively with *bone*, i.e. *induce* and *cause*, are going to be analyzed in Section 4.2.3.

The most common prepositions colligating with *bone* are *for* and *of*. They are typically positioned to the left of the noun phrase comprising *bone*. Interestingly, each colligation seems to perform a preferred grammatical or pragmatic function. For example, *for* typically introduces adverbials of purpose indicating desirable objectives pursued by the researchers (examples 1-3 in Table 6). The colligation *of* + NP comprising *bone* is often found embedded in larger noun phrases expressing quantity or measure (e.g. *the amount of*/*the degree of*/*the density of*/*the height of*/*the percentage of*/*the rate of*) in contexts where an evaluation of tested techniques is provided (examples 4-6 in Table 6).

1	The increased surface area created by a roughened surface permits more area **for bone cell attachment**.
2	Very little cancellous bone is available **for bone grafting**.
3	Although, compared with titanium, gold does not possess the good biocompatibility **for bone integration,** [...]
4	In contrast, cancellous bone harvested from the lateral proximal tibia provides the surgeon with satisfactory **amounts of bone** to graft both sinuses without the need to incorporate other graft materials.
5	The iliac crest harvest may lead to complications [...] although it can provide significant **amounts of bone volume**.
6	Today, with the introduction of advanced bone grafting techniques and the use of sophisticated bone replacement graft materials, it is possible to increase **the volume, width, and height of bone** in deficient areas [...]

Tab. 6 Expanded concordance lines for the colligations *for bone* and *of bone*

The collocational and colligational profiles of a word provide important information concerning its use in context and contribute to make learners aware of their typical pragmatic role in the construction of specialized discourse within a specific genre.

4.2.3 Verbs of causation: implied meaning

Language teachers frequently stigmatize learners' tendency to consider synonyms and quasi-synonyms listed in thesauri as interchangeable in every context. This is particularly important when some of these apparent synonyms have particular connotations which often go undetected. Learners confronted with various examples of use of these words by means of concordance lines, however, may become aware of their particular usages and increase their foreign language competence. An interesting case worth exploring is given by the two causative verbs which collocate with *bone* (Table 5). Generally speaking, both CAUSE and INDUCE share a common core of meaning, i.e. they denote the action of making something happen. In association with *bone* they indicate that a certain process affecting the patients' osseous structure was determined by a certain phenomenon or procedure. However their similarities in use stop here as each is connoted in such a way that to exchange it with the other in the same contexts is impossible. Table 7 shows their typical contexts of use.

1	Thinner widths of metal can **cause bone resorption**, wider widths may interfere with periosteal reattachment, and thicker widths may be responsible for metal dehiscence.
2	Excessive load seems to be able to **cause bone loss**.
3	Excessive load seems to be able to **cause bone loss** through the induction of bone microdamage.
4	**Bone resorption caused** by three periodontal pathogens in vivo in mice is mediated in part by […]
5	Several growth factors have been used to **induce bone formation** around titanium implants.
6	At least 7 structurally unique BMPs have been identified that can **induce bone formation** as well as accelerate the process of bone regeneration.
7	Some studies have addressed the efficacy relative to OP-1 to **induce bone formation** adjacent to dental implants.
8	Ability of commercial demineralized freeze-dried bone allograft to **induce new bone formation.**

Tab. 7 Expanded random concordance lines for the collocations *bone + CAUSE* and *bone + INDUCE*

An analysis of lines 1-4 clarifies that CAUSE is used when unpleasant processes affecting the patients' bone are mentioned. This use implies negative evaluation of the phenomena producing these undesirable states of affairs, an interpretation supported by the adjective *excessive* in lines 2 and 3. On the contrary, lines 5-8 point to the use of INDUCE in connection with positively evaluated results, which is particularly evident in line 6. Table 8 provides additional examples of use of the two verbs supporting these observations.

1	This case report demonstrates the reconstruction of a malocclusion **caused** by a congenitally missing lateral incisor […]
2	Apparently severance of these arterial branches during implant surgery, although relatively small, can **cause** exsanguination quickly, and therefore the patient's life may be threatened.
3	A food trap may occur, which can **cause** difficulty in mastication and manipulation of the food bolus by the patient.
4	Platelet-derived growth factor and dexamethasone combined with a collagen matrix **induce** regeneration of the periodontium in monkeys.
5	In the present study, our central objective was to determine if human BMP-7–derived peptides had the ability to support or **induce** biomineralization through in vitro studies. BMP-7 is a well-known member of the TGF-b superfamily capable of **inducing** bone formation and osteoblastic cellular differentiation […]

Tab. 8 Expanded random concordance lines for *CAUSE* and *INDUCE*

6	As shown in Figures 2 and 3, at both 14- and 21-day periods, peptides 6, 11, 12, and 13 were consistently able to support mineralization compared with controls. In addition, OP-1 was able to **induce** mineralization consistently greater than any peptides tested.

Tab. 8 continued

The lines in Table 8 are also retrieved from the implantology corpus and illustrate the characteristic behaviour of these causative verbs in relation to their contexts: CAUSE is negatively connoted, while INDUCE is positively connoted. It is therefore important for learners to be able to use these two verbs appropriately in order to be competent users of this particular LSP.

5 Conclusion

Corpus linguistics is an approach to language study and learning. Its corpus-driven orientation can be particularly useful for those learners with little theoretical background in linguistics as it requires them to concentrate on evidence of language use and work out representations of how words behave in their surrounding environment. Language phenomena are thus described on the basis of their recurrent, purposeful associations with their contexts. Working with corpora can thus become a favourable site of language learning via discovery and reflection.

One of the objectives of this paper has been to present corpus linguistics tools and techniques of data exploration with a particular attention to LSP learners. Indeed, the position maintained here is that being able to use these resources appropriately can contribute to improving learners' knowledge of the terminology of a certain subject matter. Furthermore, learners' competence can benefit from analysing the typical contextual associations of words and terms in order to appreciate the complex skills possessed by expert users in the construction of a certain type of specialized discourse. For this reason, another important goal has been the demonstration of how learners can exploit these techniques in studying some aspects of an LSP. In particular, the specialized vocabulary of oral implantology (a subfield of dentistry) has been initially explored to select and identify term candidates and subsequently analysed to highlight some of the purposeful connections that words have with their contexts.

References

Aston, G. (1997) "Enriching the learning environment: corpora in ELT". In Wichmann, A. Fligelstone, S., McEnery, T. and Knowles, G. (eds), *Teaching and Language Corpora*, Longman, London, pp. 51-64.

Barnbrook, G. (1996) *Language and Computers*, Edinburgh University Press, Edinburgh.

Biber, D. (1988) *Variation across Speech and Writing*, Cambridge University Press, Cambridge.

—. (1995) *Dimensions of Register Variation. A cross-linguistic comparison*, Cambridge University Press, Cambridge.

Bowker, L. and Pearson, J. (2002) *Working with Specialized Language*, Routledge, London and New York.

Gavioli, L. (2005) *Exploring Corpora for ESP Learning*, John Benjamins, Amsterdam/Philadelphia.

Hoey, M. (2005) *Lexical Priming. A New Theory of Words and Language*. Routledge, London and New York.

Partington, A. (1998) *Patterns and Meanings. Using Corpora for English Language Research and Teaching*. John Benjamins, Amsterdam/ Philadelphia.

Pearson, J. (1998) *Terms in Context*. John Benjamins, Amsterdam/ Philadelphia.

Scott, M. (1996) *Wordsmith Tools*. Oxford University Press, Oxford.

—. (2000) "Focusing on the text and its keywords". In Burnard, L. and T. McEnery (eds.) *Rethinking Language Pedagogy from a Corpus Perspective*. Bern: Peter Lang, 103-122.

Scott, M. and Tribble, C. (2006) *Textual Patterns: Key words and corpus analysis in language*, John Benjamins, Amsterdam/ Philadelphia.

Sinclair, J. (1991) *Corpus, Concordance, Collocation*, Oxford University Press, Oxford.

—. (1996) "The search for units of meaning", *Textus*, 9, pp. 75-106.

—. (1998) "The lexical item", in Weigand, E. (ed), *Contrastive Lexical Semantics*, John Benjamins, Amsterdam/Philadelphia.

—. (ed.) (2005) *How to Use Corpora in Language Teaching*, John Benjamins, Amsterdam/Philadelphia.

Tognini-Bonelli, E. (2001) *Corpus Linguistics at Work*, John Benjamins, Amsterdam/ Philadelphia.

TEACHING BUSINESS COLLOCATIONS

TEODORA POPESCU

The importance of business lexis has long been a constant preoccupation of both teachers and learners of business English, starting with the late 1960's and early 1970's, when textbook writers designed courses that focused mainly on business-related words and terminology. Later approaches have nevertheless emphasised the need for creating textbooks that pay heed to other factors as well, such as training communication skills and functions, with a real-life orientation.

The most important characteristics of the language of business English, as opposed to the language of general English, are a sense of purpose, an intercultural dimension and a need for clear, straightforward and concise communication. In order to achieve these broad objectives of business English learners, we have to find the best ways in which to teach business performance skills, such as socialising, telephoning, meetings, presentations, report writing, etc. In all these situations, a good knowledge of collocational patterns in English is of essential relevance.

Collocations are words that typically occur in association with other words. By collocational competence we understand the ability to combine lexical (and grammatical) chunks in order to produce fluent, accurate, as well as semantically and stylistically appropriate utterances. The author of the widely influential *Lexical Approach* and *Implementing the Lexical Approach*, Michael Lewis, stated the following about the lexical approach:

> "... the Lexical Approach places communication of meaning at the heart of language and language learning. This leads to an emphasis on the main carrier of meaning, vocabulary. The concept of a large vocabulary is extended from words to lexis, but the essential idea is that fluency is based on the acquisition of a large store of fixed and semi-fixed pre-fabricated items, which are available as the foundation for any linguistic novelty or creativity."
>
> (Lewis, 1997: 15)

Widdowson himself, as back as 1989, also presented a lexical view of language:

> "... communicative competence is not a matter of knowing rules for the composition of sentences and being able to employ such rules to assemble expressions from scratch as and when occasion requires. It is much more of knowing a stock of partially pre-assembled patterns, formulaic frameworks, and a kit of rules, so to speak, and being able to apply the rules to make whatever adjustments are necessary according to contextual demands."
>
> (Widdowson, 1989: 135)

The essential breakthrough of the lexical approach is that it underlines the inseparability of lexis and grammar, thus advocating an integrated approach, taking into consideration the generative power of grammatical words. The notion of *colligation*, in conjunction with *collocation* has emerged. By *colligation* we understand a typical grammatical patterning that a word may be found in. For example, we can say: "it is astonishing/suprising/amazing", but we can only say "It is not surprising that…". The other two near synonyms only colligate with the affirmative.

Teachers need to raise their students' awareness as to the way in which different collocations (and colligations) are used in business contexts. In order to do that, we may design a task-based approach to teaching/learning vocabulary. We will present in the following some methods that can contribute to the development our business students' mental lexicon.

1 Using concordancers[1] and lexical databases

There are some useful online concordancers that can be used during an English class, set in a multimedia language laboratory, with Internet access, such as:

- the *British National Corpus*, available at: http://natcorp.ox.ac.uk/lookup.html (the unsubscribed online version will only display a random selection of 50 hits);
- the *Web Concordancer*, available at: http://www.edict.com.hk/concordance/WWWConcappE.htm, with some 27 corpora to choose from; or
- the *Online BLC KWIC Concordancer* – Business Letter Corpus, available at: http://ysomeya.hp.infoseek.co.jp/, with a choice of 18 corpora.

---

[1] a concordancer = a search engine for looking through a large body of texts, i.e. a corpus

There also exist lexical databases, such as the Word.Net 3.0, provided by the Cognitive Science Laboratory, Princeton University, available at: http://wordnet.princeton.edu, which provides information about nouns, verbs, adjectives and adverbs, grouped into sets of cognitive synonyms, each expressing a distinct concept.

Sample Task 1

*1.a) Search for the word **bank** through different concordancers and fill in the table below with maximum 10 collocates under each column. Consult the WordNet database as well, in order to find supplementary lexical and semantic relations.*

vb. + bank	**bank + vb.** (both *[VN]* and *[V]*)	**adj. + bank**	**bank + noun**

1.b) Use the collocates you found in sentences of your own. Translate them into your mother tongue. What differences can you notice in terms of grammar and semantic/discourse prosody?
1.c) Can you find any idiomatic expressions?
*1.d) Is **bank** ever used as a verb? In what context and with what meaning?*
*1.e) Find examples where **bank** co-occurs with **money**.*

The first concordancer will return 1132 collocates (see Fig. 1), whereas the second only 222 (see Fig. 2). Students are advised to pay attention to the most frequent word partnerships and also to take into account the passive constructions (e.g. ***bank** will be capitalised with $50 million*, ***bank** was put on inquiry*, etc.). The information provided by the WordNet Search will add supplementary knowledge as to the other meanings of the word bank (see Fig. 3).

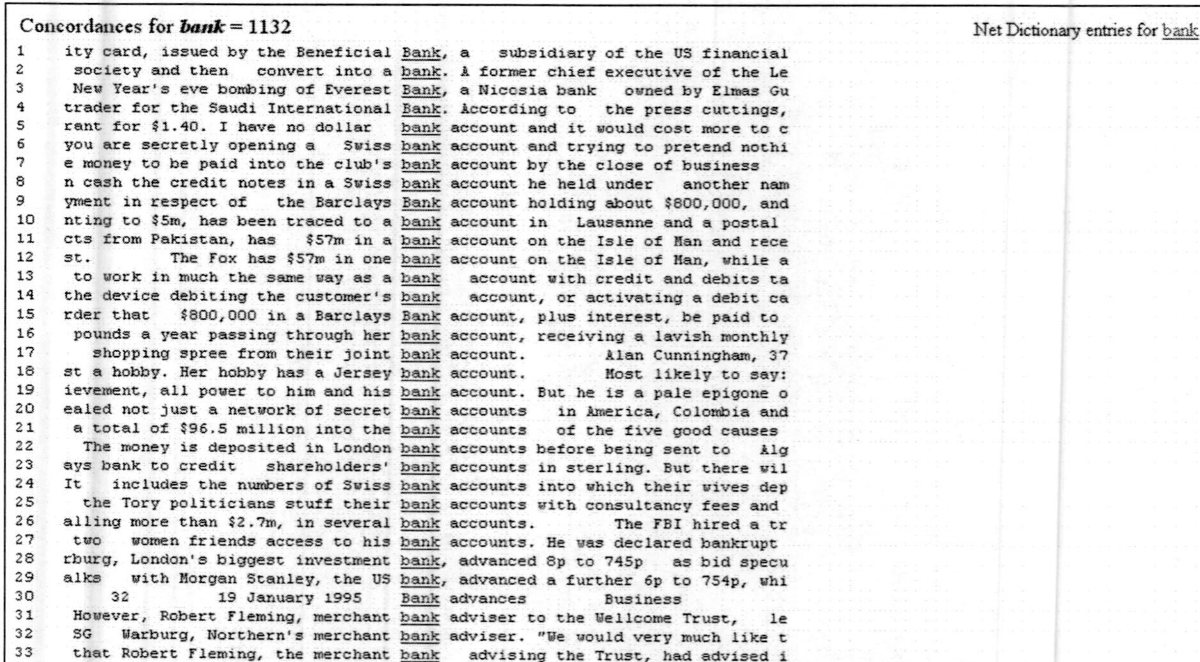

Concordances for ***bank*** = 1132 | Net Dictionary entries for bank

1	ity card, issued by the Beneficial	Bank,	a subsidiary of the US financial
2	society and then convert into a	bank.	A former chief executive of the Le
3	New Year's eve bombing of Everest	Bank,	a Nicosia bank owned by Elmas Gu
4	trader for the Saudi International	Bank.	According to the press cuttings,
5	rant for $1.40. I have no dollar	bank	account and it would cost more to c
6	you are secretly opening a Swiss	bank	account and trying to pretend nothi
7	e money to be paid into the club's	bank	account by the close of business
8	n cash the credit notes in a Swiss	bank	account he held under another nam
9	yment in respect of the Barclays	Bank	account holding about $800,000, and
10	nting to $5m, has been traced to a	bank	account in Lausanne and a postal
11	cts from Pakistan, has $57m in a	bank	account on the Isle of Man and rece
12	st. The Fox has $57m in one	bank	account on the Isle of Man, while a
13	to work in much the same way as a	bank	account with credit and debits ta
14	the device debiting the customer's	bank	account, or activating a debit ca
15	rder that $800,000 in a Barclays	Bank	account, plus interest, be paid to
16	pounds a year passing through her	bank	account, receiving a lavish monthly
17	shopping spree from their joint	bank	account. Alan Cunningham, 37
18	st a hobby. Her hobby has a Jersey	bank	account. Most likely to say:
19	ievement, all power to him and his	bank	account. But he is a pale epigone o
20	ealed not just a network of secret	bank	accounts in America, Colombia and
21	a total of $96.5 million into the	bank	accounts of the five good causes
22	The money is deposited in London	bank	accounts before being sent to Alg
23	ays bank to credit shareholders'	bank	accounts in sterling. But there wil
24	It includes the numbers of Swiss	bank	accounts into which their wives dep
25	the Tory politicians stuff their	bank	accounts with consultancy fees and
26	alling more than $2.7m, in several	bank	accounts. The FBI hired a tr
27	two women friends access to his	bank	accounts. He was declared bankrupt
28	rburg, London's biggest investment	bank,	advanced 8p to 745p as bid specu
29	alks with Morgan Stanley, the US	bank,	advanced a further 6p to 754p, whi
30	32 19 January 1995	Bank	advances Business
31	However, Robert Fleming, merchant	bank	adviser to the Wellcome Trust, le
32	SG Warburg, Northern's merchant	bank	adviser. "We would very much like t
33	that Robert Fleming, the merchant	bank	advising the Trust, had advised i

Fig. 1 Web Concordancer

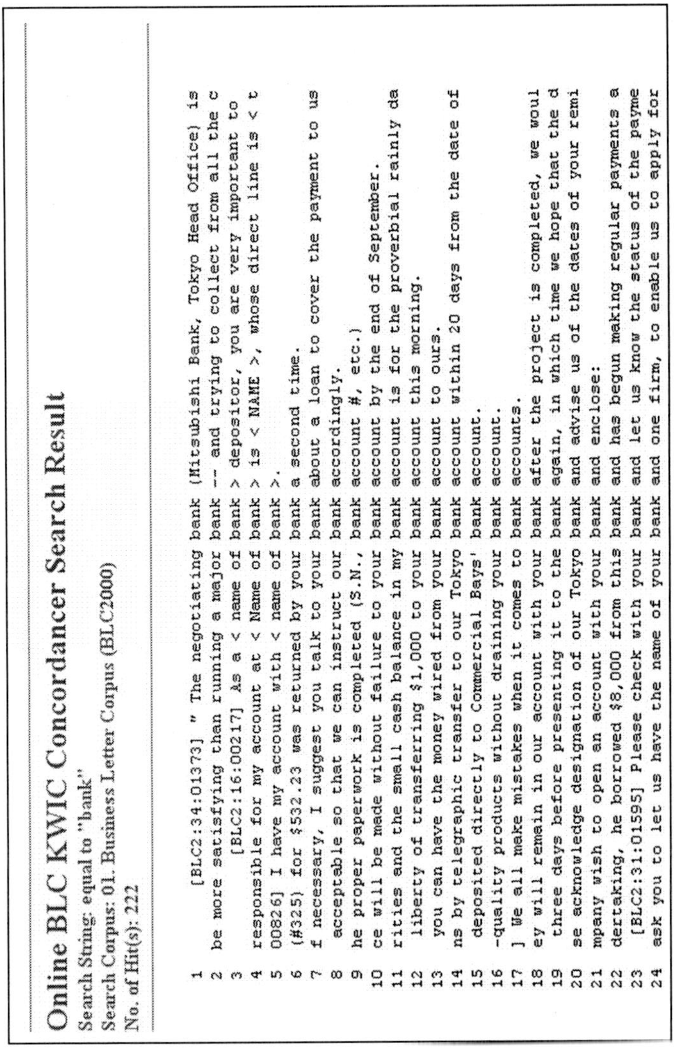

Fig. 2 Online BLC KWIC Concordancer

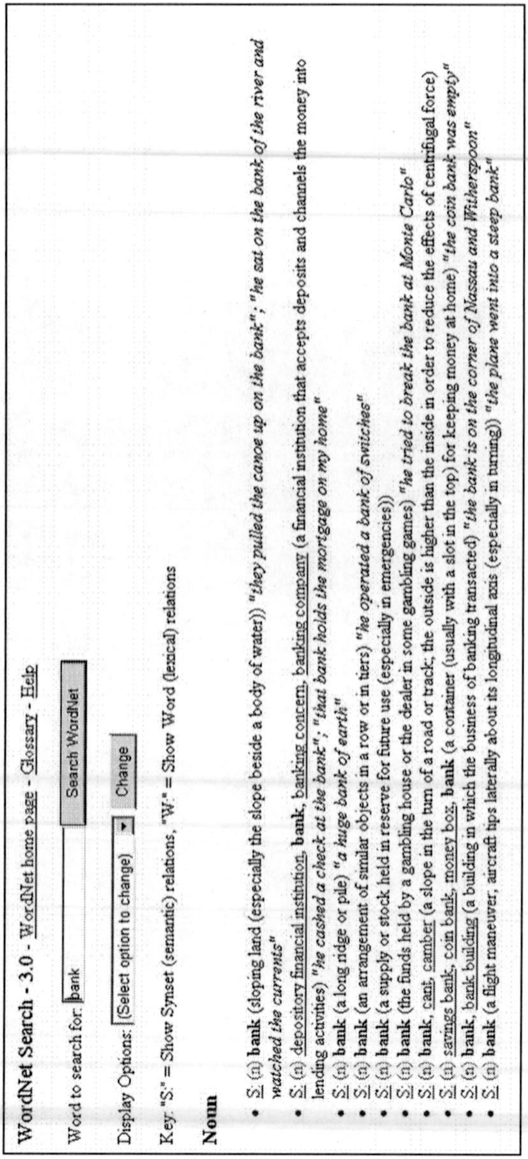

Fig. 3 Word Net Search 3.0

1.a Students work in pairs and a suggested answer is presented below.

vb. + bank	**bank + vb.**	**adj. + bank**	**bank + noun**
back	*[VN]* confirms cancellation /receipt	central	account
control	*[VN]* stops payment	commercial	balance
rob	*[VN]* refuses/returns a cheque	cooperative	charges
run	*[VN]* offers a loan	investment	cheques
sell	*[VN]* handles financing of …	leading	customers
ask	*[VN]* advises on privatisation	merchant	debt
convince	*[V]* collapsed	private	director
instruct		savings	guarantee
show to		state-run	reference
talk to			statement

Next, the students are asked to analyse some of the grammatical features of the collocations they found.

Syntagmatic / paradigmatic relationships

node	verb	DO
bank	confirms	{ cancellation receipt of draft }

verb	*DO (node)*	*to-infinitive clause object*
instruct	a **bank**	{ to accept a draft to open an account to pay an invoice }
ask	a **bank**	{ to extend an overdraft to hold a cheque }

verb	*DO*	*prep. phrase (node)*
provide	credit	with a **bank**
open	{ a letter of credit an account }	with a **bank**
{ open readjust }	an account	with a **bank**

1.b Some differences between Romanian and English are to be noted:

	Semantics	**Romanian translation**
back control run sell	an **organization** that provides various financial services, for example keeping or lending money[2]	**bancă**
rob	**building** in which this business takes place	bancă
ask convince instruct show to talk to	**people** working for the bank	a solicita **băncii/la bancă** a convinge **pe dl/dna de la bancă** a însărcina **banca** (să facă o plată) a prezenta (o situație) **la bancă** a vorbi **la bancă/cu cei de la bancă**

1.c ***Idioms***

break the bank = not break the bank (informal, humorous) if you say sth won't break the bank, you mean that it won't cost a lot of money, or more than you can afford:
We can just get a sandwich if you want – that won't break the bank.[3]

1.d ***bank v.***

147 [BLC2:23:05167] We **bank with** the local branch of the Barminster
[V] ~ (with / at...) to have an account with a particular bank:
The family **had banked with** Coutts for generations.[4]

1.e ***money*** *+* ***bank***

verb	*node1*	*prepositional phrase (node2)*	
{ borrow / bring / take }	**money**	{ from / from / to }	a **bank**
{ wire / pay / deposit }	**money**	{ from / into / in }	a **bank** account
withdraw	**money**	from	a **bank** cash point

---

[2] Oxford Advanced Genie CD-ROM
[3] Oxford Advanced Genie CD-ROM
[4] idem

2 Using business texts / creating own corpora and using dictionaries

Different online business texts

- articles from the business press: The Economist, Financial Times, etc.;
- company web pages:
  http://press.benettongroup.com/,
  http://www.marksandspencer.com/, etc.

may be used in order to extract common collocations, which may be afterwards used to design meaningful tasks.

Sample task 2

2.a) Match the words in the columns to form suitable collocations.
e.g. 1.d) ample evidence

1	ample	a)	competition	5	attract	a)	debate
2	commercial	b)	investors	6	crimp	b)	funds
3	healthy	c)	funding	7	play	c)	growth
4	responsible	d)	evidence	8	stir	d)	role

2.b) Now fill in the gaps in the texts with the collocations you found. You may want to change their form (e.g. base form to -ing form):

Commercialisation is changing microfinance—and 1. ___________ ___________. Some believe microlenders have no business making money from the poor. In many countries various rules, like interest-rate caps, have been put in place to 2. ___________ the industry's ___________. This is despite 3. __________ __________ that where there is 4. ___________ ___________ in microlending, as in Bosnia and Peru, interest rates tend to drop substantially.
Most experts in IFIs and elsewhere believe the for-profit sector must 5. ________ _ ________. Microlenders that can 6. __________ commercial ________ – deposits, loans, the capital markets – have the potential to become self-sustaining, rather than relying on the charitable instincts of others.
Socially 7. __________ __________ are already pouring in. And even the purely profit-minded have begun to open their wallets. According to a study of 200 microlenders by MIX, which collects data on the microfinance industry, 8. ___________ __________ grew to \$7.3 billion in 2005, from \$4.9 billion two years before.

(http://www.economist.com)

Answer:

1	stirring debate	5	play a role
2	crimp ... growth	6	attract ... funds
3	ample evidence	7	responsible investors
4	healthy competition	8	commercial funding

Sample task 3

3.a) Match the words in the two columns so as to form suitable collocations.
e.g. 1.h) clearing bank

1 clearing	a) management
2 crossed	b) interest
3 bearer	c) date
4 bank	d) tender
5 deferred	e) note
6 dishonoured	f) loan
7 due	g) vault
8 legal	h) bank
9 mortgage	i) worthiness
10 portfolio	j) cheque
11 promissory	k) bill
12 credit	l) securities

3.b) Now match the collocations you found above with their corresponding definitions.

1 __________ security (such as a bank note) that the issuer considers is legally owned and negotiable by the person who possesses it.

2 __________ a room with thick walls and a strong door, which is used to store money or valuable things in safe conditions.

3 __________ condition in which the payment of interest is postponed.

4 __________ a British commercial bank which is a member of a bankers' clearing house, through which cheques are cleared.

5 __________ degree to which customers are certain to pay debts promptly, degree to which they are worthy of being allowed credit.

6 __________ one which the drawee (the debtor on whom it is drawn) has refused to accept, or which the acceptor (the person who has agreed to pay it) fails to pay when it is due.

7 __________ a document which contains a promise to pay a stated amount of money to a stated person either on a fixed date or when the money is demanded.

8 __________ one with two parallel lines drawn across it, usu. by the drawer or his agent, e.g. his bank. This practice lessens the risk of loss by dishonesty.

9 __________ the date on which some debt, such as an interest payment or a bill of exchange becomes due to be paid.

10 __________ the administration of a collection of company shares and other investments that are owned by a particular person or organization.

11 __________ the form of money in which a person has a right by law to pay a debt, and which the creditor must by law accept in settlement of the debt.

12 __________ a loan to finance the purchase of real estate, usually with specified payment periods and interest rates. The borrower (mortgagor) gives the lender (mortgagee) a lien on the property as collateral for the loan. The mortgagor's lien on the property expires when the mortgage is paid off in full.

(Toma, M. and Popescu, T., 2004: 107)

Answer:

1 bearer securities
2 bank vault
3 deferred interest
4 clearing bank
5 credit worthiness
6 dishonoured bill
7 promissory note
8 crossed cheque
9 due date
10 portfolio management
11 legal tender
12 mortgage loan

Starting from the explanations given by an online dictionary, one could create a word-formation exercise. The example below was created using the information provided by the Cambridge Advanced Learners' Dictionary (the online version, see Fig. 4 below).

Definition

bank (ORGANIZATION) Show phonetics
noun [C]
1 an organization where people and businesses can invest or borrow money, change it to foreign money, etc., or a building where these services are offered:
High street banks have been accused of exploiting small firms.
I need to go to the bank at lunch time.
I had to take out a bank ***loan*** *to start my own business.*

2 A bank of something, such as blood or human organs for medical use, is a place which stores these things for later use:
a blood bank
a sperm bank

3 In gambling, the bank is money that belongs to the owner and can be won by the players.

bank Show phonetics
verb [I or T]
I used to bank ***with*** *Lloyd's* (= keep my money there).

bankable Show phonetics
adjective
likely to make money:
She is currently Hollywood's most bankable actress (= Her films make large profits).

bankability Show phonetics
noun [C]
an ability to make money:
His bankability as a pop star decreased as he got older.

banker Show phonetics
noun [C]
1 someone with an important position in a bank:
She was a successful banker by the time she was forty.

2 the person in gambling games who is responsible for looking after the money

banking Show phonetics
noun [U]
the business of operating a bank:
The intricacies of international banking remained a mystery to him.

(from Cambridge Advanced Learner's Dictionary)

Fig. 4 On-Line Cambridge Advanced Learners' Dictionary

Sample task 4

Fill in the gaps with the corresponding forms of the word ***bank.***

1 High street __________ have been accused of exploiting small firms.
2 She is currently Hollywood's most __________ actress.
3 His __________ as a pop star decreased as he got older.
4 She was a successful __________ by the time she was forty.
5 The company was forced into __________ .
6 The intricacies of international __________ remained a mystery to him.
7 "Do you think she'll come?" "I wouldn't __________ on it."
8 She was commissioned to work on a joint program __________ by the U.S. space agency.
9 The recession has led to many small businesses going __________ .

(Toma, M. and Popescu, T., 2004: 108)

Answer:

1 High street banks have been accused of exploiting small firms.
2 She is currently Hollywood's most bankable actress.
3 His bankability as a pop star decreased as he got older.
4 She was a successful banker by the time she was forty.
5 The company was forced into bankruptcy.
6 The intricacies of international banking remained a mystery to him.
7 "Do you think she'll come?" "I wouldn't bank on it."
8 She was commissioned to work on a joint program bankrolled by the U.S. space agency.
9 The recession has led to many small businesses going bankrupt.

The above tasks serve as a modest model for materials designers, and we want to underline that the list of examples may continue, and each teacher is called upon to design his/her own vocabulary tasks and activities, and to adapt different lexical-approach methods to the specific needs and individual proficiency level of his/her students. What we should always bear in mind is the necessity to design real-life, authentic tasks, which will eventually enhance our business students' mental lexicon, as well as improve their communicative performance in an English-speaking environment.

References

Brown, D. (1974) *Advanced Vocabulary Teaching: The Problem of Collocation.* In RELC Journal, Vol. 5, No. 2, 1-11.

Firth, J. R. (1957) *A Synopsis of Linguistic Theory, 1930-55*. In Palmer, F.R. (ed), (1968) Selected Papers of J.R. Firth 1952-59. London/Harlow: Longman.

Greenbaum, S. and Quirk, R. (2004) *A Student's Grammar of the English Language.* Harlow: Longman.

Kjellmer, G. (1987) *Aspects of English Collocations*. In Meijs, W. (ed) Corpus Linguistics and Beyond. Amsterdam: Rodopi.

Lewis, M. (1993) *The Lexical Approach.* Hove: Language Teaching Publications.

—. (1997) *Implementing the Lexical Approach.* Hove: Language Teaching Publications.

Lewis, M. & Hill, J. (1998) *What is Collocation?* Hove: Language Teaching Publications.

Lewis, Morgan. (2000) *There's Nothing as Practical as a Good Theory*. In Lewis, M. (ed) Teaching Collocations. Hove: Language Teaching Publications.

Nattinger, J. (1988) *Some Current Trends in Vocabulary*. In Carter, R. & McCarthy, M. (1988) Vocabulary and Language Teaching. London/New York: Longman.

Oxford Advanced Genie CD-ROM. (2003) Oxford University Press.

Popescu-Furnea, T. and Toma, M. (2003) *Business Collocations. English-Romanian Dictionary.* Cluj-Napoca: Casa Cărţii de Ştiinţă.

Toma, M. and Popescu-Furnea, T. (2004) R*eading and Vocabulary for Business Students. Part II.* Cluj-Napoca: Casa Cărţii de Ştiinţă.

Sinclair, J. (1991) *Corpus, Concordance, Collocation.* Oxford: Oxford University Press.

Widdowson, H. G. (1989) *Knowledge of Language and Ability for Use.* In Applied Linguistics, Vol. 10, No.2, 128-137.

CHAPTER III

LANGUAGES FOR SPECIFIC PURPOSES – LEXICOLOGY, TERMINOLOGY, TRANSLATION STUDIES

INTRODUCTION

ELENA CROITORU

Language varies according to the function it fulfils in communication. The variation of language according to the human activity in which it plays a part is called domain. The domains of language can be characterised according to their *domain functions*. Thus, language used in a given type of activity has a dominant communicative function, with other functions subordinate to it. In addition, there are not clear-cut distinctions between the varieties of domain. Domains vary as regards the degree in which they influence language use. The reverse also holds valid, i.e. the language chosen can itself define a domain. Thus, in a certain degree, language and situation can be considered mutually determining. Consequently, there is close interdependence between domain variation and language use.

If we were to oppose the literary domain (although it is still unclear if literature should be called a domain) to the specialized domains of functional languages, one of the contrasts would be the greater freedom in choosing the topic and language behaviour with the former, as compared to the latter.

Furthermore, the interest in the contrasts between literary and non-literary discourse has been widened to a more general interest in the empirical study of language use, which, together with a cognitive study of style and language, has gained much from a *genre –oriented* approach to discourse.

The idea is generally shared that *genre* is essential as far as the cognitive expectations of language users are concerned, especially when they belong to a certain class of language use. These genre expectations affect the production of the texts, comprehension of messages and text analysis. In other words, the cognitive genre representations help to clear up discourse aspects such as the selection and organization of the content messages, the selection of the appropriate register, on the one hand, and the foreign language teaching, translation-oriented text analysis (TOTA) and translation strategies, on the other.

The language users' cognitive representations are related to a series of parameters that correspond to genre dimensions such as domain, context and register. Thus, genre analysis makes it clear that the mental representation of genres in individual language users plays an essential role in their cognitive processing of language, whether it means text production, or the other aspects mentioned above.

Moreover, it has generally been accepted that genres range from literary to non-literary forms. A genre-based approach has been lately favoured, since genres are fundamental to the realisation of the producer's communicative intention, and determine his linguistic choices. Genres constrain the way in which register variables of field, tenor and mode can be combined in a discourse community. For example, both explicit and implicit arguments, developed about a subject matter, as utterances existing in some context, linking an arguer to an audience for the purpose of justifying the arguer's claims, belong to knowledge frames shared by the discourse participants. They are organized into schemes, plans or patterns which are controlled by the subject matter in question. In other words, the discourse community concerned with some specific subject matters will perform specific discourse operations articulated by genres. Consequently, the patterns will differ with genres. That is to say, the specific patterns of argument organization are indicative of a certain domain.

The characteristics of one of the genre dimensions, i.e. domain, are closely related to the factors of tenor and mode. One of the four factors of tenor (formal vs. informal, polite vs. familiar, impersonal vs. personal, specialist vs. popular), i.e. the *specialist/popular* distinction closely correlates with complexity and simplicity of style, respectively. The language of the texts written for *specialist readership/audience* is more complex and technical, accessible to a limited range of readers, whereas the language of a text written for popular mass readership is simple and accessible to a very wide range of readers.

Therefore, the more complex the style of a text, the less readable and accessible the text is and the greater the demands on the reader.

The language complexity can be measured by the complexity of grammatical units (e.g. nominal groups), on the one hand, and by the complexity of lexical combinations, in terms of collocability, patterns of idiomacity, in the length of words (the rough- and- ready measure), and, what is most important, in terminology, on the other. As far as the lexical complexity is concerned, terminology is the most difficult aspect in teaching language for specific purposes (LSP) and in translation.

One main role of LSP instruction is in the way it channels attention to the meanings of words, to the lexical combinations, especially collocations, and terminology specific to a certain domain, bringing them into awareness.

The challenge to methodology is determined especially by the lexical nature of language. Within *communicative* approaches, proficiency envisages *accuracy, fluency* and *complexity*. Awareness of the lexical nature of language has to be added to knowledge of a larger number of *colligational* patterns, i.e. knowledge of a word's grammar and of its accurate and fluent use in more complex patterns.

In LSP teaching, at first sight, things only seem to be easier, but they are definitely not at all easy, due to the domain specific *prefabricated* or *ready-made language* which may raise both comprehension and translation problems. On the other hand, some of these *ready-made units* may be available to the learner both for language use and as units for syntactic analysis (e.g. especially in the analysis of complex nominal groups/long noun strings in LSP). Such units form a certain stable system of linguistic means used in scientific communication. Therefore, every domain is characterized by subject-specific language which forms a shared code of the participants in that type of communication.

Syntactically speaking, it is important to mention that such lexical chunks become composite units which function as if they were single words. The degree of compositeness differs in that some of them are more closely linked than others. However, in spite of this difference, their compositeness unites them as structurally and functionally different.

It is becoming more and more obvious that the method of presenting lexis as individual words, or of practising individual decontextualized sentences is extremely inefficient. On the contrary, presenting larger text samples in class increases the possibility of learners transferring terms to their mental lexicon.

Teachers have to help learners identify the words, collocations and patterns specific to a certain domain. They know that decontextualized learning of individual words may be adequate for highly specialized terms, and that paraphrase and contextualization of more common words are usually sufficient to make the meaning of a word understood. Thus, they have to be aware of the need to incorporate co-textual information into their teaching, for example, with less lexicalized items such as collocations, considering that the wider the collocational range of a word, i.e. the more de-lexicalized it is, the more useful it will be to acquire and record it in a collocation.

Therefore, the focus is now switched to the *collocational field* of a word; that is why students use the *dictionary as an encoding tool* rather than as a decoding one, since they explore a word's collocates, not only its meanings. As a result, they are able to solve the exercises, on the one hand, and to make a summary of the text and translate it, on the other.

Consequently, a very difficult task for the teacher is to provide the appropriate collocational language in a certain domain, and a far more difficult task is to translate such combinations, especially words with very large collocational fields.

Besides dictionaries, *concordancing* helps students acquire and develop collocational ranges of words. A *concordancer* allows search for examples of a particular word or phrase in a large number of texts. It becomes obvious that sources of co-textual information which are much richer than dictionaries are provided by *concordances* which may also be a very good option for specialized terminology.

Appropriately chosen *corpora* must be designed for a particular purpose, since they provide excellent concordancing and collocational input, special terminology for a particular group of learners. The high information terms in LSP texts are easily identified by learners who only have to explore the collocates of the less lexicalized keywords in these texts. If encounters with specialized terms are left to random meetings in texts, learning will be very inefficient. Thus, teachers have to provide a more concentrated exposure to specialized terminology through careful planning of the vocabulary input to their classes. In addition, outside the classroom, students should be directed to more sources of this kind of materials.

Last but not least, the practice of glossing new words in terms of synonymy can bring about errors in second-language production. It is generally accepted that *dissonance* may occur between a lexical item and its appropriate use, which may be: stylistic, syntactic, collocational and semantic. In LSP teaching, the collocational and terminological dissonances are most frequent. As a general rule, in order to limit the range of lexical errors, the collocational and stylistic/ pragmatic dimensions to word meaning should be paid special attention.

To conclude, it as important as useful that learners should store the lexical chunks of pre-patterned language specific to a certain domain as whole composite units. Greater emphasis is laid on usefulness to the learner and frequency is no longer an overriding criterion.

As a matter of fact, the pre-patterned/pre-fabricated/ready-made language, the lexical chunks play a very important role in the interactional management of language.

THE ROLE OF MEDIATING ACTIVITIES IN TEACHING ENGLISH FOR LEGAL PURPOSES

ADÉLA BAHENSKÁ

The objective of this paper is (1) to foster discussion on positive and indeed the negative aspects of translation as one of the techniques in legal English class; (2) to suggest what could be the contribution of a foreign language (L2) teacher whose native language (L1) is the same as that of the students; and (3) to suggest why it makes sense for law students to learn to translate legal text. This paper will present some initial thoughts about the benefits of using translation and mediating activities in legal English classes. It will deal with the "setting" rather than specific techniques and types of exercises that could be designed. We will use a course of legal English for university law students with intermediate to advanced knowledge of English as a basis for the thoughts below. Nevertheless similar considerations would apply to adult courses designed for practising lawyers, and some of the ideas may be useful for other ESP classes as well, with the exception of mixed classes of learners with various native languages.

Teaching languages is a truly multidisciplinary mission and this applies twice as much to languages for specific purposes. Translation studies may be seen as one of the disciplines that can contribute to the discussion of language teaching. In the language teaching environment translation and interpreting is sometimes referred to as a fifth language skill or a "mediating activity" - using the language of the Common European Framework of Reference for Languages, which defines mediation as an activity where

> "the language user is not concerned to express his/her own meanings, but simply to act as an intermediary between interlocutors who are unable to understand each other directly."
>
> (CEFR, CUP 2001: 87)

Mediating activities, according to CEFR definition, include spoken interpretation and written translation as well as summarising and paraphrasing texts in the same language. This is the definition that will be used throughout this paper.

In the modern history of language teaching, translation and the use of native language in other language classes has been the subject of contradictory attitudes. While traditional teaching methods focused on written language and translation purely as an exercise in teaching the system of language and as means of testing, the direct method excluded the native language from teaching altogether. In the communicative method the learner becomes the core of the teaching process, and the learners' needs and objectives are the primary focus. As the main purpose why law students learn English for law is to be able to communicate within their professional community and as mediating activities form an integral part of communication, such activities must have some value in this process.

> "In considering the similarities and differences between L1 and L2 teaching, we need to ask ourselves questions about (a) the age and corresponding characteristics of the learners, (b) what the learners already know and its effects, (c) what the learners have to learn, (d) the nature of the teaching processes, and (e) the outcomes."
>
> (Mothejzíková, 1988: 24)

Let us now consider the legal English course for law students within the above framework.

(a) The age and corresponding characteristics of the learners

The students are adults, which makes them more efficient learners than children. Their ability to concentrate is better and attention span is longer. They are future professionals, and as such they expect to learn as much as possible in as short a time as possible. This reflects the main trend of the current "age of speed"; however it goes against the proven fact that learning languages is a life-long effort. Motivation as another important aspect of the learner's approach plays a prominent role in language learning because it is a long-term process and requires self-discipline on the part of learners. While games are the most natural way of motivating young children, it seems that for adults the relation to practical real-life experience is an important motivating factor - and this is where mediating activities, such as role playing (involving the role of interpreter) or translating a real contract may become an interesting link to real-life.

(b) What the learners already know and its effects

When the students enrol in the university they have completed their formal instruction in their native language. They are assumed to have intermediate or better knowledge of English. However the ability to differentiate various registers or styles in a foreign language (and sometimes the native language as well) is rather limited. At the beginning of law studies they become acquainted with the history and the basic concepts of law, which is an important condition for the ability to compare the cultural aspects of the language of law. The awareness of the system of the native language provides the possibility of contrasting foreign language elements with the native language system. Extensive exposure of students to various types of L2 legal texts, the guided process of oral translation of such texts into L1 or summarising them in L2 refines their sense of the language of their profession in L2 and indeed in L1 as well.

(c) What the learners have to learn

The students need to learn to communicate in English within their professional community. They need to become aware of the cultural differences, in our case the legal system in English speaking countries, as this has an important impact on precise interpretation of various terms and the decision whether the term is culturally specific and therefore should not be used when translating from L1 to L2 (except as a comparison), or whether the term is fairly close to L1 reality and therefore, safe to use as an equivalent. This is one of the skills they will need not just for production in L2 (for example when an L2 explanation of L1 legal concepts is required) but also for being able to critically evaluate translations of legal texts (both written and oral). This requirement stems from the real-life situation where they will necessarily be confronted with translated texts, such as EU legislation, contracts concluded in two or more languages or negotiations involving interpretation.

(d) The nature of the teaching processes

As far as the nature of teaching processes is concerned it is necessary to consider five main factors: time, objective, subject matter, methods and teaching material. We will focus here on the first four factors, as they could be considered as part of the *setting*. Time devoted to language instruction in university programmes whose main focus is not language is very limited. The outcome of the teaching process in such programmes depends to a major extent on the student's self-study discipline. Motivation plays an extremely important role in the student's decision to register for elective courses taught in English or focused on specific skills, such as legal writing.

The objective must be defined on the basis of students' needs and the needs of the society. CEFR (CUP 2001: 135-137) provides several perspectives from which the teaching/learning objectives may be identified, including (1) the development of a learner's general competencies (which translates in the case of a law student studying English as a foreign language particularly into the culture aspect and the development of the ability to put knowledge of culture in the service of their social skills); (2) the extension and diversification of communicative language competence, covering linguistic, pragmatic and sociolinguistic components (the ability to communicate, in the widest possible sense of this term, within their professional community, ranging from knowledge of specialised vocabulary down to awareness of various registers); (3) better performance in one or more specific language activities, covering reception, production, interaction or mediation (Future lawyers should strive to improve in all of these activities. Mediating activities additionally seem to be quite close to the role of a facilitator or a negotiator, which are found among the skills a lawyer should have. The lawyers will often find themselves translating between individual registers of a single language, when converting the language of a statute, contract or a judgment into plain language so that their clients understand.); (4) optimal functional operation in a given domain – public, occupational, educational or personal domain (In our case the emphasis will be placed on occupational and educational domains, because the students will need to use the language for professional purposes and for expanding their knowledge when studying abroad.); and (5) the enrichment or diversification of strategies or the fulfilment of tasks (which, in case of law students, translates into discovery and experience of other cultures). The objectives will differ for individual students; nevertheless the overall goal should be for the students to achieve Effective Operational Proficiency (using CEFR terminology), which is described as follows:

> "Can understand a wide range of demanding, longer texts, and recognise implicit meanings. Can express him/herself fluently and spontaneously without much obvious searching for expressions. Can use language flexibly and effectively for social, academic and professional purposes. Can produce clear, well structured, detailed text on complex subjects, showing controlled use of organisational patterns, connectors and cohesive devices."

The subject-matter should cover those aspects that are specific to legal English, taking into account that the time of the course is always limited and the choice of topics to be covered is of essence. In the case of legal English the principal distinctive factor would be the vocabulary, not just from the point of view of specific legal terminology (mainly specialist terms and descriptive terms or taxonomies, Chromá 2004: 19) but also from the viewpoint of extensive synonymy of English legal terms as a result of English being spoken in various parts of the world. The language of acquis communautaire being yet another challenge for the law student. Marta Chromá defines LSP as

> "a subsystem of the general language system which consists of (describing and analysing) the selection, combination and use of existing morphological, lexical and syntactic units, structures and patterns that would best serve the specific social context."
>
> (Chromá, 2004: 13)

In the field of subject-matter the native language will assist in identifying potentially problematic aspects in the foreign language class.

There are numerous possibilities of using mediation techniques within the scope of method. It will be the subject of further research to identify such techniques and to verify in the case of Czech law students what are the advantages and disadvantages of individual techniques and what combination of them appears to be the most efficient under particular circumstances. Mediating activities, such as pointing out appropriate translation equivalents in a student's native language or asking students to explain a term in English using their own words or paraphrasing, as well as oral translation of difficult passages in complex written texts into L1 to verify reading comprehension, can save time, and the students learn to work around the terms they do not know when speaking L2 or using the context to make a qualified guess of the meaning of unknown expressions when reading. One of the factors that must be taken into account in the case of using native language in L2 class is transfer, which is defined as

> "influence resulting from similarities and differences between the target language and any other language that has been previously (and perhaps imperfectly) acquired."
>
> (Odlin, 1989: 27)

On the one hand native language is seen as the culprit of negative transfer; on the other hand researchers admit that knowledge of the native language and other languages enables positive transfer and thus assists in the learning process.

> "Along with social factors, a number of pedagogical factors may have an important effect. For example, teachers who know the native language of their students may provide information about native-target-language contrasts that other teachers cannot provide. Similarly, textbooks and other materials that present analogies between the native and target languages may promote or inhibit some kinds of transfer."
>
> (Odlin, 1989: 136)

Whether the involvement of native language promotes positive transfer and helps to address negative transfer will depend, among other things, on the choice and application of teaching techniques. The approach of the teacher in drawing the students' attention to lexical issues, such as false cognates (e.g. English evidence /meaning proof/ and Czech evidence /meaning record-keeping/) will be extremely important as well as the type of materials to be used. The method considerations could also cover the potential for cooperation between a native speaker of English and an English teacher whose native language is the same as that of the students, as well as making sure that the students have a possibility to attend integrated courses on particular aspects of the legal systems of English speaking countries taught by lawyers who are native speakers of English.

The issue of teaching material is closely related to the method and respective techniques as well as to subject-matter. It would need to be covered with specific reference to individual language elements, with emphasis on vocabulary for law, in structure according to individual language skills or activities and mediating activities; would need to be broken down with respect to the direction of translating or interpreting. But this is beyond the scope of this paper.

(e) The outcomes

The outcomes, as already indicated above, will depend on numerous factors including the skills of the teacher - as a mediator opening the gates to knowledge and skills that may be of benefit to the student - and on the student's informed decision as to how much time he/she wants to devote to studying the language.

We believe that there is a strong case for future lawyers and speakers of "small" languages to develop a critical approach to translated material, and that translation studies have a lot to offer in making as efficient as possible use of native language and mediating activities in foreign language class. A graded approach, starting with the English teacher whose native language is the same as that of the students, later involving a native English teacher and then exposing students to lectures in English could represent a good way forward for most LSP settings.

References

—. (2001) *The Council of Europe Common European Framework of Reference for Languages*, Cambridge: Cambridge University Press.

Chromá, M. (2004) *Legal Translation and the Dictionary,* Tübingen: Niemeyer.

Mothejzíková, J. (1998) *Methodology for TEFL Teachers,* Praha: Státní pedagogické nakladatelství.

Odlin, T. (1989) *Language Transfer, Cross-linguistic influence in language learning*, Cambridge: Cambridge University Press.

ISSUES IN ON-LINE LEGAL TRANSLATION TEACHING

MIGUEL ÁNGEL CAMPOS PARDILLOS

Why an online course in legal translation?

For the past two decades, translation has been one of the most popular degrees in Spanish universities. In spite of the wide range of studies and the ever increasing array of universities offering graduate programmes, Translation and Interpreting still ranks among those with the greatest number of applicants, and to date it still appeals to the students with the highest qualifications, either via general university entrance examinations (in which Translation and Interpreting attracts the students with the highest grades) or through specific admission tests. In all cases, all this leads to a number of students who, either because the programme did not exist as such until the early nineties, or because they were unable to study the degree of their choice, request some kind of translation training at post-graduate level, usually after completing degrees in Languages or English Studies (the usual student profile), but also in Law or Economics.

This was the reason which, more than a decade ago, led the Department of English at our University to start a post-graduate course in translation and interpreting, initially aimed at non-specialists who wished to re-orient their careers (quite a usual occurrence worldwide, as described, amongst others, by Lung, 2005). The course was taught for over a decade, and has only been modified due to a general restructuring process of Spanish university degrees, which includes both graduate and postgraduate options. However, what we did observe over the last editions was a declining interest for translation in general, perhaps due to the increasing number of institutions where the degree is offered. Conversely, this decline was offset by a growing number of requests from all over Spain and abroad which enquired about the possibility of specific training in Legal Translation which did not require the students' physical presence in Alicante; this was due to the fact that our Institute for Applied Modern Languages is one of the most widely known sources of English-Spanish legal translation theory and materials in Spain. Until three years ago, nevertheless, it was felt that the time was not ripe yet for online teaching, for despite the generalization of Internet use; it is only for the past three-four years that Spanish Internet providers have ensured the availability of reliable connections at an affordable price. Also, present postgraduates have a degree of computer / Internet literacy which was not so widespread only four or five years ago, although some students, as will be pointed out below, still resist working with the Web (as noted, amongst others, by Uschi, 2007).

At first, the course was addressed at postgraduates in English Studies, although applications were also accepted from other postgraduates providing some evidence of sufficient domain of English (i.e. at Cambridge Proficiency level). Indeed, the first edition only attracted applicants from English Studies and Law, but to our surprise, in the second and third edition we have had an unexpected number of applications (20 per cent) from postgraduates in Translation and Interpreting. We personally contacted each and every one of them, informing them that they might already be familiar with part of the contents of the course, and even with the fragments proposed for translation, for the textbook used is indeed the most popular in Spain for English-Spanish legal translation (five editions to date).[1] However, in all instances the applicants confirmed their interest, for in their opinion the lessons they had received in legal translation had been insufficient (something that merits further discussion elsewhere), or they were interested in obtaining further training and extra practice.

The course structure

The technical specifications of the course were adapted for students to be able to use all features with no need for a high level of computer literacy. For reasons of brevity, which preclude a detailed discussion of all the characteristics of the course, emphasis shall be made on the following components: (a) the teaching units, (b) the self-correcting exercises, (c) the online tutorials, (d) the forums, (e) the compulsory written papers, and (f) the final examination.

---

[1] A month before the beginning of the course, the students are sent a copy of the textbook (Alcaraz, 2003), plus a bilingual English-Spanish legal dictionary (Alcaraz & Hughes, 2003).

(a) The teaching units

As is often the case with English for Legal Purposes and Legal Translation courses (Candlin et al., 2002; Northcott & Brown, 2006), a content-based syllabus was chosen, divided into 15 units: two on translation strategies ("An introduction to translation" and "An introduction to legal translation"), four on introductory topics in legal language and procedure ("The language of English law", "The English court system", "Criminal Procedure" and "Civil Procedure") and eight on specific legal topics ("Sale-Purchase contracts", "Lease contracts", "Labour contracts", "Company Law", "Family and Probate Law", "Alternative Dispute Resolution", "Insurance Law", "EU Law" and "Lawyers, solicitors and representation before the courts").

Out of these units, the first two have a specific structure, for they are intended for students who have received no training in translation as such. The purpose is to provide a number of simple translating techniques beyond the literal version, based on the strategies proposed by Vinay and Darbelnet in the late fifties, and adapted to English-Spanish translations by Vázquez-Ayora (1977). The interface for Lesson 1 is shown below.

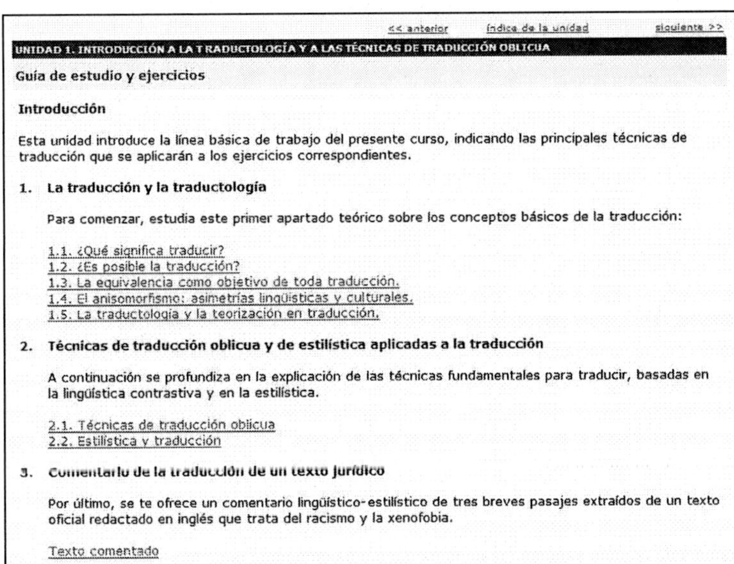

<< anterior   índice de la unidad   siguiente >>

UNIDAD 1. INTRODUCCIÓN A LA TRADUCTOLOGÍA Y A LAS TÉCNICAS DE TRADUCCIÓN OBLICUA

Guía de estudio y ejercicios

Introducción

Esta unidad introduce la línea básica de trabajo del presente curso, indicando las principales técnicas de traducción que se aplicarán a los ejercicios correspondientes.

1. **La traducción y la traductología**

   Para comenzar, estudia este primer apartado teórico sobre los conceptos básicos de la traducción:

   1.1. ¿Qué significa traducir?
   1.2. ¿Es posible la traducción?
   1.3. La equivalencia como objetivo de toda traducción.
   1.4. El anisomorfismo: asimetrías lingüísticas y culturales.
   1.5. La traductología y la teorización en traducción.

2. **Técnicas de traducción oblicua y de estilística aplicadas a la traducción**

   A continuación se profundiza en la explicación de las técnicas fundamentales para traducir, basadas en la lingüística contrastiva y en la estilística.

   2.1. Técnicas de traducción oblicua
   2.2. Estilística y traducción

3. **Comentario de la traducción de un texto jurídico**

   Por último, se te ofrece un comentario lingüístico-estilístico de tres breves pasajes extraídos de un texto oficial redactado en inglés que trata del racismo y la xenofobia.

   Texto comentado

Fig. 1

The documents are in .html format, and can be either viewed online or downloaded into the students' computers; by means of hyperlinks, the student can browse around the unit. The theoretical contents are supplemented by simple, self-correcting exercises (usually gap-filling), such as those in Figure 2 (the answers are shown in lighter type).

Units 3-15 have a theoretical and a practical section. In all the units, the students are asked to carefully read both the on-screen introduction and the corresponding lesson in the textbook. Then, a number of self-correcting exercises are proposed (see following section), in which the main ideas are clarified and reinforced. Following a usual trend in materials integrating language and law (Candlin et al. 2002: 299-320), each unit is self-contained.

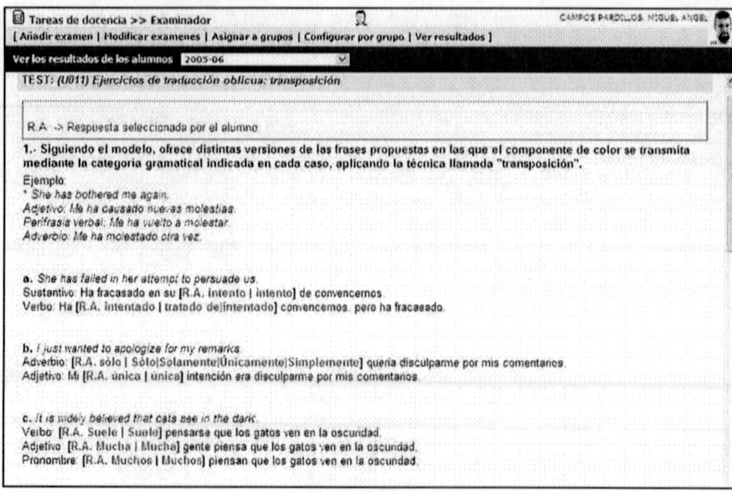

Fig. 2

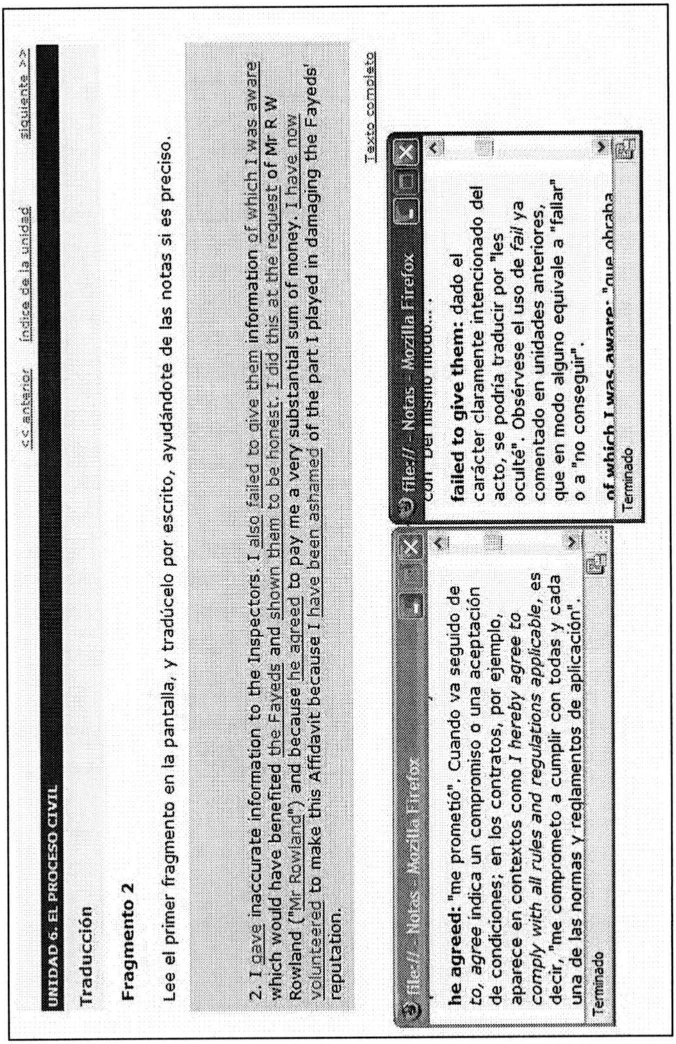

Fig. 3

However, what the students have found most useful, and rightly so (for such is the purpose of the course) is the second part of the unit, containing the translation exercise. Except for two units, the text is the same as that contained in the textbook, with two types of translation aids: the footnotes in the book (which offer a number of options for the translation into

Spanish of potentially difficult words or phrases), and those available online.

The text is shown on-screen, divided into six fragments. By clicking on each of them, the relevant paragraph is shown with a number of hyperlinks, which in turn lead on to specific comments on the translation, dealing with potential false friends or emphasizing the correct usage in the target language. What is more interesting with a view to actually learning to translate any text (versus learning to translate only one given text, and being unable to extrapolate), sometimes there is a discussion of potential alternatives in other texts or for other users.

Every two fragments, there is a small section in which students are asked to render sentences from their language into English; the purpose here is not, strictly speaking, to translate, but rather to consolidate the specific vocabulary and phrases corresponding to the topic in each lesson, usually as a reminder of the footnotes. For example, in the exercise shown below the purpose is, on the one hand, to reinforce the topic-related terminology (tenant, tenancy, without notice), and on the other, to emphasize general notions on legal translation (in this case, the equivalent of fail as an "empty" negative form, or the conditional meaning of where). The exercises allow for two "levels" of difficulty, whereby students are offered an "intermediate" version in which they can fill in the gaps:

> En aquellos casos en que el arrendatario y el titular no se ponen de acuerdo en las condiciones, el inquilinato puede resolverse sin previo aviso.
>
> *Ayuda para la traducción.*
>
> Where a ___ and an ___ fail to ___ terms, the ___ may be ___ without ___.
>
> *Solución.*
>
> Where a tenant and an owner fail to agree terms, the tenancy may be terminated without notice.

Finally, the main points in each unit are summarized by means of a checklist (Figure 4), followed by a multiple-choice test, with both topic- and translation-based questions.

(b) The self-correcting exercises

Each unit in the course contains a whole set of exercises, aimed at testing the way students have actually systematized the contents and techniques, with a special emphasis on confidence-building. Such exercises are based on a software tool included in the Virtual Campus at the University of Alicante, the so-called "Examiner". The system allows, amongst others, for gap-filling or multiple choice tasks, but also allows tutors to check if their respective students have done the exercises and the results obtained.

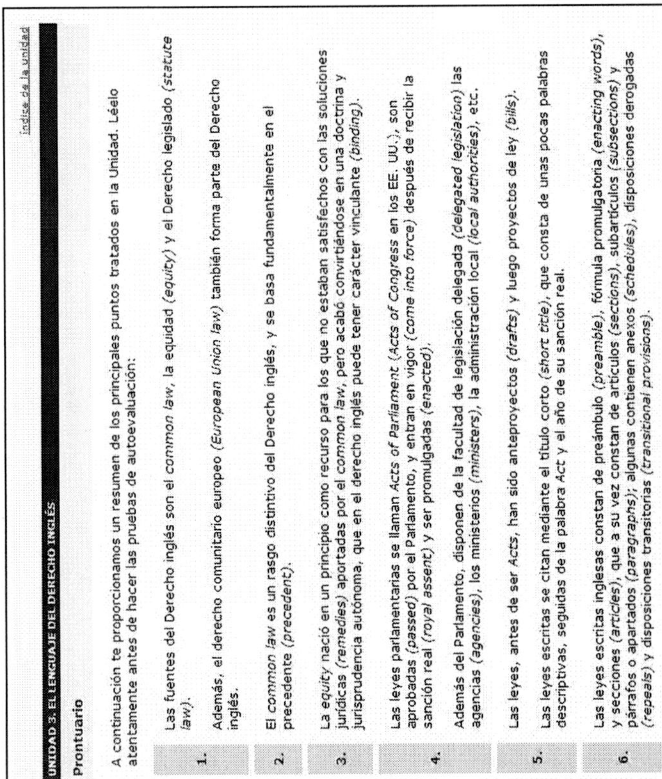

Fig. 4

In those units dealing with texts with a very stable macrostructure (as defined, amongst others, by Alcaraz, Campos and Miguélez, 2003: 118), a genre-based approach is combined with the content-based one, and students are encouraged to use parallel texts as a source of equivalent terms or phrases. For instance, in Unit 8, dealing with lease agreements, the students are asked to compare similar clauses of lease agreements in English and Spanish:

3. Damage Deposit Upon the due execution of this Agreement, Lessee shall deposit with Lessor the sum of eight hundred dollars ($800) receipt of which is hereby acknowledged by Lessor, as security for any damage caused to the Premises during the term hereof. Such deposit shall be returned to Lessee, without interest, and less any set off for damages to the Premises upon the termination of this Agreement.	***SÉPTIMA***: en este acto, los ARRENDATARIOS hacen entrega a la ARRENDADORA de TRESCIENTOS NOVENTA EUROS CON SESENTA Y SEIS CÉNTIMOS (390,66 €.), en concepto de fianza por posibles deterioros que pudiesen ocasionarse en la vivienda durante el periodo de alquiler, o por incumplimiento, por parte de los ARRENDATARIOS, del plazo del presente Contrato. Dicha cantidad será devuelta a los ARRENDATARIOS, menos los gastos que pudiesen ocasionarse por reparaciones, después de revisar la vivienda a la conclusión de este contrato y simultáneamente a la entrega de llaves a la propietaria.

A careful examination of the equivalent formulae in these clauses allows students to find translations which are perfectly suitable for the same genre in the target language:

1. en este acto *(upon the due execution of this Agreement)*
2. a la conclusión de este contrato *(upon the termination of this Agreement)*
3. posibles deterioros que pudieran ocasionarse en *(any damage caused to)*
4. durante la vigencia del presente Contrato *(during the term hereof)*
5. Dicha cantidad será devuelta a *(Such amount shall be returned to)*
6. and less any set off for *(menos los gastos que pudieran ocasionarse)*

(c) The online tutorials

The Virtual Campus also contains an online tutorials tool, which makes it possible to address either the webmaster (in case of technical problems) or each personal tutor (for any questions regarding the contents of the course). Although it might be possible to use e-mails for these questions, the advantage of this system is twofold: on the one hand, it has almost unlimited storage capability for messages and attached documents (which it automatically classifies into folders). On the other hand, it offers the possibility to transform any reply into a FAQ or to choose from a list of ready-made answers; these can be short remarks, such as "the answer can be found in the textbook", "both versions are correct", or even long explanations (e.g. on the use of capitals in English and in Spanish, etc.) including, where appropriate, references to websites. Whenever possible, tutors try not to provide direct answers, but rather to guide the students so that they can find the answer by themselves.

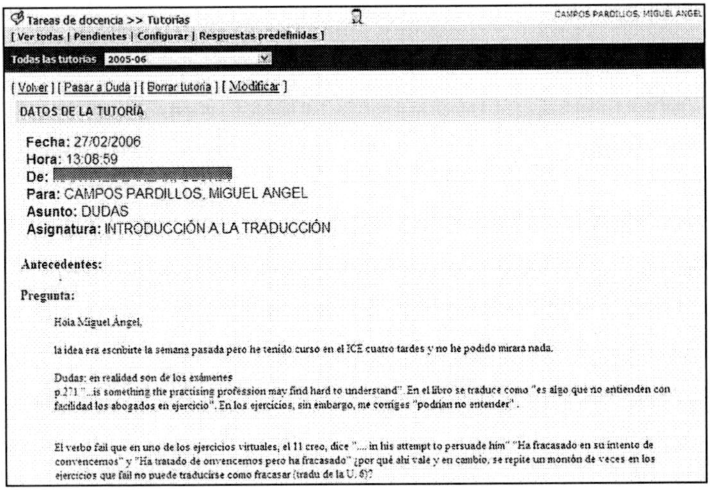

Fig. 5

The Virtual Campus tool is also used in order to send and return the compulsory written papers, which will be discussed in greater length below.

(d) The forums

Undoubtedly, the greatest challenge in all online language and translation courses is the lack of peer presence. Deprived of contact with other students, the learner may fall easy prey to discouragement or disorientation, for it is not possible to know if problems are unique or usual ones, and in the worst cases some students may feel that everybody is doing well out there except them. In order to avoid this isolation, and provide the much-needed "group feeling" and "human touch" (see, for example, the University of Illinois 1999 Report) the students are, at the beginning of the course, encouraged to introduce themselves, in such a way that both all participants share a virtual space in which they express their hopes and expectations concerning the learning process.

In addition to these introductions, which profit from an adult learner environment in which a "learning contract" is explicitly entered, any of the tutors can start a thread on any topic at any stage. For example, one of the students once sent her tutor a message asking for advice on dictionaries. Instead of providing a simple answer, or even creating a FAQ for everybody to receive the same information, it was decided that perhaps a small debate on the usefulness of dictionaries and how practical they seemed to the students, could be more productive in terms of helping them to become aware on how much can be expected from a dictionary. Such debate, as seen below, was extremely popular, because at this stage learners already have some experience on the use of dictionaries, and if any misconceptions emerge, they are rapidly debated (see Fig. 6).

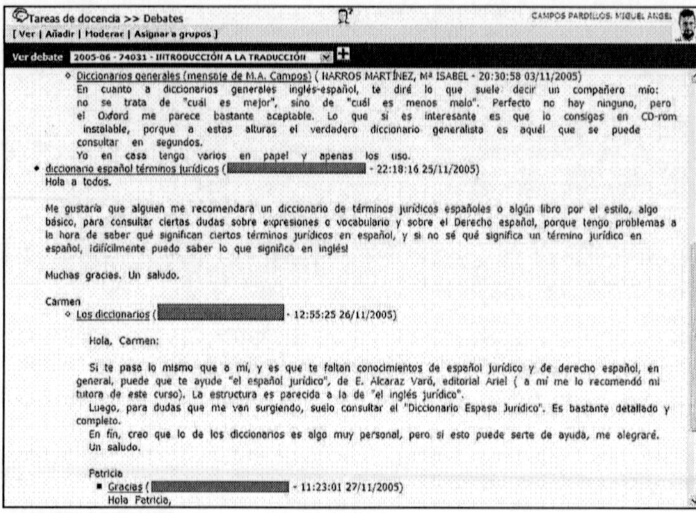

Fig. 6

In addition to these uses, an additional purpose of the forum was the so-called "for gourmets only" section. In order to cater for all levels in legal translation (some of the students in the course are already practicing translators), it was decided to add a little "extra", under the shape of a text for advanced translation. Initially the idea was to hand it out to the students as an optional task which they could send to their respective tutors; however, it was felt that the whole activity could become more collaborative and attract various levels of participation if the forum was used. Out of the several options available (e.g. A translates one paragraph, then B and C agree or disagree, the tutor moderates the debate and comments on the pros and cons of each version, etc.), a format was chosen in which the tutor simply proposes a potential translated version, without saying whether it is acceptable or not (though intentionally introducing controversial options and usual mistakes), and the students give their opinions, suggest alternatives, etc. (see Fig. 7).

As can be seen, the students feel free to express their emotions on the translation and the course; for example, one of them admitted that she felt discouraged because, as she put it herself, she would not have been able to produce a version like the one proposed, "not in a month of Sundays"; in addition to the tutor offering some words of encouragement, other colleagues of hers said that they had also found it difficult, at times even impossible. The student was persuaded by the combination of all voices, and continued to strive for better and better translations. Of course, the debate also becomes an amplified, public version of the student-teacher tutorial, in such a way that comments are "overheard" by other students who might not be bold enough to ask.

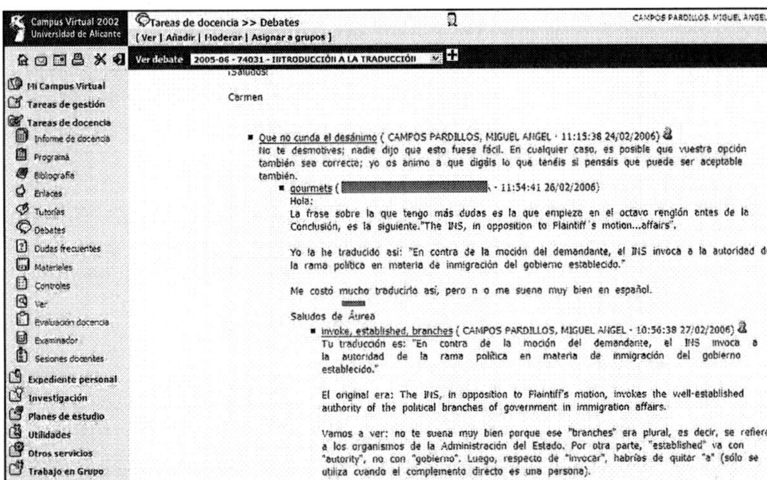

Fig. 7

(e) The compulsory written papers

However, as one can imagine, translation cannot be simply taught and assessed by means of self-correcting exercises and debates; the only way to accurately monitor the students' progress is by means of compulsory, periodic translation papers, accounting for 40% of the final mark. In order to better prepare the learners for the final examination discussed in (f) below, the usual format for written papers in specialist translation was chosen, i.e. fifty per cent of the marks for "known" subject matter (vocabulary and content questions, and translation of fragments from the units) and another fifty per cent for an unknown translation. The first part, for which neither dictionaries nor textbooks are allowed, attempts to encourage students to do the exercises in the units, for they know that by working hard on such materials they can reasonably expect to prepare for the written examination.

We are aware that some teachers are against allocating such a high percentage of the mark (50% of each paper) to materials that may simply have been committed to memory; however, it is our belief that memory does play a role in legal translation, in the sense that it is impossible to rely on dictionaries and research for all the vocabulary and structures needed at a certain stage, for two reasons. Firstly, availability: in certain situations the dictionary is simply not an option (e.g. in court appearances, at least in Spain). Secondly, regarding time organization, excessive dictionary use results in low quantitative performance, which in turn precludes meeting deadlines and, what is more serious in the case of translators (who usually work freelance), accepting a number of jobs sufficient to obtain a reasonable income (and pay social security contributions) every month.

Papers are corrected by the tutors and returned to the students via the Virtual Campus, with comments on mistakes and suggestions for improvement. In general, students have found this extremely useful, and mentioned this as one of the most salient features of the course, especially since it leads sometimes to interesting and illustrating debate; in some cases, the tutors have gained extensive knowledge about Spanish legal vocabulary from Spanish judges taking the course.

Students who fail any of these papers are allowed to try again during the first two weeks of June; should they not do this, they are still legally allowed to take the final examination, but in this case the grade obtained therein is the only mark.[2]

(f) The final examination

As required by University regulations, and also following the usual strategy against cheating, there is a compulsory written examination which

[2] To date only two students have taken the final examination without submitting the compulsory papers, and failed. In principle, given the dynamics of Spanish university education, the student might have felt that the mark was a sort of "punishment" for not complying with some requirements of the course, but none of them perceived it as such.

students have to take in designated venues (the host university, but also other cooperating institutions in other Spanish cities and abroad). The structure of the examination is similar to the ones taken during the year, and the results in general have been positive so far; in fact, the marks have been found to deviate very little from those obtained in the papers. This agrees with the remarks by McNett (2002), who points out that making the final examination an on-campus test may increase the chances for cheating in intermediate exams, but students are aware that this will be of little help if passing the final exam is a compulsory requirement.

Looking ahead: problems and potential solutions

Once the course has been running for almost three years, the following problems have been detected: (a) technical problems; (b) content-derived problems; (c) others.[3]

(a) Technical problems

Online learning may present a number of difficulties related to the platform used, or simply due to technical problems which are greatly disappointing for students (see, for example, Towndrow [2004]). In this respect, some of the students encountered problems because of lack of computer literacy, especially in the case of those over the age of 40. In other some cases the problem did not come even from the system itself, but from the students' computers, which were sometimes faulty due to poor maintenance.

We believe that the situation will greatly improve as, over the years, candidates become more and more students familiar with the use of computers (the Eurostat figures issued in June 2006 are quite optimistic for the ages between 16 and 24 years old); for urgent cases, in future editions we shall consider the possibility of providing telephone assistance, whereby the webmaster may sit before a screen and take the student through all the necessary steps. Also, some contingency plan might also come in handy for total failure of the virtual campus

[3] The problems discussed in this section come from three basic sources: my experience as the coordinator of the course, the remarks by the tutors, and the comments made by the students in a written survey which all students in postgraduate courses must fill in at the University of Alicante, as part of our quality control programme. Thanks are due to all of them, especially to the students, for their time, and also for their words of praise.

(sometimes unavailable due to maintenance reasons), in the shape of Internet group pages.

(b) Content-derived problems

Some of the students found the units too short, especially the ones on the language of civil and criminal law, respectively. This is certainly true, if we consider that both the contents and the vocabulary in these units are comparatively much greater than those in other units. We are currently studying the possibility of subdividing these units into two (i.e. Civil Law I, Civil Law II), although that might prolong the course, or re-allocating part of the contents to other, related units.

Other students have commented on the need for general lessons on Law in general (especially those coming from language degrees). Again, the duration of the course appears to be an obstacle, for introducing units on legal topics would make the course too long, and might not appeal to students already possessing such background (i.e. lawyers, but also translators who have studied some kind of introductory subject at university). The solution seems to lie in using the Internet as a source of general knowledge, and for future editions we plan to introduce optional exercises and quizzes (in the Webquest format[4]) based on information that may be obtained online.

(c) Others

We have also detected that in some cases there was cheating among the students; this occurred in the compulsory exercises sent every six weeks, in which learners were supposed to do the first part of the examination without using the textbook. In order to verify this, small variations were introduced in the fragments for translation included in the papers: in some cases the students' translation corresponded to the textbook version. In further editions, it is our intention to explore some of the strategies suggested by Varvel (2005), starting from an emphasis on the practical nature of the course and the importance of the contents versus the academic certificate.[5]

---

[4] On the extremely successful Webquest tool, see http://webquest.org/.

[5] This is one of the examples of what is known in Spain as "own" courses (*títulos propios*), i.e. those diplomas which are not recognized by central government, but simply issued by individual universities and accepted (or not) by firms and institutions on the basis of their reputation (vs. an official degree in Modern Languages, which in principle could allow the holder to work as a teacher regardless of one's knowledge, but simply because one holds the relevant degree).

In addition to this, at the end of the fourth edition it is our desire to carry out a quantitative and qualitative survey, to gauge both perceptions on the course (which are also collected yearly in anonymous surveys at the end of the year) and the implications on the professional careers of the students who have taken the course. One specific area we are interested in is whether the course has led students to move into a career in translation, or whether legal English and translation have been added to their skills as an added feature for professional practice (i.e. for lawyers) or as part of their areas of language teaching.

References

Alcaraz, E. (2003) *El inglés jurídico. Textos y documentos.* Barcelona: Ariel.

Alcaraz, E. & Hughes, B. (2003) *Diccionario de términos jurídicos inglés-español, Spanish-English*. Barcelona: Ariel. 7th edition.

Alcaraz, E., Campos, M.A. & Míguélez, C. (2006) *El inglés jurídico norteamericano*. Barcelona: Ariel. 3rd edition.

Candlin, C.N., Bhatia, V.K. and Jensen, C.H. (2002) "Developing legal writing materials for English second language learners: problems and perspectives". *English for Specific Purposes* 21: 299-320.

Eurostat (2006) "More than a third of EU25 population have no basic computer skills". Report issued on 20 June 2006. Retrieved March 15, 2007 from the World Wide Web *http://*epp.eurostat.ec.europa.eu.

Felix, U. (2007) "The Impact of the Web on CALL". Retrieved March 12, 2007 from the World Wide Web *http://users.monash.edu.au/~ufelix/finalWebCall.htm.*

Lung, R. (2005) "Translation training needs for adult learners". *Babel* 51:3: 224-237.

McNett, M. (2002) "Curbing Academic Dishonesty in Online Courses". *Pointers and Clickers*, Retrieved 29/03/2007 from the World Wide Web
http://www.ion.uillinois.edu/resources/pointersclickers/2002_05/index.asp.

Sifakis, N.C. (2002) "Applying the adult education framework to ESP curriculum development: an integrative model". *English for Specific Purposes* 22: 195-211.

In this kind of programme one might expect that students might pay more attention to what they may learn and less to the certificate itself, but cheating has been found to be present as well.

Towndrow, P. (2004) "Reflections of an on-line tutor". *ELT Journal Volume*, 58/2: 174-181.

University of Illinois Teaching at a Distance Seminar. (1999) *Teaching at an Internet Distance: The Pedagogy of Online Teaching and Learning.* Retrieved March 21, 2007 from the World Wide Web *http://www.vpaa.uillinois.edu/reports_retreats/tid_final-12-5.pdf.*

Vázquez-Ayora, G. (1977) *Introducción a la traductología: curso básico de traducción.* Washington: Georgetown UP.

Varvel, V.E. (2005) "Honesty in Online Education". *Pointers and Clickers*, Vol 6(1). Retrieved March 15, 2007 from the World Wide Web *http://www.ion.uillinois.edu/resources/pointersclickers/2005_01/VarvelCheatPoint2005.pdf.*

Vinay, J. P. and Darbelnet, J. (1977) *Stylistique comparée du français et de l'anglais: méthode de traduction.* Paris: Didier. (originally published in 1957 in Montréal by Beauchemin).

EXPLICITATION AND DELETION FROM THE PERSPECTIVE OF TEACHING LSP TRANSLATION

ELENA CROITORU[1]

Text, the teaching of ESP and translation strategies

With the emergence of translation studies as an independent discipline in its own rights, the awareness of the text as a complex, multi-dimensional structure has increased. This points out once again the importance of the *top-down text-analysis* which is essential to translation, as well as the *communicative function* of the text as a unit embedded in a given *situation*, against a certain *socio-cultural background*. As a matter of fact, the suggestion has often been made that the translator's first task in making the text analysis is to identify the text in terms of culture, situation and text-type. The next level of the text analysis is related to the text *structure*: the top-down analysis starts from the macro structure going down to the level of lexical cohesion. All this considered, on the basis of the conclusions reached from the analysis of the source text (ST), the strategies to be used in translating the text should be established.

The fact must be mentioned that such an analysis usually focuses on a *web of relationships*, except for the situations in which the analysis is concerned with certain items, due to their relevance and function in the text.

Generally speaking, literary texts involve the *creative extension* of the language norm. Therefore, with literary texts, translation involves *recreating language dimensions* and the result will be *a shift of perspective* in the target text (TT).

However, we should suggest that this statement holds valid not only for literary texts. Special language translation requires *knowledge of terminology* and experience in handling it. Nevertheless, there may be

[1] I owe the suggestion of this challenging topic to some of my MA students in "Translation and Interpreting" at "Dunărea de Jos" University of Galați.

aspects of specific relevance in translating English specialized texts, and in teaching ESP translation.

The teaching of ESP takes into account the complexity and the various functions of the specialized languages. A very important practical requirement is the description of some special language at text level including both intralingual and interlingual comparisons. This lays stress on the combination of special subject and translation exercises included in the curriculum: learners translate specialized texts later in the degree programme.

The basic principle is that the target text (TT) is not completely identical with the conventions of the source text (ST); neither is it identical with the conventions of the (quasi) parallel texts in the target culture (TC) (cf. Schäffner, 1998: 89). Thus, opposed to the utopian view on translation as the pursuit of textual identity, there is the opinion that it is seldom possible to change the language without changing other elements.

The changes that occur in a translation are determined by the differences between the two languages in contact. According to Popovič, these differences "determine the major components of the translation's structure" (Popovič, 1970: 79). The major changes are shifts in structure. Furthermore, he argues that the translator

> "resorts to shifts precisely because he is endeavouring to convey the semantic substance of the original in spite of the differences separating the system of the original from that of the translation, in spite of the differences between languages [...]."
>
> (id. ibid.)

Thus, the translator tries to render the original as faithfully as possible. This leads to a sort of tension between the semantic substance of the ST and the shifts occurring in the linguistic structure of the TT. Such a way of looking upon translation reminds us of the "faithful-free" dichotomy. The idea is that the greater the differences between the two languages, the greater and the more numerous the shifts occurring in the TT.

In order to create an adequate TT, an adaptation of the TT to the typological conventions of the TC must be achieved.

A comparative analysis of the ST and TT will point out the shifts occurring in translation and the strategies used in the translating process.

The *explicitation strategy* (ES) involves shifts in the TT and expansion of TT by inserting words which are not found in the ST. The term explicitation was first used by Vinay and Darlbernet (1958, 1995) who defined it as the introduction in the TL of the information which is only implicit in the SL. The most frequent changes made through this strategy are: additions, expansions of condensed structures and passages, insertion of explanations, repetitions of previous words (usually nouns) for the purpose of clarity, more accurate descriptions, change of punctuation marks (see Appendices 1 and 2), using (very) long explanatory syntagms for words especially in technical English (see Appendix 3). There are many words that have a specialized and "protected" meaning (Sinclair 2004:151) in a discipline; most of them are granted the status of terms, others are not. For example, for scientific and technical language there is a well organized terminology that "seeks to maintain the semantic isolation of the terms, and to counter the natural pressures of usage" (id. ibid.). A large number of such terms are translated by using the explicitation strategy (see Appendices 1 – 3).

According to the *explicitation hypothesis* (EH) put forward by Blum-Kulka, the level of explicitness in the TT is increased by the explicitation strategy, which is "a universal strategy inherent in any process of language mediation, including translation" (Blum-Kulka, 1986: 21). It "postulates" an observed cohesive explicitness from the SL to the TL texts in spite of the differences between the two linguistic and textual systems involved (id. ibid.) According to the EH the translator/interpreter renders implicit forms more explicitly.

K. Klaudy (1996, 1998) identifies four types of explicitation strategies: *obligatory* (due to the structural differences between the two languages), *optional* (attributed to differences in text building strategies and stylistic preferences), *pragmatic* (due to the cultural differences between source culture (SC) and TC), and *translation-inherent* (specific to the translation process).

The opposite strategy is that of *deletion* by which something irrelevant is dropped. That word which is considered unnecessary for the meaning of the sentence will not occur in the surface structure of the TT. Deletion takes place at the syntactic and semantic levels. In D. Katan's opinion, by deletion "the meaning of a sentence may be implied, vague or even ambiguous" (Katan, 2004: 133).

The strategy of deletion must be used in such a way as to preserve the co-textual and contextual clues, also considering the linguistic expectations and the contextual constraints.

In Chitra Fernando's opinion,

> "deletion is a process common to all levels of language though different sorts of levels require that other terms (e.g. elision, contraction) be used to describe its effects: the absence of an element normally present".
>
> (Fernando, 1996: 51)

The structures or syntagms in which some element has been deleted, i.e. those with permuted

> "compressions, indicate the fluency of the language user. However, non-native speakers may consider deletion to be impeding identification and interpretation of such structures".

To all this deletion is frequently used and is based on the principle of least effort, common in most language use.

In teaching, deletion is frequently used for purposes of testing language proficiency. If it is too frequently used, it means that there is too much redundancy in the text.

Deletion is usually associated with the *cloze* procedure in teaching used for measuring the readability of textbooks, a reader's degree of comprehension of a text, and as a means of teaching and testing language proficiency in foreign language teaching.

An extension of cloze activities from random deletion to *discourse cloze* was suggested by Deyes:

> "If a truly discourse cloze is to reflect the reader's ability to follow information through the text and use contextual clues as well as co-textual ones then, it is argued, theme and rheme, as units of information, provide criteria for item deletion".
>
> (Deyes, 1984: 128)

Deletions represent a variety of communicative values; moreover, syntactically speaking, they represent the full range of syntactic units (S, O, P, A).

In ESP texts most often nouns, adverbs, comparatives are deleted (see Appendix 1, STs 3, 4, 6, 7, 10, and Appendix 2, ST 6).

A teaching experiment

In the following sections, an experiment will be presented which I made to include the strategies of explicitation and deletion in the teaching of translation to MA students in *Translation and Interpreting* at the "Lower Danube" University of Galați and to students in the last year of study, before taking their BA degree.

The courses I was responsible for were called *Interpretive theories and techniques of translation* and *Theory and practice of translation*, respectively. Generally, the students who select these courses have certain expectations and needs. They want to know how to handle translation problems like equivalence, non-equivalence, untranslatability, how to solve problems in translating collocations, idioms, culture specific elements, and especially how to overcome translation traps. They also want to identify and discuss situations of misinterpretation, mistranslation, undertranslation and overtranslation, and translation strategies like the two under discussion. Given the fact that a large number of them, especially the MA students, are practising translators and their works are to be assessed by their superiors and clients, and others are high-school teachers themselves and have to correct and assess their students' translations, they are interested in the problem of evaluation, in finding solutions as regards assessing works of translation.

As a rule, within the MA programme, and the optional course of theory and practice of translation taught to BA students in the last year of study, theoretical aspects of translation theories, techniques and strategies are introduced before text analyses, commentaries and translation practice proper. In our case, aspects of the explicitation strategies were presented, on the one hand, and of the opposite strategy, i.e. that of deletion, on the other.

Usually, the curricula in translation courses concentrate on the translation of a number of specialized texts in one field at a time, in subjects like scientific and technical translations, legal translations, translations from the field of economics, public administration, etc.

I consider that after having explained the theoretical aspects referring to a translation problem, technique or strategy, it may be more productive to offer students text samples of a group of such specialized texts for them to understand the problem better for each type of text. (see Appendices 1, 2, 3). Learners are not aware of all the research involved in the translating process. Thus, the first step is to make them aware of it.

As a general working method, while comparing the (ST) and (TT), our main concern is not whether the TT is equivalent to the other texts in the TL, but what *degree* of equivalence the two texts compared show (cf. Toury, 1991: 113). Linguistic units of different types and levels participating in the textual relationships and carrying textual functions (textemes) are analysed within the TT-ST comparison. The units selected for comparison are ST based.

It is a well-known fact that when confronted with the observational data in the product of the translating process, students *intuitively* realize the translator's reasons for having made one choice or another. According to Hofstede's model, mental processes can never be observed directly; "their investigation is always based on the products of such processes" (Hofstede, 1991: 76).

Moreover, texts are usually identified as translations when linguistic, stylistic, textual, pragmatic shifts from the TC norms are perceived. When such deviations are found out, a kind of "adjustment mechanism" is set in motion which ensures the "correct" interpretation of the texts studied (Weizman and Blum-Kulka, 1987: 72; Toury, 1991: 55).

Furthermore, as C. Schäffner points out, the translator has to

> "comply with cultural norms, i.e. to decide which norms take priority, whether the cultural norms of the SL community as reflected in genre conventions, the cultural norms of the TL community, or perhaps a combination of the two [...]".
>
> (Schäffner, 1997: 329)

Considering Hofstede's model, we chose types of translated texts which "told" something relevant in terms of the two translation strategies under discussion.

A working model

The working model I devised for my students involved: 1) comparisons between TT and ST units; 2) identification and discussion of the shifts from the ST units; 3) giving explanations and making generalizations about the degree of non-equivalence between TT and ST. The translated texts were also rated in terms of the degree of acceptability, i.e. acceptability of the *translation as a TL text*, or as a *translation in the TL*. The student- translators were let to know that the samples were translations.

Having been given the specific guidance, the subjects could conduct the analysis of specific points in both texts. A discussion followed about the ways in which some linguistic units were rendered in the TTs.

(a) Students' task

Students were supposed to answer some questions such as:

1 What are the situations where the TT deviates from the ST?
2 Are there additions and deletions in the TT?

3 How frequent are: a) the additions, and b) the deletions?
4 Are the additions and the deletions: a) haphazard, or b) necessary due to the differences between the two languages? Give reasons for your interpretations.
5 Which of the four types of explicitation strategies may be used in each text? Explain your point of view.
6 Are the additions and the deletions effective in conveying the message of the ST? To what extent?
7 Which do you prefer: a) a ST-oriented method of evaluation? , or b) a TT-oriented analysis? Give your reasons for that.
8 Do you consider a translator's note necessary to mention the deliberate deviations from the ST?

(b) Findings

There were 108 students of all. 72.4 % of them pointed out shifts from the ST to the TT, but only 59.8% could give satisfactory answers as regards the reasons for each of the translation strategies. However, the experiment proved to be quite challenging. It was worthwhile. It helped me convince the students that such activities viewed both as research and as translation practice varied according to the specialized field the text was taken from.

One of the most important conclusions was that the theoretical aspects of the working model must be explained in advance, which usually helps students understand the problems much better, ask theoretical questions and put such knowledge in practice.

All this will lead to increasing the importance of the translation courses at university level during the three years of study before taking the BA degree. I would even consider that greater attention needs to be paid to translation practice during high school years as well.

The students got aware of the need to read the preface/translator's note referring to the deliberate shifts from the ST to TT, where there was no such note.

Moreover, they realized they had to be more careful about the *translational norms*[2] when the ST-TT comparisons showed such shifts.

Last but not least, the students appreciated the translator's choice of an *acceptable* instead of an adequate translation, especially when the aims set

---

[2] There were cultural, historical, political, ideological, literary or social reasons for the translator to have translated the way (s)he did; these make up the translational norms.

out in the preface were achieved without subjecting the translation to any rigid criteria necessary in attaining adequacy[3].

Devising questionnaires, comparative analyses and cloze tests

A very useful way of studying translation problems focussing on the translated text, particularly on the addressees' responses to it (by empirical methods) is that of devising a questionnaire and having groups of subjects answer the questions, then analyze their reactions. I devised the following questionnaire:

1. Is the application of explicitation strategy (ES) by language learners different from its application by professional translators?
2. Are there differences in the application of the ES in oral vs. written translation? If there are any, what do they consist in?
3. Are there differences in the application of the ES in translating from L1 to L2 and from L2 to L1?
4. Are there differences in the application of the ES in translating literary vs. specialized texts?

Due to the relationship between explicitness and readability, the *explicitation hypothesis* (EH) may be tested by means of *cloze method* which can modify EH by exploring the circumstances under which it is prevailing.

As the EH claims,

> "it might be the case that [a rise in the target text's level of explicitness] is a universal strategy inherent in the process of language mediation, as practised by language learners, non-professional translators and professional translators alike".
>
> (Blum-Kulka, 1986: 21)

The subjects, who were student-translators, had to establish translation relationships on the highest possible level. Their spontaneous *reactions* were decisive in measuring the readability of the TT and in establishing the degree of its acceptability on the part of the target readers (TRs), considering the fact that the translator *constructs* the TT. (Nida and Taber, 1969; Snell-Hornby, 1983; Toury, 1991, 1995).

Thus, one way of dealing with explicitation and deletion strategies may be to devise *comparative analyses* of the readability of the TT vs. the ST.

---

[3] Readers interested in further details are referred to E. Croitoru (2006).

Such comparisons yield interesting and useful insights into similarities and dissimilarities between the two texts in terms of grammatical structures, lexical units, discourse and stylistic features. Together with other research methods, *cloze tests* offer even greater insights into the ways addressees *process* and realize the shifts or deviations from ST to TT.

The subjects were divided into three groups: 1) graduates of English (either teachers of English in high schools or part-time translators), 2) graduates of engineering, and 3) professional (experienced) translators.

During the second stage of our experiment, the subjects were divided into three groups based on the type of BA degree: 1) teachers of English and part-time translators with a philology BA degree, 2) professional translators with a BA degree and 3) professional translators with an engineering BA degree.

Full awareness of the translation problems and strategies under discussion was the basic requirement.

The rate of reliability of the subjects was not the same considering their BA degree in philology, and engineering, respectively.

The subjects who were professional translators with an engineering BA degree "felt" and understood the specialized text better and had intuitive knowledge of the explicitation and deletion strategies used in the TT, making an intuitive assessment of the TT, whereas the two groups who had basic knowledge of translation theory and practice could give substantial explanations referring to the grammatical, structural and lexical differences between the two texts in terms of the translation strategies under discussion.

Conclusions

We consider that more instructive conclusions could be drawn by working with mixed groups, i.e. groups made up of graduates with a philology BA degree and graduates with an engineering BA degree, for texts in their field of expertise. The latter may be considered "better" representatives of the ordinary reader.[4]

The prevailing conclusion was that the responses were different with the subjects who had previous knowledge of translation studies, as compared to the subjects who had no such training.

A very important conclusion is also that the shifts from ST to TT as well as the deviations from the TL cultural norms "are not judged as

---

[4] cf. Toury's (1991: 57) comment on Tirkkonen Condit's (1986:60) experiment.

intentional, and therefore are not assigned any hidden meaning". (Toury, 1991: 56)

As Toury argues,

> "it is precisely deviations which have become *habitually associated with translation* on the basis of previous encounters with translated texts which trigger that '*adjustment mechanism*'."
>
> (Toury, 1995: 57, italics in the original)

References

Blum-Kulka, S. (1986) *Shifts of cohesion and coherence in translation*. in House, J. and Blum-Kulka, S. (eds.) (1986) *Intercultural Communication: Discourse and cognition in translation and second language acquisition studies*. Tübingen: Narr.

Croitoru, E. (2006) *Explicitation in translation*. in *The Fellowship of Cultural Rings*. Proceedings of the International Conference Galati, October 20-21, 2005, pp. 146-154, Bucureşti: Editura Didactică şi Pedagogică R.A.

Deyes, A. (1984) "Towards an authentic discourse cloze" in *Applied Linguistics*, vol. 5, No. 2, pp. 128-137.

Fernando, C. (1996) *Idioms and Idiomacity*. Oxford: OUP.

Hofstede, G. (1991) *Cultures and Organizations: Software of the Mind*. London: McGraw Hill.

Katan, D. (2004) *Translating Cultures*. Manchester, UK and Northampton MA: St Jerome Publishing.

Klaudy, K. (1996) Back Translation as a Tool for Detecting Explicitation Strategies in Translation. in Klaudy, K., Lambert, J. and Sohar, A. (eds.), *Translation Studies in Hungary*, pp. 99-114, Budapest: Scolastica.

Nida, E. and Taber, C. R. (1969) *The theory and practice of translation*. Leiden: E.J. Brill.

Popovič, A. (1970) The concept "Shift of Expression" in Translation Analysis. in Holmes, J. (ed.) and de Haan, F. and Popovič, A. (associate eds.). *The Nature of Translation*. Mouton. The Hague, Paris: Publishing House of Slovak Academy of Sciences, Bratislava.

Schäffner, C. (1997) Translation as intercultural communication – Contact and conflict, pp. 325-337 in Snell-Hornby, M., Jettmarová, Z. and Kaindl, K. (eds.) (1997) *Translation as Intercultural communication*. Amsterdam/Philadelphia: John Benjamins Publishing Company.

—. (1998) Parallel Texts in Translation. in Bowker, L. , Cronin, M. , Kenny, D. and Person, J. (eds.) *Unity in Diversity? Current Trends in Translation Studies,* pp. 83-90, UK: St Jerome Publishing.

Sinclair, J. (2004) *Trust the Text.* London: Routledge.

Snell-Hornby, M. (1983) *Metaphorical thought and translation: Taking a stand on P. Newmark.* Trier: L.A.U.T [Series A, Paper No. 108]

Tirkkonen-Condit, S. (1989) Professional vs. non-professional translation: A think-aloud protocol study. in Sequinot, C. (ed.) *The translation process.* York University.

Toury, G. (1980) Communication in translated texts: A semiotic approach. in Wills, W. (ed.) *Semiotik und Űbersetzen,* pp. 99-109, Tübingen: Narr.

—. (1991) What are the descriptive studies into translation likely to yield apart from isolated descriptions. in van Leuven-Zwart, K. and Naaijkens, T. (eds.) *Translation Studies: The State of the Art. Proceedings of the First James S. Holmes Symposium on Translation studies.* Amsterdam/ Atlanta. Ga: Rodopi, pp.179-192.

—. (1995) *Descriptive Translation Studies and Beyond.* Amsterdam/ Philadelphia: John Benjamins.

Weizman, E. and Blum-Kulka, Sh. (1987) *Identifying and interpreting translated texts: On the role of pragmatic adjustment.* in Toury, G. (ed.) *Translation across Cultures* , pp. 61-73, New Delhi: Bahri Publications

Corpus

Antell, G. (1985) *Economics: Institutions and Analysis*, New York: Amsco School Publications in Croitoru, E. (coord.) (2004).

Croitoru, E. (coord.) (2004) *English through Translations*. Galati: Editura Fundatiei Universitare "Dunarea de Jos"

—. (1991) *English for students in machine building technology.* University of Galati, Romania.

Dima, G. (2004) *Answer key* in Croitoru, E. (coord.).

Popescu, F. (2004) *An English-Romanian Selective Vocabulary*, in Croitoru, E. (coord.) (2004).

Leonte, M. (2002) *Vinul – aliment, tonic si medicament* translated by Croitoru, E. and Popescu, F. (2004), Galati: Pax Aura Mundi.

APPENDIX ONE

Text samples translated from English for Technology (naval architecture and machine building technology)

ST1: As no space can be **wasted** and weight must be kept as **low** as possible, the **structural design** has developed in such a way that most of the **parts** serve at least two purposes, **and** sometimes more.	TT1: Deoarece nici un spaţiu nu trebuie **lăsat nefolosit**, iar greutatea trebuie păstrată pe cât posibil la **valoarea minimă**, **proiectul structurii navei** a fost conceput astfel încât majoritatea **partilor componente** să aibă cel puţin două întrebuinţări, uneori chiar mai multe.
ST2: [...] the **sides** [of the ship] are composed of the **shell plating** and the decks. [...] To appreciate the ship as a whole, it is well to understand **the function** of each of the **parts**.	TT2: [...] **învelişul metalic al corpului navei** si puntile constituie **partile exterioare ale navei**.[...] Pentru a privi nava ca pe un întreg, este necesară înţelegerea **modului in care funcţionează** fiecare dintre **partile componente**.
ST3: [...] These are formed by a second **complete** layer of watertight plating, located a few feet above the outer bottom and extending **from bilge to bilge**. Any **grounding** or similar damage which **pierces** the outer bottom plating will flood one or more of these tanks [...].	TT3: [...] Acestea sunt formate de un al doilea strat de bordaj etanş situat la câteva picioare deasupra carenei şi care se întinde **de la o gurnă la alta**. Orice **coliziune cu fundul apei** sau cu un obstacol asemănător care **ar duce la perforarea** bordajului exterior al carenei ar produce inundarea a unuia sau mai multora dintre aceste tancuri [...]
ST4: In order to provide sufficient **headroom** for the propelling machinery, it is **usually** necessary to omit one or more of the decks in this region.	TT4: Pentru a oferi destul **spaţiu pe verticală** pentru instalaţia de propulsie, este necesară omiterea uneia sau mai multor punţi în această zonă. Translated by Croitoru, E. and Velica, M. in Croitoru, E. (coord), 2004
ST5: Almost every type of machine capable of rotating a tool or a workpiece has been used for drilling. When only a few parts are involved, when accuracy **is not critical**, or when **workpieces** are too large to be transported, hand drills are often used. Engine lathes also are often used for drilling, particularly of **large or long**	TT5: Aproape orice tip de maşină care poate să rotească o unealtă sau o piesă, **în procesul de prelucrare**, este întrebuinţată **în procesul de găurire**. Când în procesul de găurire este nevoie numai de câteva piese, când acurateţea **nu constituie o cerinţă importantă** sau când **piesele ce trebuie prelucrate** sunt prea mari pentru a fi transportate, se

holes.	folosesc aparatele manuale de găurit. De asemenea, strungurile cu motor sunt folosite deseori pentru găurire, mai ales **în cazul** găurilor **cu diametru mare sau al celor adânci**.
ST6: […] the process is usually employed only for **high** production. Some part configurations, however, are **practical** to produce only by broaching; for parts of this type, the broaching of **low production quantities** may be warranted. Croitoru, E., 1991: 78-79	TT6: […] procedeul este de obicei utilizat în producția **pe scară largă**. Totuşi, anumite configurații ale piesei pot fi produse numai prin broşare; pentru acest gen de piese, broşarea unor **cantități mici de piese** poate fi garantată. Translated by Dima, G. in Croitoru, E., 2004
ST7: Although **the greatest use of** hand-feed drill presses is for drilling only a few pieces at a time, they are often preferred regardless **of the size** of the production lot.	TT7: Deşi masinile de găurit cu alimentare manuală sunt **cel mai frecvent folosite** pentru găurirea în acelaşi timp doar a câtorva piese, ele sunt deseori preferate indiferent de lotul de producție.
ST8:O pârghie principală o reprezintă reglementarea corectă a falimentului, cu un rol important în curățirea economiei de factorii de influență neeconomici şi neproductivi, **respectiv productivitatea muncii scăzută**, lipsa piețelor de desfacere, producția pe stoc, management slab, **slaba tehnologizare** etc. Cone, S., 1996: 6	TT8: One of these main tools is the correct settling of bankruptcy, which plays an important role in excluding the non-economic and non-productive influential factors from economy. **Such factors may be a low coefficient of the productive capacity**, the lack of dispatch markets, surplus production, inefficient management, a **low level of technology development**, etc. Translated by Dima, G. in Croitoru, E., 2004
ST9: **Băut cu moderație**, vinul întăreşte vederea şi nervii, dar în cantitate prea mare, **acestea slăbesc**. ST10: Vinul face să apară, **treptat**, acel duh al ospeției şi **acel fir invizibil care leagă indivizii şi societățile, unindu-le în jurul unor sentimente, idei şi /sau interese comune**; Leonte, M., 2002	TT9: **In reasonable quantities**, it reinforces sight and nerves, but in large quantities, **it makes them grow weaker**. TT10: Wine also makes hospitality feelings, **ideas and/or mutual interest occur**; Translated by Croitoru, E. and Popescu, F., 2002

APPENDIX TWO

Text samples translated from English for Economics

ST1: New methods of production and the development of **a fine transportation system made it profitable** for industry to grow in size and expand its markets.	TT1: Noi metode de producţie şi dezvoltarea unui **sistem de transport bine pus la punct** au permis industriei să se dezvolte şi să-şi extindă pieţele **într-un mod profitabil**.
ST2: As the **scale of production** grew, so did the cost of **doing business**. In many **industries**, firms that could no longer afford to expand lost **their ability to compete** and were forced to bankruptcy. [...] Sometimes the severe competition led to *price wars*, in which firms **took turns cutting** pieces in order to **undersell** their competitors.	TT2: Pe măsură ce creştea **producţia**, au crescut şi costurile **afacerii**. În multe **ramuri industriale**, firme care nu şi-au permis să se extindă şi-au pierdut **competitivitatea** şi au fost împinse la faliment. […] Uneori competiţia acerbă a dus la un război al preţurilor, în care **firmele au redus alternativ** preţurile pentru **a vinde mai ieftin decât** concurenţa.
ST3: […] some business owners thought it better **to cooperate with one another** than to compete. […] The most **notable of these strategies**, known as ***business combinations***, are described below. A number of **industries** established pools in the 1870s and 1880s, but the railroads **made the greatest use of them**.	TT3: […] unii proprietari de firme au considerat că este mai bine **să coopereze** decât să concureze. […] Cele mai **demne de menţionat dintre acestea**, cunoscute sub numele de ***asocieri în interes de afaceri***, sunt descrise mai jos. O serie de **ramuri ale industriei** şi-au format monopoluri în anii 1870-1880, dar căile ferate **au profitat cel mai mult de pe urma acestora**.
ST4: Since they [pools] were informal **agreements, they** could not be enforced. When one or more of the member firms broke the rules by **underselling** the pool or invading the territory **of the other members**, the pool ceased to exist.	TT4: Întrucât erau neoficiale, **aceste acorduri** nu puteau fi impuse. Când una sau mai multe dintre firmele membre încălcau regulile **vânzând sub preţul stabilit** de monopol sau invadând teritoriul **celorlalte**, monopolul înceta să mai existe.
ST5: The former **stockholders** received their share of the profits in the form of dividends on the trust certificates they held.	TT5: Foştii **deţinători ai pachetelor de acţiuni de control îşi** primeau partea **lor** de profit sub formă de dividende, pe baza certificatelor de depozit pe care le deţineau.
ST6: By limiting production to an agreed level, the cartel seeks to gain the same kind of control **over prices** as a monopoly. This kind of collusion is	TT6: Prin limitarea producţiei la un nivel stabilit, cartelul caută să deţină, **asemenea monopolului**, acelaşi tip de control. Acest tip de asociere este

generally illegal in the United States, but it is legal in most other countries.	considerat ilegal în Statele Unite, dar este legal în majoritatea celorlalte țări.
ST7: **Mergers** have been the most common form of **business combination** in recent years. Antell, G., 1985 in Croitoru, E. (coord.), 2004	TT7: **Companiile create prin fuzionare** au fost cea mai răspândită formă de **asociere in interes de afaceri** in ultimii ani. Translated by: Raluca, A., Velică, M. and Velică, C., in Croitoru, E. (coord.), 2004

APPENDIX THREE

From explicit to highly explicit TL "equivalents" of words, collocations and pre-fabricated/ready-made language used to render higher precision to the TL structures

adapter: 1. piesă de ghidare/cuplare. 2. manşon de reducţie pentru adaptarea broşei la dimensiunile capului de fixare.
air brake: frână pe bază de/acţionată cu aer comprimat.
adjustable ram/block: placă de strângere pentru fixarea mecanismului de deplasare a berbecului (la şeping).
align reaming: alezare concomitentă a găurilor co-axiate la piese de asamblat/care urmează să fie asamblate.
aligning reamer: alezor lung pentru prelucrarea concomitentă a două găuri coaxiale.
allowable maximum pull: efort/forţă de tracţiune maximă admisă la broşare.
argon arc welding with consumable electrode: sudare cu arc electric cu electrod fusibil în mediu de argon.
argon arc welding with non-consumable electrode: sudare cu arc electric cu electrod de wolfram în mediu de argon.

COMPUTER SCIENCE NEOLOGISMS AND THEIR TRANSLATION

IVANKA FERČEC

Introduction

Even before the advent of the Internet, which opened up new horizons and enabled virtual contact of (almost) all world languages, the English language strengthened its position as the largest of the modern languages and the language of world communication (the so-called *lingua franca*). The Internet as well as the birth and rapid development of new technologies, primarily in English-speaking countries, resulted in frequent linguistic changes as new things, concepts and ideas emerging day by day need to be termed appropriately. The problem of gaps in the vocabulary of any language can be solved by using one of the following three procedures; i.e. a new word is coined by using the existing elements in the language in question, a word is borrowed from a foreign language (this represents the simplest and most frequently used procedure of linguistic borrowing), and either the original meaning of the existing word in the language in question is changed or a new, additional meaning is added to the old one (Filipović, 1990).

This paper discusses computer science related new words and illustrates a strong influence of English as a source language on Croatian as a receiving language exemplifying the fact that the lack of standardised terminology enhancing that constantly changing field causes a discrepancy between translations offered by bilingual dictionaries and expressions used in actual practice.

Neologisms and computer science

Every period of time brings some novelties, but due to rapid development of all branches of science and especially technology, it is linguistically almost impossible to respond well to so many changes. The birth and achievements of new technologies that are constantly being updated have a significant influence on every language, which is in turn subject to changes and tries to find most suitable ways how to integrate new concepts invented in English into the existing native communication system. Croatian newspapers and magazines are full of (head)lines like *Gdje možete pronaći uskrsni wallpaper te screensaver za vaše računalo? (Where can you find Easter wallpaper and screensaver for your computer?)*, *Dodatni linkovi na uskrsne web stranice (Additional links to Easter web sites)*, or *Blogeri, nemajte straha (Bloggers, don't be afraid)*. Words like *linkovi* or *blogeri* are called neologisms. These specific ones are also known as *Internet-*, *computer-* or *technology-related neologisms*, *science and technology neologisms* or *neologisms of the www*, indicating that computer science is just one of the fields in which neologisms constantly emerge.

Sometimes the inventors of new concepts coin new words, but what happens more often is that the usage and meaning of already existing lexical items, either single words or multiple forms, are shifted, changed or extended (*new-born* vs. *recycled* word forms, cf. Volz, 1995). Or according to Sager (1990:80), "Regarding their form, neologisms essentially take two, either they are totally new creations or they are borrowed from other languages". Appearing typically in cultures and fields subject to fast and frequent changes and a rapid propagation of information, neologisms[1] (from Greek, neos = new and logos = word) are characteristic of all modern languages.

(a) Neologisms and word formation

Computer science neologisms undergo more or less the same linguistic formations as non-technology related neologisms. According to Tattersall (2003), in English derivation, compounds and acronyms represent most frequently used tools for the creation of technology-related neologisms. However, there are also some other common procedures referring to the formation of new words.

Derivation or affixation is the addition of a prefix or a suffix to an existing word. Most productive prefixes in this particular context are *cyber-* (e.g. *cyberspace*[2], *cybercafé*) and *e-* (as in *e-business* or e-*ticket*),

---

[1] Bearing in mind that every word used to be a neologism when it first came into existence, the word *neologism* was a neologism itself for some time after its coinage (around 1800).

[2] *Cyber* can function as the first element of some compounds but also as an independent word in a compound (e.g. *cyberspace, cyber economy*).

with its alternative forms *e*, *E*- and *E*[3], and thus the following variants co-exist as to electronic mail: *e-mail*, *email*, *E-mail* and *Email*, the first one being most frequently used. Neologisms can also exist as compounds formed by combining two or more existing words (e.g. *online*, *newsgroup*, *webmaster*). Clipping refers to abbreviating or cutting off words at the beginning (e.g. *phone*), at the end (as in *net*) or at both ends of a word (e.g. *flu*). New words are also formed by blending or joining part of one word to part of another, which results in the so-called Portmanteau words (e.g. *netizen* = *Internet* + *citizen*, *emoticon* = *emotion* + *icon*), or by changing the grammatical class of the word in question, i.e. conversion (e.g. a verb like *to back up* → a noun *a back up*). In the field of science and technology terms or expressions are frequently shortened by means of acronyms. As to their pronunciation, acronyms can be pronounced either as sequences of letters (e.g. *HTML*, *DVD*) or as single words (e.g. *WYSIWYG*, *BASIC*). Extension of the semantic field, i.e. addition of a new meaning to already existing words, has resulted in semantic neologisms (e.g. *chat*, *bug*).

Some neologisms have emerged as a result of playing with words. In analogy to the term *couch potato* denoting TV-addicts, those (usually young) people who spend an excessive amount of time at their computers are turning into *mouse potatoes*. *Macintrash*, an offending notion used in conversation, refers to a Macintosh PC. *Nybble* (the original spelling) or *nibble*, half a byte or four bits, is said to have been coined on the basis of a pun on the English word bite (i.e. byte)[4].

(b) Computer science neologisms and their translation into Croatian

Due to constant and fast improvement of ICT, introduction of related concepts and terminology into other receiving languages has always been a must. Since most of those new concepts come from English-speaking countries, predominantly the USA, Croatian usually borrows the original English terms/words, i.e. anglicisms[5]. A strong influence of English is present in all languages, not only “small” languages like Croatian, but also some other so-called world languages like French or German. As a result,

---

[3] A feasible explanation for this phenomenon might be the following. At first e- was just an abbreviation standing for *electronic*. Later on, as e- became very popular, many users were uncertain whether it was an abbreviation or a prefix, whether to write it with or without a hyphen.

[4] Stern gives an interesting overview of etymology of some neologisms of the World Wide Web including an extensive list of examples.

[5] On anglicisms in the Croatian language see Filipović, 1990.

blends like Denglish (Deutsch, i.e. German + English) or Hrenglish (hrvatski, i.e. Croatian + English) came into being pointing out a possible overuse of English words in respective languages.

The Croatian language has always been open to accepting foreign words, adapting them at different levels and integrating them into its phonological and morphological system. Due to various historical, political, economic, social and cultural conditions, those were mostly borrowings of German and Italian origin. Since lately the omnipresent English language has become dominant in all fields of science and technology, the number of words used in Croatian but originating from English has increased rapidly. Although Croatia does not record a strong puristic tradition aimed at preventing integration of new words of foreign origin into the Croatian language, such words were not desirable at the beginning of 90-ies. According to Muhvić-Dimanovski,

> "linguistic purism which often comes as a reaction to a (too) large inflow of foreign words also generates neologisms; these neologisms, however, are built from native elements but are novelties in the language as well."
> (Muhvić-Dimanovski, 1998: 499)

Although strenuous efforts were undertaken at that time to replace undesirable foreign words in Croatian and provide Croatian variants instead[6], this was only a trend which did not last for a longer period of time, since Croatian variants for numerous foreign computer-related words coming predominantly from English simply did not seem to be natural and most of them sounded at least strange if not funny. A typical example is the term *hardware* for which *očvrsje* was coined in Croatian (čvrst = hard), but gained no widespread acceptance[7]. Since the word *očvrsje* has never been really adopted, it is questionable how well it will be understood now by Croatian-speaking persons, especially the ones not involved in this field.

Every neologism undergoes three fundamental evolutionary stages:

1 proposed by an individual or being used by a very small group of people;
2 reaches a significant audience, but no wider acceptance;
3 gains recognition and widespread acceptance.

---

[6] As to this matter, Croatian is not an exception. More details on French efforts against anglicisms can be found in Tattersall, 2003.

[7] According to Stojaković (2004:85), linguistic borrowings from English into Croatian, especially in a broad field of computer science, often co-exist in several forms: *hardware* vs. *hardver* vs. *sklopovlje*. In addition, terms like *sklopovlje* and *fizičke komponente računala* are also used.

Thus, the result is clear: If a neologism is not accepted first by the public and then by language prescriptivists who are supposed to recognise it as such and incorporate it into dictionaries, it disappears from common usage. This is what happened to *očvrsje*, *znakovnik* (i.e. a code), *sklopnjak* (i.e. a chip), *ulazište* (i.e. a port) and some other Croatian neologisms of the 1990s.

Unlike the 1990s, the Croatian language is quite open to adoption of foreign words, which are "imported" in line with new concepts denoting them. Since computer science terminology has not been standardised yet, in the same newspaper or magazine a reader might find several expressions used for one particular word in English; e.g. *prijenosnik* and *prijenosno računalo* (i.e. a laptop) or *kompjuter*, *kompjutor* and *računalo* (i.e. a computer), proving that usage of such computer-related words is mostly inconsistent and depends solely on the author of the corresponding article. Due to a constant change and rapid development in the field in question, neither monolingual nor bilingual (paper-printed) dictionaries can timely and adequately update their entries. Therefore, it might be understandable but maybe not acceptable why so many different words are used in Croatian for one English word.

Deliberately or not, young people all over the world are under constant influence of the English language, while listening to the music, watching films, surfing the Internet, playing games. This might be the reason why most of them use English words/variants of any type. In Croatian they either use a phonological form of a neologism based on the pronunciation of the model (e.g. *čet* from chat) with typical Croatian endings (e.g. the verb *četati* from *to chat*, or the noun *četanje* from *chatting*)[8] or even retain the original English orthography (e.g. *hardware*), whereas only a few give Croatian translations (e.g. *hardware* is translated as *sklopovlje*, *fizičke komponente* and *dijelovi računala*). Generally speaking, some computer-related neologisms can be perfectly translated into Croatian, like *download* = *učitati*, *e-mail* = *elektronička pošta*, *burner* = *pržilica*, some remain the same as in the original language, e.g. *blog*, *on-line/online*[9], whereas some

---

[8] Forčec, I. (2006). A questionnaire was conducted with 60 students of the University of Osijek. They were given 30 computer science related neologisms and were asked to provide answers to three questions (1. If the following expressions are familiar to you, please explain their meaning.; 2. How would you translate the given expressions into Croatian?; 3. Which form of the given expressions do you use most frequently?).

[9] It must be pointed out that *online* is always both written and pronounced in Croatian the same as in English.

are borrowed, only phonologically adapted, and then used as such, e.g. *hacker* = *haker*, *scanner* = *skener*, *domain* = *domena*.

Although the meaning of certain neologisms is entirely transparent, it is usually very difficult even to propose an acceptable translation equivalent. For example, how can we translate into Croatian the compound *a technology butler*, "a hotel staff member who performs computer-related tasks and helps guests with software and hardware problems"? How is this new job translated into other languages? Or the aforementioned *mouse potato*? Most computer-literate people know what *egosurfing* denotes, but in Croatian there is no suitable translation of that term. Is the only acceptable solution to give its definition or description in the text that is being translated? What if a couple of or ten other similar terms are given in the same text? These three neologisms exemplify that translation is in general a challenging and demanding task, which requires a good grasp of overall and specific knowledge and great efforts.

Conclusion

Computer science related neologisms represent nowadays a constantly growing field within vocabulary of every language. Due to the fact that technology is mostly developed in English-speaking countries like the USA, English has become the source language from which recipient languages borrow neologisms, which after some time and suitable modifications either become parts of the language or fall into disuse. Problems with translating such neologisms into Croatian are twofold: lack of standard terminology and inconsistent usage.

In the process of finding an appropriate term for a new concept language experts and non-experts might agree or disagree to a certain degree, accept a new word quickly, object to it, delay its acceptance or refuse its recognition causing it to die out. Whether officially recognised as neologisms or not, they are omnipresent and require translation into languages other than English. However, for the purpose of communication, there is no need for translation, because English is the means of global communication. And for the purpose of understanding, there is no time for translation, because keeping up with technological development in terms of new words is almost impossible.

References

Ferčec, I. (2006) *Neologizmi u računalnim znanostima.* In: Granić, J (Ed.). *Jezik i mediji.* Zagreb – Split: HDPL, 223-229.

Filipović, R. (1990) *Anglicizmi u hrvatskom ili srpskom jeziku: porijeklo razvoj – značenje.* JAZU – Školska knjiga, Zagreb.

Muhvić-Dimanovski, V. (1998) *Neologizmi na razmeđi jezične otvorenosti i jezičnog purizma. Filologija* 30/31, 495-499.

Sager, J.C. (1990) *A Practical Course in Terminology Processing.* John Benjamins Publishing Company, Amsterdam/Philadelphia.

Stern, D. *Cyberlanguage; Neologisms of the World Wide Web.* Available at http://www.digicult.net/mt/neologisms.htm

Stojaković, B. (2004) *Hrvatsko računalno nazivlje u društvenoj interakciji. Strani jezici* 33, 1-2, 83-92.

Tattersall, A. (2003) *The Internet and the French Language.* Centre for Language in Education: Occasional Paper No. 65, University of Southampton.

Volz, N. (1995) *CORDON – A Joint Venture Case Study.* In: *Language Resources for Language Technology: Proceedings of the TELRI,* Tihany, 160-168.

DEVELOPING LEXICAL AND SOCIOLINGUISTIC COMPETENCE IN BUSINESS ENGLISH, GERMAN AND POLISH

MONIKA KOWALONEK

Introduction

The Common European Framework divides learners into three broad divisions (Basic User A, Independent User B and Proficient User C) which can be divided into six Levels: Breakthrough A1, Waystage A2, Threshold B1, Vantage B2, Effective Operational Proficiency C1 and Mastery C2.[1]

The aim of this paper is to discuss the role of communicative language competence in teaching Business English, German and Polish at the Levels B2, C1 and C2. In the beginning there will be made an attempt to explain the term "Language for Specific Purposes". The main part will be devoted to surveying both lexical and sociolinguistic competence as components of communicative language competence. Since language is a sociocultural phenomenon the special emphasis will be put on teaching and learning economic lexis and the culture background of the community in which a language is spoken.

Language for Specific Purposes

Although there have been many attempts to point out and characterise Language for Specific Purposes (LSP), it is not easy to give its explicit definition. While trying to skim the opinions presented by many scientists, one could easily discover that the most popular description – a starting point – was made by Hoffmann (1985: 53) who considers LSP as a combination of particular lexical and syntactical elements of Language for General Purposes (LGP). A conclusion can be drawn that these elements of LGP operate in a bit different way in the case of LSP, in other

[1] Common European Framework of Reference for Languages: Learning, teaching, assessment (2001). Cambridge, p. 23.

words they differ in choice and frequency of some areas of grammar and lexis. For example in Business English the use of present perfect progressive is likely to be often used. As far as vocabulary is considered, numbers or currencies seem to be of importance.

In addition, especially relevant to the teaching process are the following business language features:

- typical collocations: złożyć ofertę/to make an offer/ ein Angebot machen;
- a lot of metaphors: ceny idą w górę/prices go up/Preise gehen rauf;
- internationalisms: leasing/a leasing/das Leasing;
- typical texts: e.g. list handlowy/a business letter/der Geschäftsbrief.

Lexical competence

Communicative language competence consists of three main components: linguistic, sociolinguistic and pragmatic.

Lexical competence can be defined as the ability to use and the knowledge of the vocabulary of a language. Being an essential joint factor of communicative competence, it should be accurately taught throughout the whole language acquisition process.

Lexical elements include:

- sentential formulae, including direct exponents of language functions such as greetings, e.g. Miło mi Państwa poznać/Nice to meet you/Nett, Sie kennen zu lernen
- phrasal idioms, metaphors: ceny idą w górę/prices go up/Preise gehen rauf
- fixed frames, learnt and used as unanalysed wholes, into which phrases or words are inserted to form meaningful sentences, e.g.: Zwracam się z uprzejmą prośbą o/ I am writing to request/Hiermit erbitte ich von Ihnen
- other fixed phrases, such as, e.g. : w odpowiedzi na/in response to/als Antwort auf
- fixed collocations: wygłosić przemówienie/to make a speech/eine Rede halten
- single word forms, e.g. rynek/a market/der Markt. This particular word can have a few meanings, e.g. a market- can be understood both as a place at which people gather in order to sell and buy things and as the business or trade in a particular product.

As far as the lexis is concerned, an independent user (B2) should have a good range of vocabulary to be able understand the main ideas of complex texts on both concrete and abstract topics, including technical discussions in his/her field of specialisation. Proficient users (C1, C2) should have a very good command of a broad vocabulary repertoire including colloquialisms and idiomatic expressions. Moreover, he or she should use language effectively for professional purposes and express him/herself precisely and fluently, differentiating finer shades of meaning.

As the above description shows, students need to meet high requirements concerning lexis, for this reason it is of great importance to introduce it in an interesting way.

Teaching idioms, colloquialisms and metaphors makes the lesson attractive and may encourage learners to expand their vocabulary storage. Business language very good reflects the theory of Lakoff and Johnson[2] that "our ordinary conceptual system in terms of which we both think and act, is fundamentally metaphorical in nature" (1988: 25).[3]

As a consequence, in business language there are many so-called orientational metaphors which have to do with spartial orientation (up-down or in-out). Furthermore, many ontological metaphors (those in which an abstraction can be represented as something concrete such as an object or person) are present The increasing availability of corpora[4] made it possible to analyse metaphors in Business Polish and to introduce them then in the classroom. An important consideration for planning lexis work is the distinction between visual, auditory and kinesthetic learners. There are many ways to convey the meaning of different lexical items and it is crucial to find their best presentation technique. In view of the fact that the vast majority of the learners in the target group had a visual memory, following metaphors were presented visually to meet students' needs.

- ceny idą w górę/ Preise gehen rauf/ prices go up
- w biznes można wejść/ man kann in ein Geschäft einsteigen/ you can go into business
- biznes rośnie, rozwija się/ das Geschäft wächst, entwickelt sich, boomt/ business grows, develops, booms
- biznes można kręcić,rozkręcić/ man kann das Geschäft beleben/ you can turn a business around/round
- biznes można prowadzić/ man kann das Geschäft führen/ you can operate a business

---

[2] Lakoff, G., Johnson, M. (1988) Metafory w naszym życiu (translated by Krzeszowski, T.P.). Warszawa: Państwowy Instytut Wydawniczy.

[3] translated from Polish by the author of this article

[4] www.korpus.pwn.pl (15.05.06)

– polski biznes wychodzi z epoki siermiężnej (comes from "siermięga" in English: "a smock-frock", in German "der Bauernkittel")

Sociolinguistic competence

LSP teaching and learning means not only focusing on linguistic elements, but also on skills required to deal with the social dimension of language use, which is of great importance especially in the business communication between representatives of different cultures. To meet the requirements of the sociolinguistic appropriateness a language learner at Level B2 should be able to sustain an interaction with native speakers and do it in a clear, confident and polite way in a formal or informal register. Furthermore, the expressions he or she uses should be appropriate to the person and situation concerned. A proficiency user's knowledge of idiomatic expressions and colloquialisms at Level C1 should be extensive and the way of expressing him/herself flexible and effective for professional purposes, including joking and allusive usage. A proficiency user at Level C2 is seen as a mediator between speakers of the target language and his or her mother tongue who takes account of both sociolinguistic and sociocultural differences. His or her command of idiomatic expressions and colloquialisms is excellent.

Therefore, developing sociolinguistic competence seems to be a crucial element in foreign language teaching. This competence consists of following components:

(a) linguistic markers of social relations

It is significant to stress that these are different in various languages and cultures. The examples for use and choice of greetings or address forms are not universally applicable. By way of illustration, if we write a formal business letter in English to someone holding a PhD or other doctorate and whose name we know, we use the form: Dear Dr Smith, in German: Sehr geehrter Herr Doktor Schmidt, whereas in Polish we say: Szanowny Panie Doktorze (no surname). This example demonstrates many intercultural differences and these problems should not be either overlooked or neglected by a foreign language teacher.

(b) politeness conventions

The conventions to show "positive" or "negative" politeness are divergent in various languages and cultures and may lead to misunderstanding. In the process of teaching Business Polish, English or German these differences are not big, because these are all European languages.

(c) expressions of folk wisdom

These are, in other words, fixed formulae, which make a significant contribution to a popular culture as: proverbs, idioms, expressions of attitudes. It should be highlighted that these formulae may not have equivalence in other languages. For instance there are some phraseologisms connected with business in Polish: neapolitańskie sumy, wyjść jak Zabłocki na mydle, bajońskie sumy, narobić bigosu. It is almost impossible to translate these expressions into English or German, without knowing their cultural origin. As an example an expression: "wyjść jak Zabłocki na mydle" can be translated into English as: "to lose a lot of money"; into German: "bei etwas schlecht wegkommen". It is essential to know that Franciszek Zabłocki was a Polish nobleman who carried on trade and did it honestly. Once he decided to avoid paying tax and hid soap he wanted to transport by ship below decks. To his surprise, after reaching the opposite bank, there was no soap – just soapsuds.

(d) register differences

Register differences are defined as: "systematic differences between varieties of language used in different contexts" (Common European Framework 2001, 120). In other word, the way a learner expresses his or herself can be: frozen, formal, neutral, informal, familiar or intimate. It is important to proceed with some caution while using more formal or more familiar registers, because their inappropriate use may be a source of misunderstanding. There is a neutral word "zasiłek dla bezrobotnych" (English: unemployment benefit, German: das Arbeitslosengeld) which can be replaced by an informal expression "kuroniówka".[5] It is obvious that introducing more and more familiar registers means not only transmission of different language elements, but also culture items. Polish

[5] Jacek Kuroń (1934-2004) was a Polish historian and opposition leader with the Solidarity movement

"kuroniówka" is a colloquial expression used in tribute to Jacek Kuroń's legacy as Minister for Social Welfare.

To summarise, from Level B2 learners should use language socioliguistically appropriate to the situations and persons involved and be able to deal with variation of speech and have better and better control over register and idiomatic expressions. This competence relates also to the awareness of culturally different appropriate behaviour. In Poland it is typical that a man often kisses woman's hand as a sign of respect. This tradition is unknown in other European communities and may cause confusion. Introducing culture items can enhance and strengthen students' manners and behaviour during interpersonal and business communication. Furthermore, it can give learners an impulse to extend their vocabulary.

Conclusions

In order to carry out different communicative activities required to deal with the professional situations in which LSP learners are involved, they need to use a number of competences. All human competences contribute to the learner's ability to communicate, but one of the conclusions that can be drawn is that developing lexical and sociolinguistic competence constitutes an especially important factor in the teaching process, because it is of great significance for business communication. The presented didactic suggestions on how to deal with certain issues in LSP teaching are likely to be treated as a starting point for creating new materials and programs.

References

—. (2001) Common European Framework of Reference for Languages: Learning, teaching, assessment, Cambridge: Cambridge University Press.

—. (2003) Europejski system opisu kształcenia językowego: uczenie się, nauczanie, ocenianie, Warszawa: Wydawnictwa Centralnego Ośrodka Doskonalenia Nauczycieli,

Hoffmann, L. (1985) *Kommunikationsmittel Fachsprache. Eine Einführung*. Tübingen: Gunter Narr Verlag.

Kątny, A. (red.) (2001) *Języki fachowe-problemy dydaktyki i translacji*. Olecko: Wszechnica Mazurska.

Lakoff, G., Johnson, M. (1988) *Metafory w naszym życiu*. (tłum. Krzeszowski, T. P.). Warszawa: Państwowy Instytut Wydawniczy.

Pfeiffer, W. (2001) Nauka języków obcych. Od praktyki do praktyki. Poznań: Wagros.

Skowronek, B. (2001) *O nauczaniu języków specjalistycznych*. in Kątny, A. (2001) Języki fachowe-problemy dydaktyki i translacji 115-121.

Szulc, A. (1984) *Podręczny słownik językoznawstwa stosowanego*. Warszawa: Państwowe Wydawnictwo Naukowe.

LIST OF AUTHORS

Adéla Bahenská
Law Faculty, Charles University
Czech Republic
bahenska@prf.cuni.cz

Isabel Balteiro
University of Alicante
Spain
balteiro@ua.es

Noémia Bárbara
Escola Superior Agrária de Coimbra
Portugal
nbarbara@esac.pt

Jana Bérešová
Trnava University
Slovak Republic
jberes@truni.sk

Nina Bexaeva
Linguistic Center, Saratov State Technical University
Russia
006023@saronline.ru

David Brett
University of Sassari
Italy
dbrett@uniss.it

Miguel Ángel Campos Pardillos
University of Alicante
Spain
ma.campos@ua.es

Elena Croitoru
Dunarea de Jos" University of Galati
Romania
elena_croitoru@yahoo.com

Rosana Dolón Herrero
Filologia Anglesa i Alemanya, Facultat de Filologia, Universitat de València
Spain
dolon@uv.es

Svetlana M. Fedyunina
Linguistic Center, Saratov State Technical University
Russia
lunc@sstu.ru, aef@bk.ru

Ivanka Ferčec
Faculty of Electrical Engineering, University of Osijek
Croatia
ivanka.fercec@etfos.hr

Dita Gálová
Faculty of Mechanical Engineering, Brno University of Technology
Czech Republic
galova@fme.vutbr.cz

Nataša Gajšt
Faculty of Economics and Business, University of Maribor
Slovenia
natasa.gajst@uni-mb.si

Dana Hanesová
Faculty of Education, University of Matej Bel in Banská Bystrica
Slovak Republic
dhanesova@pdf.umb.sk

Yasemin Kirkgoz
English Language Teaching Department of Çukurova University
Turkey
ykirkgoz@cu.edu.tr

Monika Kowalonek
Institute of Applied Linguistics, Adam Mickiewicz University Poznań
Poland
monika.kowalonek@wp.pl

Antonio Pinna
University of Sassari
Italy
ap_dedalo@hotmail.com

Teodora Popescu
"1 Decembrie 1918" University of Alba Iulia
Romania
teo_popescu@hotmail.com

Nadežda Stojkovič
Faculty of Electronic Engineering, University of Niš
Serbia
snadica@elfak.ni.ac.yu

Francisca Suau-Jiménez
Filologia Anglesa i Alemanya, Facultat de Filologia, Universitat de València
Spain
suau@uv.es

Božena Zavadilová
Faculty of Mechanical Engineering, Brno University of Technology
Czech Republic
zavadilova@fme.vutbr.cz

INDEX